STUDIES IN AMERICAN POPULAR HISTORY AND CULTURE

Edited by
Jerome Nadelhaft
University of Maine

A ROUTLEDGE SERIES

Studies in American Popular History and Culture

Jerome Nadelhaft, *General Editor*

Narrative, Political Unconscious and Racial Violence In Wilmington, North Carolina

Leslie H. Hossfeld

Routledge
New York & London

Published in 2005 by
Routledge
270 Madison Avenue
New York, NY 10016
www.routledge-ny.com

10 9 8 7 6 5 4 3 2 1

Library of Congress Cataloging-in-Publication Data
Hossfeld, Leslie H., 1961–
    Narrative, political unconscious, and racial violence in Wilmington, North
Carolina / Leslie H. Hossfeld.
        p. cm.—(Studies in American popular history and culture)
    Includes bibliographical references (p.) and index.
    ISBN 0–415–94958–0 (hardback : alk. paper)
    1. Wilmington (N.C.)—Race relations. 2. Wilmington (N.C.)—Race relations—
Sources. 3. Riots—North Carolina—Wilmington—History—19th century—Sources.
4. Riots—North Carolina—Wilmington—History—19th century. 5. African
Americans—North Carolina—Wilmington—History—19th century. 6. African
Americans—North Carolina—Wilmington—Interviews. 7. Whites—North
Carolina—Wilmington—Interviews. 8. Subconsciousness—Political aspects—North
Carolina—Wilmington. 9. Narration (Rhetoric) 10. Discourse analysis, Narrative—
Case studies. I. Title. II. Series: American popular history and culture (Routledge (Firm))

F264.W7H67 2005
305.896'073'0975627—dc22   2005005118

For my son, Cassius Modisana Leeuw Hossfeld

Contents

Foreword

In this informative, exciting, and well-theorized book, Leslie Hossfeld explores uncharted terrain in the history of racial oppression. She examines some major atrocities perpetrated by whites in the 19th century—the terroristic murders and other violence directed against the black community in Wilmington, North Carolina, in 1898. As part of this probing analysis, she traces the impact that whites' ideological construction of these atrocities has had on the people of the Wilmington area in subsequent decades.

Hossfeld takes on a difficult task, for data on this forgotten history are hard to find, buried as they often are beneath long years of neglect and destruction. In this task of racial archeology Hossfeld has done well, for she has dug deeply into an extensive array of archival materials, including letters, public speeches, and newspaper articles, to get at the events and the ideological narrative developed to explain them. She brings this history up to the present using recent interviews with 42 black and white Wilmingtonians of various generations and classes. She discovers how these citizens learned about the 1898 events and how they view them today, as well as how they see new interpretations of the events.

Finding a historical project that illuminates the country's white-racist history is not difficult, for there is much about U.S. history that is intentionally neglected by most white Americans, including most of the white experts who dominate social science disciplines. One reason for this neglect is that the past is brimming with atrocities like the 1898 white terrorism in Wilmington. This bloody, often genocidal, past is hard to accept for those whites, the substantial majority, who still celebrate themselves and their ancestors as being especially ethical, religious, generous, and "good" people. From the founding fathers to present-day whites, whites have had a strong tendency to view themselves as what historian Ronald Takaki calls "virtuous republicans." In the past and in the present, most whites have seen their racial group as a special repository of great virtues—including high morality, hard work, family commitment, frugality, reason, and intelligence. From this virtuous republican perspective, whites have viewed African Americans and other Americans of color as the opposite: immoral, lazy, oversexed, profligate, irrational, and unintelligent.

Historical data show that the virtuous republican view of highly moral whites illustrates the *hypocritical ethic* that whites have long preached but have often failed to live by. Hossfeld's book provides hard evidence of the frequent lack of virtue, even of basic decency, among *many* white Americans in one important place in the 19th century. The white assaulters, murderers, and arsonists described herein are not a few isolated bigots, but much larger groups of "good white citizens"—numbering more than a thousand men in one murderous mob alone. Ordinary white men were often led by those from the area's well-off white elite.

Hossfeld tells an intriguing historical story. Most Americans are not aware that in the last few decades of the 19th century and the early decades of the 20th century *numerous* southern cities had thriving black communities with many black businesses and numerous black officeholders, such as council members, coroners, and magistrates, as well as a fair number of black mail clerks, police officers and firefighters. Wilmington was such a city in the late 19th century, with blacks in these aforementioned positions and in positions of lawyers, tailors, barbers, restaurateurs, and skilled crafts workers. The reality of thriving black communities moving out from under the oppression of slavery and peonage was too much for most southern whites. As elsewhere, North Carolina whites at this time were intent on destroying the progress black Americans had made during the progressive Reconstruction period. Using terroristic tactics—which whites pioneered in during the late 19th century—tens of thousands of whites in towns and cities across the South drove blacks from elected office, killed and mauled black men, women, and children, and burned homes and businesses. While many spontaneously participated in the violence, others joined in organized white-supremacist groups–including the world's oldest terrorist group still in operation today, the Ku Klux Klan—to destroy thriving black communities.

White fears of black progress were intense in the 1890s, particularly since black Republicans joined with poor white farmers in the Fusion alliance in North Carolina to maintain significant participation in local politics. Violent threats against Wilmington's black voters came to a head in the election of November 1898, and many did not show up at the polls. This resulted in a victory for Democratic Party candidates, in a fashion similar to what had already happened in most areas across the South. Wilmington was one of the last areas where the Reconstruction progress of African Americans was ended by white violence, in this case aided by a white supremacist Democratic Party. White celebrations of their reasserted political control in the November election turned into violent atrocities. The day after the election a "White Declaration of Independence" was signed by hundreds of whites, and the next day a mob of one thousand white men marched on a black newspaper's offices and burned them down. Prominent black officeholders and other leaders were driven out of the city, and many black citizens were shot. The whites' goal was get rid of the black middle class and political influence in the Republican party. Many blacks hid from the violence in a cemetery or fled the city in fear. Soon after this white riot, whites threw blacks out of office (even before their terms were up—in effect, a coup d'etat), and not long thereafter the area was thoroughly segregated by Jim Crow laws put into full effect.

In addition to presenting a clear-eyed view of these events, Hossfeld explores in depth the historical development of the "dominant narrative," the white interpretation of the 1898 atrocities committed by whites. She examines the development of this ideological narrative for more than a century. The 1898 atrocities have major effects that persist into the 21st century. Why this is the case, and what the effects are, constitute key questions addressed in this book.

What then was the dominant narrative that lasted until its reinterpretation in the late 1990s? After the 1898 atrocities, whites created a narrative of events that was highly biased and ideological, serving the interests of white supremacy. Whites used fabrication, exaggeration, and blaming-the-victim strategies to rationalize the terroristic actions that they had participated in. A key feature of this narrative, as Hossfeld shows well from the White Declaration of Independence, is the virtuous-republican view that whites are far superior to blacks in morals, industry, and intelligence. The dominant narrative viewed African American participation in the pre-1898 government not only as politically threatening but also as socially and sexually threatening. Even into the 1950s and 1960s some local whites were defending the 1898 riot as necessary to "protect" white women from dangerous black men. An associated theme in the dominant narrative was that during the white riot the local Cape Fear river was "running red with blood" and "choked with bodies" of allegedly threatening black citizens.

Another critical aspect of this dominant narrative was the way it played up racial categories (that is, African Americans) as the source of the area's socioeconomic problems and played down the class differences among whites that were the real cause of whites' poverty and underdevelopment in the area. The reason the elite aggressively pressed the ideological of white supremacy was that class differences among whites had led to the growth of the Populist Party in North Carolina and other southern areas in the 19th century, and to Fusion alliances between the blacks in the Republican Party and white farmers and workers in the Populist Party. By articulating a strong racist narrative accenting superiority of whites, the elite in Wilmington and across the South was successful in splitting white farmers and workers off from alliances with black workers and farmers, thereby reducing political democracy and enhancing oligarchical rule by descendants of the old slaveholding class. In his brilliant 1930s book, *Black Reconstruction,* sociologist W. E. B. Du Bois explained that for centuries, ordinary white farmers and workers had bought into a racist ideology because it facilitated their access to privileges and opportunities that come from being labeled as "white." These ordinary whites accepted a "public and psychological wage" of whiteness, instead of greater material incomes they would likely have had if they had joined with black Americans in workers' and farmers' organizations and alliances like those in Wilmington. Southern white elite, in effect, bought off ordinary white farmers and workers with a racist ideology that made whites of all classes feel racially superior—and which spurred supremacist violence against African Americans.

Reviewing archival materials for the decades since the invention of this substantially fictional white narrative of the 1898 violence, Hossfeld shows how later generations of whites have periodically accented the dominant narrative of the 1898 violence to control the black population during periods of social change. For example, during World War II, the dominant narrative was used to caution blacks against pressing too hard for civil rights and better jobs in the area's war industries. In the early 1950s, black citizens started pressing the Wilmington school board to equalize conditions in white and black schools. In meetings with black citizens, white officials alluded to the "good racial relations of the last fifty years," and by implication the 1898 white-riot, in trying to counter pressures for improved schools. Whites have periodically resurrected the dominant white narrative and its threats to local black citizens.

Gradually, over the next few decades, a new dominant narrative has developed, one accenting a version of the national white-shaped ideology of colorblind liberalism. During the 1980s and 1990s major books criticizing the older narrative about the 1898 violence were published, and their critique helped to stimulate development of a new narrative about the violence. Central to this process was creation in the mid-1990s of a 1898 Centennial Foundation to prepare for activities to commemorate the 1898 events in an what was termed an "appropriate" way. The local commemoration of the violence in 1998 helped to generate a new dominant narrative of the 1898 events. The new view combined aspects of the older narrative with some elements of the black viewpoint to create a more liberal narrative, yet one that still, in effect, sustains racial inequality and white social, political, and economic dominance in the area.

Today, the preferred narrative, especially among Wilmington's whites, is an ideological perspective that imbeds elements of the color-blind liberalism accented nationally by whites, especially those in the elite. This perspective argues that "we" need to forget the past's racial violence and move on to reconciled relations today among racial groups. This new dominant narrative emphasizes that, while there once were highly racist whites and violent events, now most whites do not discriminate. Equal opportunity and individual achievement are accented in this ideology, which in Wilmington as elsewhere rejects the idea of significant reparations for the great harm done in white atrocities against black individuals and communities. While admitting whites were in 1898 aggressors against Wilmington's black community, this new white-shaped narrative accents the fact that "no one living today" took part in the violence and offers a history of the events that does not name those responsible. As Hossfeld puts it, "In not assigning blame . . . the belief in individualism and meritocracy–that privilege is not passed-on but earned–is sustained." The accent of the narrative is now on the future, on "moving forward together," rather than on dealing with damage from past atrocities and with large-scale reparations that are morally due.

There is great and continuing damage from the many white atrocities that were perpetrated against millions of African Americans who themselves, or whose parents and grandparents, lived under the near-slavery of segregation from the late 1800s to the late 1960s. The Wilmington atrocities constituted only a small number of the hundreds of white atrocities, massacres, and riots that targeted significant segments of black communities in the South (and sometimes in the North) in this period. Mobs of whites killed an estimated 6,000 African Americans in lynchings in this long era, and often these mobs included white men, women, and children who celebrated the atrocities with picnics and dismemberment of the bodies of those tortured and lynched. Significant areas of black residence, sometimes whole communities, were destroyed in towns and cities across the South. Atrocities like those in Wilmington in 1898 were perpetrated by large mobs of whites in hundreds of black communities. Thus, in Helena and Phillips, Arkansas at least two dozen black citizens were killed and many others were driven out by whites fearful of blacks' organizing for change. During 1921 in Tulsa, Oklahoma, hundreds of African

Americans were killed by white mobs, including some deputized by authorities, and a vital black business sector and community were substantially destroyed. In 1923 in Rosewood, Florida, white mobs killed dozens of blacks and drove others out of town. In these latter cases, state legislatures considered reparations for survivors or their families, and the Florida legislature paid reparations. Clearly, in these cases the idea of reparations was considered, so there are precedents for such actions in the Wilmington case and many others. The often extreme brutality and constant terrorism of this long oppression period has yet to be fully documented and dealt with by local and national policymakers.

Among Hossfeld's respondents, who were interviewed recently, black citizens were more likely than white citizens of Wilmington to have grown up with stories of the 1898 violence, and they were more likely than whites to have heard accounts of the atrocities inflicted on the black community. One also sees in her interviews much fear and anger over the long years of oppression during legal segregation in Wilmington. Many whites will wonder why it is that African Americans today cannot forget the past. Indeed, that notion is part of the colorblind liberalism that pervades the latest dominant narrative of the 1898 violence. The reason is simple: The memory of atrocities is passed along generations of African Americans because they feel that it is necessary to present cautionary lessons for their children—that is, one lesson is to be wary of whites who still cause much harm to black individuals and communities.

Today, across the United States, there is still a significant level of fear of whites in most black families and communities. This fear is realistic, given not only the recent past history of white atrocities, but also given the high level of discrimination—which is well-documented in my research and that of many other scholars—still faced by African Americans in areas like employment, housing, and public accommodations today. One of my African American undergraduate students, Ruth Thompson-Miller recently interviewed forty elderly African American women and men in the South about their experiences under legal segregation. One of the striking aspects of the interviews is the high level of fear that they report for themselves and their communities during the era of legal segregation. Most of them talk painfully about the reality, severity, and causes of this fear of whites. They had to live not only with routine racial discrimination in most areas of their lives, but also with the possibility of their, or their relatives,' being molested, attacked, or killed by whites *every day* of their lives under legal segregation. Sadly, they had *no way out* of this constant fear-generating situation except to leave homes and families and move to other regions or countries, or by death. Thompson-Miller conducted one especially memorable interview with an elderly woman who today still lives in a darkened house where she keeps lights dim and shades drawn. The reason is that during the segregation period such actions were often necessary to reduce the damage that might be done by violent white marauders who periodically rampaged through her and similar neighborhoods. She today remains fearful of whites and the damage they might do.

As Hossfeld's analysis shows, the damage of legal segregation and its many atrocities is incalculable and far exceeds the 2–4 trillion in economic losses to African Americans from slavery and legal segregation that some economic historians have documented. How does one compensate African Americans for the hell that whites brought on them for 13 generations, and for the reasonable fear and anger that still pervades their lives and cautionary teachings to their children and grandchildren? Clearly, the rejection of reparations by whites in Wilmington and elsewhere makes no ethical sense given the extent of the atrocities perpetrated by whites over centuries and the long-term damage that such nefarious actions have long caused.

Joe R. Feagin
Graduate Research Professor
University of Florida

List of Tables

Acknowledgments

I am extremely indebted to the many people who helped make this book possible. The people I interviewed in Wilmington who shared their stories with me provided valuable insight into social relations and told stories that were often difficult to share. Dr. Margaret Mulrooney graciously allowed permission to reprint her essay "1898: A Brief History."

I owe special thanks to Michael Schulman, Don Tomaskovic-Devey and Jeff Leiter, who helped focus and refine my thinking and whose insightful observations and expertise have made this a better piece. Their skill and love of their craft provide the exemplar that has helped me become a better sociologist. Anne Schiller, Gail O'Brien, and Jammie Price have contributed to this project through well-timed suggestions and encouragement. My conversations and friendship with Andre Brown have been invaluable; his acumen on race and white privilege has helped me fine-tune my thinking on the ways in which race impacts our lives. More importantly, he reminds me daily that ideals should not be compromised.

Lastly, I want to thank my family. My brother Chip Hossfeld and my cunada Chong Kang have provided love and support, and most importantly good humor, through this long journey. My brother Mark Hossfeld and his wife Maureen have been great support. Mark never grumbled at the constant barrage of questions I threw at him and always calmly made suggestions and provided answers. I want to thank two extraordinary people—my parents, Betty and Herman Hossfeld. They constantly amaze me at the depth of support and love they provide. And finally, I want to thank my son, Cassius Hossfeld, who came along at just the right time and provides the greatest source of joy for me and who has known, all along, that I could do it.

Chapter One
Introduction

I grew up in a town in which stories had tremendous power. I was always puzzled by this, as it often seemed that the stories told were more important than the lives being led. People were identified by their recipes as well as by what their mothers and fathers had or had not accomplished. It was a southern town, indeed a Deep South delta town, yet this quality did not make it unique. The new lore about the U.S. South stakes claims on the geography of storytelling—that the defeated Confederacy has a richer storytelling tradition full of myths and lore unlike other parts of the United States—and that by virtue of its defeat and oppression has greater rights to storytelling. Yet stories, collected stories, potentially have tremendous power in any community, anywhere on the globe. Events and their actors' actions are often retold in communities over many generations, frequently setting the stage for the way future events and actors should behave. Certainly the South offers numerous examples of such collective memory–the mythological power of stories about the Civil War are immediate examples that come to mind. Similar forces around folklore concerning events and actors exist in communities all over the world. In Spain, I heard stories in small towns about their Civil War and the actors and events in their communities. In Zimbabwe, Botswana and South Africa, stories I heard about the liberation movement and actors and events take on a collective quality, passed down by community members over time. These stories often mark the path for future action or expectations about the "way things ought to be."

Since stories can have this kind of power to frame expectations and paths of future action it is important to know how this comes about. What are the mechanisms that frame some stories about events and people in communities yet ignore or even suppress other stories about events and people in the same community? Who has the power to frame and manipulate stories, and to ensure their reproduction over time? To examine these questions sociologically, I researched the stories told in one community in North Carolina with a violent racial past.

In the autumn of 1998, I attended a lecture at an African-American church in Wilmington, North Carolina. The lecture was given by a white academic on an ex-slave, Abraham Galloway, whose successful career after Emancipation led him to a position as a senator in the state legislature in Raleigh from 1868–1870. Galloway's home town was Wilmington, North Carolina. During the question and answer session after the lecture, an African-American member of the audience stood and asked, almost in an accusatorial tone, why he had never heard of Abraham Galloway. Why were there no monuments or plaques dedicated to Galloway? Wilmington is an historical city where one can find plaques and monuments devoted to important local figures strewn throughout its historic district. Why, he wondered, were no African Americans honored in his city so rich with history and one so interested in preserving its historical figures? He felt it had to do with the racial violence that took place in Wilmington in 1898 and provided an example from his own past as evidence. He told the group assembled in the church that when he was a child, his grandmother would caution him and his siblings in a firm whisper to: "Stay away from whites. They'll throw you in the river if you don't watch out." As if on cue, sunlight beamed in through the enormous windows of the chapel, illuminating the speaker. His voice changed as he remembered his grandmother's words and he spoke in an alarming manner. As an onlooker, it was a powerful moment. As a researcher already interested in the events surrounding 1898, it was a moment that focused my research: How do historical events impact social relations long past the event itself?

The reference he alluded to from his grandmother's warnings went back to racial violence in 1898, where local lore has it that African Americans were thrown into the Cape Fear River en masse. It was clearly a potent forewarning for this child, now an adult, as in his telling he evoked the fear his grandmother either felt or wished to instill. For me, as a researcher, it was an illuminating moment, literally and figuratively, as it directed my thoughts to the function of stories. I knew from research on the 1898 violence that the story of blacks drowning in the Cape Fear River was commonly used by whites to intimidate blacks. Why does an event in the past resonate in current discourse? What function does it serve when it is used? How does this event impact current relations among various groups? Intuitively one might think that these stories would have powerful consequences for social relations in a community. I wanted to investigate this empirically.

I directed my research focus to the function of stories that circulate in communities–stories that linger over years and often appear to serve interests of the dominant groups in society. In terms of race relations, U.S. history is inundated with accounts of dramatic confrontations between dominants and subordinates. Examples include places like Elaine, Arkansas; Tulsa, Oklahoma; and Wilmington, North Carolina, all cities with violent racial pasts. In each, researchers have noted longstanding lore, myths, or narratives about violent racial events that often serve as localized explanations about the way things used to be, or still are today (Nash 1972; Ellsworth 1982; Thomas 1992; Cody 2000; Stockley 2001).

What is remarkable about Wilmington is the pervasiveness of references to the violence in public and private meetings, newspaper articles, and local television news reports. Here are a few examples:

- On 12 November 1999, Mr. E.B. Davis Sr., told local television reporters that the recounting of votes for a City Council election between white councilman Quinn and newly elected black councilwoman Spaulding-Hughes . . . "goes back to 1898 when the powers that be tried every way they could to keep their control."

- In a February 1999 newspaper article about the lack of black representation on the Azalea Festival executive committee, Reverend Johnny Calhoun said . . . "these problems we're dealing with are a lot older than you and I."

- Sociologist Christopher Mele's (in Rose 1998) research on resident mobilization in a Wilmington housing project found that activists attribute the apathy and lack of mobilization among local blacks to the 1898 violence, quoting one resident as saying "you have to fight the past all over again."

- In a 2000 public meeting in Wilmington, a community member said, "The problems we have in Wilmington are not new. We are fighting battles that my great, great-grandmother and grandfather fought."

While these examples offer recent references, both direct and oblique, to the 1898 violence, narratives generated in earlier decades also point to a persistent story about the violence in 1898:

- On July 11, 1943, North Carolina Governor Melville Broughton reminded his audience at the banks of the Cape Fear River in Wilmington, North Carolina, of the racial violence that had occurred nearly a half century earlier: "Forty-five years ago . . . blood flowed freely in the streets of this city . . ." (Tyson 1998)

- During a 1951 New Hanover County School Board Meeting, Dr. Hubert Eaton petitioned the school board for desegregated schools. Dr. Eaton explains in his autobiography: "Near the close of the meeting, the school board attorney, Mr. Hogue, alluded to the race riots of 1898. However innocuous his intention, his statement was inescapably interpreted as an effort to intimidate–to warn that it could happen again." (Eaton 1984)

- An interview by Leon Prather of a Wilmington resident in the early 1980s explains: "My grandparents told me the Cape Fear was saturated at the mouth with dead Negroes. And you know what? The Cape Fear is a very large river." (Prather 1984)

Wilmington, North Carolina offers a rich resource for examining the role narratives play in maintaining power in communities and for studying the link between narrative and ideology. An analysis of narratives is useful for an inquiry into ideology. As Thompson (1984) put it,

> . . . ideology, in so far as it seeks to sustain relations of domination by representing them as 'legitimate' tends to assume a narrative form. Stories are told which justify the exercise of power by those who possess it, situating these individuals within a tissue of tales that recapitulate the past and anticipate the future (1984:11).

Stories about the violence in 1898 have circulated in Wilmington for 100 years. Today, it is common to hear reference to 1898 as an explanation for racial tension in the city, or why blacks have not fared well over the years.

RACIAL VIOLENCE IN WILMINGTON, 1898

The November 1898 violence was the local culmination of a white supremacy campaign sweeping the South at the time. Democrats in the state of North Carolina had convened early in the year to ensure victory, by whatever means, in the 1898 elections. They had lost the 1894 elections to the Fusion Party, a coalition of Republican and Populist parties that combined tickets to ensure victory. The Fusion coalition represented a cross-race coalition: blacks formed a large percentage of the Republican Party. And according to Edmonds (1951:37), "while some Populists opposed the Negro as an officeholder, there was some degree of unity in 1894 for the sake of holding a ticket together." Wilmington represented a particularly sore point for the Democrats. The success of Fusion and Republican parties in Wilmington hampered Democrats. Wilmington had a black majority (56 percent) that supported the Republican Party. In addition, Wilmington was considered a place where African Americans were doing well and could succeed, holding political office, as magistrates, police officers, and firemen. African Americans were also successful as business entrepreneurs (Prather 1984).

The Democrats worked feverishly through the summer of 1898 with propaganda and race-baiting campaigns supported by state and local newspapers. In August 1898, the Wilmington newspaper, an organ of the Democratic Party, resurrected a speech by Rebecca Fulton of Georgia from the previous year that advocated lynching a thousand Negroes a day to deter black men from making sexual advances toward white women. As part of the race-baiting white supremacy campaign, the newspaper neglected to provide the dateline of the year before, so the editor of the black-owned Wilmington Daily Record, Alex Manly, thought he was responding to a recent lecture by Mrs. Fulton. Manly's editorial denounced Mrs. Fulton's speech, arguing that white men should keep better watch over their property and that black men "were sufficiently attractive for white girls of culture and refinement to fall in love with them as is very well known to all." Democrats seized the moment, ran Manly's editorial throughout the state, and anti-black sentiment grew. The Democrats used Manly's editorial to spearhead the white supremacy campaign, and to attract poor and working class whites. The editorial proved to be the catalyst for the November 10th violence.

Blacks stayed away from the Wilmington voting booths on November 8th and Democrats easily won local elections. On November 9th, a "White Declaration of Independence" was signed by 457 white male citizens on the steps of County Courthouse, who declared that Wilmington would no longer be run by Negroes and that white labor would henceforth be the desired labor in the county. On November 10th 1898, a mob of approximately 1000 white men marched through the streets of Wilmington to the offices of the Daily Record and burned it down. The leaders of the violence then proceeded with a political coup d'etat: the newly elected Democrats were placed in office immediately after the elections. Under normal circumstances officials assumed their duties in late spring. In this case, individuals serving out their terms were thrown out of office. Prominent black and white Republican and Fusion leaders were escorted out of town and put on trains. Many blacks were shot. Scores of black citizens spent days and nights hiding in the local cemetery on the edge of town. For days following the violence local newspapers reported that trains were full of black citizens leaving Wilmington; additional trains were provided to accommodate the exodus (Edmonds 1951; Prather 1984; McDuffie 1979). Over the next two years, Jim Crow laws effectively disenfranchising blacks were created at both the local and state level (Edmonds 1951). In one decisive event, African-Americans in Wilmington were effectively marginalized from both political and economic arenas.

Immediately following the violence, an account of the events that justified white leaders' violent actions on November 10 and the political coup d'etat emerged. This white version of the November 10 violence was distributed by local and state newspapers. The white account of events in 1898 would become a common thread over the years to come. It persisted in public dialogue and private narrative in tandem with the social and economic inequalities that continued to mark relations between black and white communities in Wilmington. The intractability and persistence of the white account suggests that it may have been sustained purposively and used as a tool by the dominant group in Wilmington as a reminder to the subordinate group of their social position, playing a key role in shaping and maintaining racial inequality in Wilmington.

If reality comes to us in the form of narratives, narrative is a crucial medium that connects subjects to social relations (Jameson 1981). Narratives about critical events can reveal how social actors understand social relations and how social groups sustain these interpretations over time. The general sociological question of this research is: How do events in the past impact present day social relations long past the event itself? Specifically, this research examines the role and function of narrative in bolstering and sustaining hegemonic dominance in communities. Ultimately it poses the question: How does fundamental social change occur over time? Whereas some social science research focuses on the role of institutions in fostering social change (Sampson, Squires, Zhou 2001), this research points to and illuminates the role of narrative and ideology in averting constitutive social change.

ORGANIZATION OF THE BOOK

In Chapter Two, I examine the theoretical literature relating to ideology, narrative, hegemony and political unconscious and collective memory. I follow this with a chapter on research questions and methods. In Chapter Four, I provide what I call a 'baseline' narrative. In essence, I walk through public reference to the 1898 event over a hundred-year period. I examine archival data and describe the context in which public reference to 1898 surfaces over the years, paying close attention to the speaker, the audience receiving the public reference, and the material conditions of black and white Wilmingtonians at the time of the reference. I suggest that there is both a dominant narrative about the 1898 event as well as subordinated narratives about the event, and these mutate over time. Tracing this 'mutation' is an important part of understanding the function of narrative in communities. The research question guiding this chapter is: How and in what ways has the dominant narrative been used to maintain a hegemonic ideology and suppress other narratives?

In Chapter Five, I describe the development of the new narrative that emerged in 1998 during the centennial commemoration of the event. The analysis in this chapter identifies the mechanisms by which narratives combine elements of the dominant ideology with subordinate narratives to produce new narratives which, in this case and I suspect usually, sustain rather than challenge ruling hegemony.

Chapter 6 turns to contemporary narratives about 1898. I interviewed black and white Wilmingtonians from various age, sex and class categories and examined their 'narratives' about 1898 using the concept of political generations (Zeitlin 1970). I wanted to know when and how they learned about 1898, how they view it today, and whether they support the new narrative that emerged in 1998 about reconciliation. I compare and contrast these findings based on the expectations about generational cohort effects and collective memory.

In Chapter Seven I examine the findings presented in the previous chapters and draw conclusions using the concept of political unconscious. I close with a discussion concerning the ways narratives deny or repress history, and the implications for sociological research on race.

Chapter Two
Theoretical Context

In *Coffee and Power* (1997) Jeffrey Paige uses narratives to elucidate the underlying structure of social relations in El Salvador, Costa Rica and Nicaragua, and the ideological mystification that obscures these relations. He explores the transformation of ideas as well as the political-economic transformation that led these three Central American countries to parliamentary democracy and neo-liberalism despite their varied political pasts. Paige's analysis of narratives collected from members of coffee dynasties in the three countries employs three related concepts to understand the ideological transformation among elite. He utilizes Marx's concept of ideology, the concept of narrative developed in literary criticism and now used by social scientists, and the concept of the political unconscious developed by Frederic Jameson. I, too, seek to understand the link between narrative and ideology and like Paige use the concepts of ideology, narrative and political unconscious. For the purposes of this study I add the concepts of political generations, hegemony and counter-narratives.

Ideology. Paige employs Marx's notion of ideological mystification as described in *The German Ideology,*

> Ideology is that set of beliefs that is a product of a particular social process of inversion in the realm of reality, and second in the realm of ideas. The production of ideology is an attempt to resolve in the realm of ideas contradictions that are unresolvable in the realm of social reality (Paige 1997:340).

As Marx points out in *The Eighteenth Brumaire,* ideology is not simply false consciousness–an illusive depiction of reality. Marx's concept of ideological mystification involves the inversion or 'camera obscura' of reality. So, to use Paige's example, the inversion of the workings of capitalism mystifies the real social relations between capitalists and workers. The commodity form

and realm of 'exchange' presents the 'freedom' of the market while concealing the subordination of workers to capital. Zizek (1989:21) argues that this
is where Marx detects the 'symptom': a crack or a

> "certain 'pathological' imbalance which belies the universalism of the
> bourgeois 'rights and duties' . . . The symptom . . . is a particular ele-
> ment which subverts its own universal foundation, a species subverting
> its own genus . . . In this sense we can say that the elementary Marxian
> procedure of 'criticism of ideology' is already 'symptomatic': it consists
> of detecting a breakdown . . ."

For both early and late Marx, ideology involves inversion and concealment
of the fundamental contradictions of capitalism.

Narrative. Narrative analysis has been the domain of literary criticism
and only recently has the 'narrative turn' occurred in the social sciences
(Polkinghorne 1988; Mishler 1991; Mishler 1995; Maines 1993; Riesman
1993; Denzin 2000; Andrews, Sclater, Squires and Treacher 2000).
Consequently, narrative analysis in the social sciences has lacked a clear research methodology, although recent steps to address the broad range of research labeled 'narrative research' have been taken (see Polkinghorne 1988;
Reisman 1993; Lieblich, Ruval-Mashiach and Zilber 1998; Andrews,
Sclater, Squires and Treacher 2000). The tendency has been to blend methods of literary criticism, subjectivism in the social sciences and cultural studies (Andrews, Sclater, Squires and Treacher 2000:5). Mishler (1995)
however, does not believe that narrative studies is a

> . . . separate and distinctive discipline . . . rather . . . a problem-centered
> area of inquiry. From that perspective, it will always include a multiplic-
> ity and diversity of approaches. However, I believe we can learn from
> one another and thereby strengthen our separate directions of work.

The many directions of narrative research are seen in the varied defini-
tions of what narratives are. Lieblich, Rubal-Mashiach and Zilber (1998:2–3)
define narrative research as "any study that uses or analyzes narrative materials" and propose a model that can be used for the "analysis of a wide spectrum
of narratives, from literary works to diaries and written autobiographies, conversations, or oral life stories obtained in interviews." For Polkinghorne (1988)
and Craib (2000), narratives are stories. Craib believes narrative research "can
be defined so broadly that the term applies to any and everything a sociologist
or psychologist might want to study (quoted in Denzin 2000: xi)." Narratives
are to be found in, "novels and epic poems, but also in movies, comic strips and
ballets and puppet shows and anecdotes told at cocktail parties (Dowling

1984:24)." For social scientists narratives are "provoked by researchers' interventions, such as oral histories, interviews and written life stories (Steinmetz 1992:490)." Also important are "naturally occurring" personal documents, including working-class autobiographies, letters and diaries. While the emphasis in the social sciences has been on narrative as a source of data, a recent shift has situated narrative as a "fundamental category of human consciousness" (see for example Steinmetz 1992; Maines 1993; Somers 1992; Personal Narratives Group 1989; Hall 1985).

A common theme in all the social science literature on narrative analysis is the important focus on the organizing principle of narratives and the evaluative structure narratives contain (Linde 1986; Mishler 1991; Steinmetz 1992; Somers 1992; Lieblich, Tuval-Mashiach and Zilber 1998; Andrews, Sclater, Squire and Treacher 2000; Jacobs 2000). Linde identifies three structural features of narratives: event structure (employment), evaluative system, and explanatory system. These features govern the selection process in narratives, how events are defined, and which events are included. Important tools in narrative analysis include examining events that are selected for narration and those that are omitted, as well as the organizing principle of narrative. Linde (1986:187) argues that the evaluative structure passes normative judgment about, "the way things are, the way things ought to be, and the kind of person the speaker is." It is in this sense of the organizing and evaluative features that narratives bond so closely to ideology, particularly to the way real events are converted into an "ideologically mystified story" via what is omitted or what normative judgment is passed. As Storey (1996) puts it, "All narratives contain an ideological project."

For Andrews, Sclater, Squires and Treacher (2000), Walters (2000) and Wolkowitz (2000), narratives often "hide the operation of power relations" and "mask powerful hidden relations of subjection and coercion" (Andrews, Sclater, Squires and Treacher 2000:8–9). Mishler (1995) identifies this area of narrative research as the 'politics of narrative.' To examine the link between narrative and ideology and the operation of power relations hidden in narratives, I examine public and private narratives and operationalize these as dominant and subordinate narratives. The dominant narrative in my research is represented in public narratives found in newspapers and speeches over a hundred-year period. Subordinate narratives in my research are generally private narratives located in letters, diaries, and the contemporary interviews I conducted. Bradbury and Sclater (2000) note a distinction between public and private narratives:

> Narrators, especially those in the public domain, deploy discourses and
> construct stories in a way that may be regarded as rhetorical; they estab-
> lish, challenge, consolidate or otherwise give weight to the sense of iden-
> tity and the social relations they wish to claim or promote. Stories in the
> private domain tend to be more concerned with description, explanation
> and understanding, justification or perhaps, rationalization (2000:196).

As Bradbury and Sclater (2000) point out, the production and function of
private and public narratives differ. In this research, I draw on the concept
hegemony discussed below to illuminate the power that a dominant group
has to control narrative, particularly in the public domain.

Hegemony. I add to Paige's model Gramsci's concept of hegemony
and the role ideology plays in maintaining hegemonic control. For Gramsci
(1971), the cultural terrain is a social site in which hegemonic control is continuously demonstrated and disputed–a site which allows us to theorize
about the role narratives play in maintaining hegemonic power. Hegemony
represents the battle for ideas and consent to the dominant ideas; it represents an aspect of social control arising out of social conflict. Hegemony differs from coercive domination in that it is a cultural and ideological means
whereby dominant groups secure their control via consent from subordinate
groups. Hegemony exists in the capacity of the dominant group to maintain
their dominance by ensuring the consent of subordinate groups.

Gramsci makes a distinction between coercive dominance and hegemonic 'leadership.'

> The supremacy of a social group manifests itself in two ways, as
> "domination" and as "intellectual and moral leadership." A social
> group dominates antagonistic groups, which it tends to "liquidate" or
> to subjugate perhaps even by armed force; it leads kindred or allied
> groups (Arrighi & Silver 1999: 26).

Gramsci explains that domination relies on coercion, yet hegemonic 'leadership' relies on the dominant group to cast itself as the carrier of society's
overall interest.

> It is true that the State is seen as the organ of one particular group, destined
> to create favorable conditions for the latter's maximum expansion. But the
> development and expansion of the particular group are conceived of, and
> presented as, being the motor force of a universal expansion, a develop-
> ment of all the "national" energies (Arrighi & Silver 1999: 26).

Hegemony, then, is this added power that a dominant group amasses by its
leadership ability as well as the ability to control narrative. Arrighi and Silver

(1999:26) call it the inversion of Parson's notion of "power deflation"—hegemony consists of "power inflation" that allows the dominant group to acquire and maintain leadership capability with the support of the subordinate groups.

Counter-narrative. The concept counter-narrative has been developed by feminist theory and addressed in the work of the Personal Narratives Group (1989). It is defined simply as narratives that "reveal that the narrators do not think, feel, or act as they are 'supposed to'" (Personal Narratives Group 1989:7). The Personal Narratives Group argues that counter-narratives are particularly useful as they provide alternate ways of understanding conditions, and can:

> Serve to unmask claims that form the basis of domination . . . Personal narratives of non-dominant social groups are often particularly effective sources of counter hegemonic insight because they expose the viewpoint embedded in dominant ideology as particularist rather than universal, and because they reflect the reality of a life that defies or contradicts the rules.

Political Unconscious. The concept of political unconscious was developed by Frederic Jameson in his book *The Political Unconscious: Narrative as a Socially Symbolic Act* (1981). Jameson's theory is based on the epistemological assumption that reality comes to us in the form of narrative: it is not that we make up stories about the world to understand it, but "the much more radical claim that the world comes to us in the shape of stories" (Dowling1984: 95). Given that reality is in the form of narratives, narratives require interpretation, and indeed for Jameson narrative and interpretation are inseparable. Drawing an analogy with Freud's theory of psychological life, narratives are a symptom of the work of political repression. Jameson finds that every narrative hides the underlying contradictions of history—and as a Marxist—these have to do with the reality of exploitation. Narrative,

> simultaneously *presents* and *represents* a world, that simultaneously creates or makes up a reality and asserts that it stands independent of that same reality. Or similarly, that narrative seems at once to reveal or illuminate a world and to hide or distort it.

Whenever there is a latent meaning behind something that is manifest, interpretation is imperative. Jameson offers a mode of interpretation called *symptomatic analysis* that reveals the specific ways in which narratives deny or repress history. An important part of Paige's analysis of elite narratives rests on Jameson's notion of *strategies of containment,* or ideology. For Jameson, ideology is

> not merely a limitation, a premature closing-off of thought to the truth about History, but as the *repression* of those underlying contradictions that have their source in History and Necessity . . . in short . . . an idea of History intolerable to the collective mind, a mind that denies underlying conditions of exploitation and oppression much as the individual consciousness denies or shuts out the dark and primal instinctuality of the unconscious as Freud discovered and described it.

The idea of political unconscious, for Jameson, is "the collective denial or repression of underlying historical contradictions by human societies" (Dowling 1984: 132).

> For Jameson, as a Marxist this is not, of course some dark paranoid fantasy: it is the nightmare of history itself as men and women have always lived it, a nightmare that must be repressed as a condition of psychological survival not only by the master but also by the slave, not only by the bourgeoisie but also by the proletariat (Dowling 1984:118).

Paige finds Jameson's concept particularly powerful primarily because, "it makes narrative ideological representations its central focus without losing sight of their grounding in material human experience." In Paige's findings, the Central American elite narratives of "Liberty, Progress and Democracy" concealed the contradictions of the suppression of revolutionary movements in the 1930s and 1980s in Central America. The ideological transformations of Liberalism and Neo-Liberalism in the narratives of the coffee elite leave out or repress significant pieces of Central American reality: the immiseration and proletarianization of the rural population.

A cursory glance at the Wilmington, 1898 narratives shows a similar pattern of repressing or denying history. By using the concept of the political unconscious, my research will illuminate the contradictions that the narratives mask and the ways in which the narratives deny or repress history. The concept of political unconscious points to the historical determinants of ideology in the Wilmington narratives and the material base in which these narratives have developed.

Political Generations. I borrow a concept from the work of Maurice Zeitlin's (1970) *Revolutionary Politics and the Cuban Working Class*, called "political generations." Zeitlin's thesis is that:

> a) different political generations were formed among the Cuban workers as a result of the impact on them of distinct historical experiences, and b) that the differential response of these generations to the revolution is understandable in terms of these experiences (211).

Zeitlin defines political generations as

... those individuals of approximately the same age who have shared, at the same age, certain politically relevant experiences. Formulated in this way, the concept leaves open to empirical investigation the decision as to a) which age groups to isolate for analysis and b) which experiences to delineate as having decisive political relevance for that age group (219).

Zeitlin determines the years 18–25 as appropriate years for forming normative expectations about political thought. I knew from Larry Thomas' research on the Wilmington Ten (1980) that many of the leaders and activists during that time fell into this age range. As Zeitlin argues, general sociological knowledge about cohorts tells us that age-based social norms influence political thought. Research by Schuman and colleagues finds that collective memories are often cohort memories. Expanding on Mannheim's (1952) ideas on personal experience and generational effects as well as Halbwach's (1992 [1925]) ideas on collective memory, Schuman et al. conduct survey research to measure generational effects and knowledge of historical events across different national populations (Schuman and Scott 1989; Schuman, Belli & Bischoping 1997). Schuman, Belli & Bischoping (1997) find that historical events are most meaningful to people when they are in their formative years of adolescence and young adulthood. Yet, what about events that happen before people were born? Are there generational effects on collective memory? Paez, Basabe and Gonzales (1997) study the process of remembering, rumination and intergenerational oral transmission of collective events. They examine the way events that occurred prior to subjects' birth affect them, often because the event affected their grandparents and parents. Paez, Basabe and Gonzales (1997:170) find these generational forms of "submerged informal history" a rich source of collective memory that "generates intragroup loyalties and intergroup hate."

The archival analysis of the Wilmington narratives demonstrates that the public narrative about 1898 violence changed over time. One assumption in this research is that narratives about 1898 violence have been used over time as a coercive tool for the dominant group, especially during periods when the subordinate group tested the hegemonic control of the dominant narrative. By placing contemporary informants in categories of 'political generations' I gauge the way in which the narrative changed over time based on historical epoch in which the dominant narrative was made public.

Collective Memory. Research on collective memory provides useful tools to examine generational effects as well as tools for analysis of the way in which narratives become part of social memory. Research on collective memory stems from the work of Maurice Halbwachs, a French sociologist and student of Durkheim's whose seminal work, *The Social Framework of Memory*

(1925) argues that memory operates in a social framework, " . . . it is in society that people normally acquire their memories" with society itself, not the individual, providing the framework for memory. For Halbwachs, shared memories are "powerful markers of social differentiation." Halbwachs examines how memory is constructed, shaped and sustained by groups. His research analyzes the differences between individual and collective memory, arguing that groups provide the material for memory and prompt individuals into recalling some events and forgetting others. In addition, groups can even produce memories in individuals of events that they never "experienced" in any direct sense. Over time, Halbwachs' argues, memories become generalized "imagos" and such imagos require a social context for their preservation. "Memories, in this sense, are as much the products of the symbols and narratives available publicly as they are the possessions of individuals." Rituals, ceremonies, monuments and social events provide reference points for social memory varying spatially and temporally by group.

Contemporary research on collective memory expands on Halbwachs' original work, with two areas in particular having relevance for the Wilmington research. The first examines the way in which past events have been manipulated and/or 'invented' to serve present-day interests (Swidler & Arditi 1994; Paez, Basabe & Gonzales 1997; Pennebaker & Bansik 1997). Baumeister & Hastings (1997) survey examples of motivated distortions of collective memory and theorize about collective 'self-deception techniques,' suggesting that group memories are systematically "distorted in a variety of ways to maintain a positive image of the group" (Baumeister & Hastings1997:278). Selective omission, fabrication, exaggeration and embellishment are some of the strategies and mechanisms used in collective self-deception.

The second area examines the elements that permit negative and repressed events to be retained as facets of collective memory, what Iniguez, Valencia and Vazquez (1997:237) call the "construction of remembering and forgetfulness." They examine the construction of memories about the Spanish Civil War through analyzing the way 'ordinary' people remember history. Drawing a distinction between *remembering* and *history*, remembering is "not a simple process of evoking and recovering elements fixed in a historical moment, but rather a remembering that produces narratives legitimizing, maintaining, ordering and conditioning social life" (Iniguez, Valencia and Vazquez 1997:237). History "corresponds to the process of conversion of these narratives into the reified, institutionalized history of the period" (Iniguez, Valencia and Vazquez 1997:237). After collecting narratives of remembering about the Spanish Civil War from a range of individuals, many of whom were too young to have been alive at the time of the War, their findings target the variations and interests of different social groups in remembering, suggesting a correspondence between narratives and social groups or categories: "different social groups, categories, and collectives each with its own past, will surely have different social memories that shape and are shaped by their own intersubjectivity (Iniguez, Valencia and Vazquez 1997:237)." Remembering has to do with both ideology and political action. In the case of remembering the Spanish Civil War the fundamental relationship they find is related to legitimization of the democratic order (Iniguez, Valencia and Vazquez 1997:237).

Investigation into remembering, forgetting and suppressing events is found in the work of collective memory researchers working with traumatic events. Marques, Paez and Serra (1997) and Pennebaker and Banasik (1997) examine institutional forgetting and voluntary informal silencing of negative events. Pennebaker, Paez and Rime (1997) finds that in the case of traumatic events like torture, mass killings and rape, people suppress talking openly about them for several reasons: fear of repression; because of painful reminders of what transpired; or reinforcing group stigmatization. Pennebaker and Bansik (1997) examine the collective memory of 'silent events,' "where people actively avoid talking about a major shared upheaval" and repress the traumatic event or displace its meaning.

Marques, Paez and Serra (1997) found that silence was the common response that veterans of the Portuguese colonial wars in Africa adopted upon return, as did Vietnam veterans in the United States. Institutional forgetting of traumatic events was also a feature of both these wars. Collective silence reinforces the power of the collective memory. Lira (1997) examines collective memories of atrocities in Chile, as well as 'collective forgetfulness' surrounding the dictatorship's human rights violations from 1973 to 1990. She finds that human rights violations in Chile transcend issues surrounding individual abuses and created an atmosphere of collective 'chronic fear.' As the psychological literature points out, traumatic events in which collective violence and repression are present, psychological disorders materialize like intrusive memories (Horowitz 1986) and cognitive and behavioral avoidance symptoms (Davidson and Baum 1986). Silence or forgetting may be instilled through repressive governments or authoritarian institutions (Bellelli & Amatulli 1997). The guilt and/or shame associated with traumatic events may create voluntary forgetfulness (Iniguez, Valencia & Vazquez 1997). As Lira (1997) finds, some social groups in Chile prefer to avoid talking about the atrocities in that country. Or as Marques, Paez and Serra (1997) note during the transition in Spain from Franco's dictatorship to monarchic democracy reference to the Franquist era was repressed.

Like Jameson's work on political unconscious, collective memory research focuses on Freud's argument that "individuals repress that which is negative, or if they do remember it, they do so in a distorted way" (Marques, Paez, Serra 1997:258). As argued in the Marques, Paez, and Serra (1997:258) research, "these processes of forgetting, distorting and reconstructing allow individuals to parallel the memory of traumatic events with the social frames of reference built around the dominant values and beliefs."

SUMMARY

The basic theoretical premise of this research is that the white power structure has hegemonic control of the means of fostering and reproducing ideology of domination via narrative; that narrative then embeds and perpetuates white ideology. This study elucidates this premise by looking at the case of Wilmington, where I examine public and private documents, as well as interview contemporary residents, to explore how they portray the 1898 events and tap collective memory in Wilmington from various social groups. An examination of narrative over time, through political generations, shows the mutation of the white ideology from an overt white supremacist version to a liberal version—both of which repress opposing perspectives. The political unconscious is the repression of the narratives of subordinated groups. I expect to see evidence of the original political unconscious in contemporary accounts of respondents from various political generations. In addition, my expectation is that white ideology is still present, but that it has mutated across political generations to accommodate small, but real, changes in power relations. The accommodation seen in the Wilmington case seems to have been provoked by the emergence of previously suppressed narratives.

Chapter Three

Research Questions, Methodology and Analytical Strategy

RESEARCH QUESTIONS

This research investigates the way some narratives are used to maintain hegemonic ideology and suppress other narratives during times of contestation. Six concepts–hegemony, ideology, and narrative, political generations, political unconscious, and collective memory–provide a systematic theoretical perspective to analyze narratives about Wilmington 1898.

Analysis of Wilmington 1898 consists of three distinct, though related, empirical areas. The first centers around the following research question: How and in what ways have dominant narratives been used to maintain a hegemonic ideology and suppress other narratives? Wilmington experienced violent racial episodes surrounding the death of Martin Luther King, Jr. in 1968 and the desegregation of local schools (also known as The Wilmington Ten). I analyze pre-and post-Civil Rights era narratives to illuminate the changing functions of narratives over time. A close examination of the narratives and the time-period in which they publicly surface reveals that public reference to 1898 occurs especially during times of contestation. The relationship between narrative and hegemonic ideology is explored by examining when the hegemonic ideology was contested and the ways in which dominant narratives are parts of the process of maintaining white power. I place the narratives on a time-line with 1898, 1941–43, and 1968–1971 as key points which illuminate the process by which ideas are contested and become dominant.

The second area of inquiry overlaps with the first and involves the examination of a new narrative that emerged in Wilmington. In 1998, Wilmingtonians experienced a 'cultural intervention'–a centennial commemoration of the 1898 racial violence. The dominant ideology was challenged as a grass roots organization "retold" the story of the 1898 violence. Interestingly, a new narrative emerged, consistent with the dominant hegemonic ideology of the United States–that of liberalism and democracy. The new narrative calls for reconciliation and absolves those living today of the deeds of their ancestors. While the new narrative invokes 'inclusiveness,' it has effectively silenced alternative counter-narratives calling for reparations. It prompts the question: What are the mechanisms by which narratives combine elements of the dominant ideology with subordinate narratives to produce new narratives that, for the most part, sustain rather than challenge the ruling hegemony? This question implies an inquiry into white racism.

Racism is understood as a system of racial oppression including ideas, institutions and practices that develop into lasting structures and widespread relations of domination (Feagin & Vera 1995). The initial violence in 1898 that generated the narratives represents the era of white supremacy, an overt, bald-faced form of racism. I investigate the ways in which the narratives in Wilmington mutated from an overt white supremacy campaign to a refined liberal version of white racism as embodied in the new narrative of 1998. The new narrative directs attention away from the systemic quality of white-created and white-maintained racism. These patterns of highly racialized thought are long lasting and deeply entrenched in our society. I couple this with an examination of the material base in which ideology is situated, elucidating the system of oppression and the way it is embedded in the culture and institutions of not only the white-controlled community of Wilmington, but the white-controlled American society in which Wilmington is situated.

The third area of inquiry involves examining the ways in which narrative denies or represses history using Jameson's concept of political unconscious to read the narratives symptomatically. What is the manifest and latent content in these narratives? In what ways do these deny or repress history? In research on coffee elite in Central America, Jeffrey Paige says, with astonishment, "All societies and their ruling elite construct historical fabrications, but few go to the lengths of removing all newspapers referring to an event from public libraries" (1997:344). Similarly Wilmington gatekeeper hid under 'lock and key' in a secret cache at the public library evidence of Wilmington's unpleasant, violent past. Paige continues, "This positively Orwellian construction of an official narrative of Salvadoran history was so successful that analysts refer to a "political culture of silence"–one that so thoroughly expunged all traces of the counter-narratives of the 1930s that the left virtually had to begin from scratch in the 1970s" (1997:344). As the Wilmington narratives attest, a 'culture of silence' has made research on the Wilmington violence difficult. The narratives also suggest that the 'culture of silence' is present today. Even after a public commemoration of the event, people in Wilmington are reluctant to talk about what they were told as children about the violence in 1898.

METHODOLOGY

I began this research puzzled by the routine recalling of an event that took place over 100 years ago. This puzzle led me to the general sociological question: How do events in the past impact present-day social relations? I wanted to know: Why do residents in Wilmington, North Carolina summon a heinous event in the past to explain contemporary social relations? Why does this event resonate in current discourse? What function does it serve when it is used? Has this changed over time? In order to answer these questions, both historical and contemporary research is required.

Historical Research—Archival Analysis

My first task was to establish a 'baseline' that traced narrative development since 1898, so I turned to archival data to determine how the narrative of 1898 had changed over the years. I worked with the assumption that reality comes to us in the form of narrative (Dowling 1984). As discussed in Chapter Two, I delimit the term narrative to mean "the organizational scheme expressed in story form" (Polkinghorne 1988:12), therefore looking primarily for emplotment and relationality of parts (Somers 1992; Hart 1992; Maines 1993). Thus I assume that narrative is central to peoples' lives, performing meaningful functions both at the individual and cultural levels.

Two secondary sources provided excellent insight into the historical context in which 1898 developed: Helen Edmonds' 1951 publication *The Negro and Fusion Politics in North Carolina 1894–1901;* and Leon Prather's 1979 publication *We Have Taken A City: The Wilmington Racial Massacre and Coup of 1898.* Edmonds conducted interviews in the late 1940's with several of the elite blacks who had fled the violence. Prather obtained several interviews, one from the son of Alex Manly, the editor of the Wilmington black newspaper whose editorial was the catalyst for the November 10, 1898 eruption. The findings in these two books directed my archival research to newspaper articles, personal letters, public speeches, monographs, personal accounts, interviews and other primary and secondary sources. I consulted local biographies looking for references to 1898, as well as local family archives and papers available at the New Hanover County Public Library and the University of North Carolina collections.

Family papers at the Southern Historical Collection at the University of North Carolina at Chapel Hill, the North Carolina State Archives, and the Governor Broughton letters and papers were also useful.

I also read the handful of masters' theses and dissertations on the 1898 violence or containing references to it. Few researchers conducted interviews, however the authors described the difficulty they had in obtaining access to 1898 data in Wilmington in the late 1960's -1970's. Several discussed the way in which their research was regarded suspiciously by whites and blacks in the community and the unwillingness of both whites and blacks to discuss what they knew about 1898. A journal article by June Nash that appeared in *The Journal of Black Studies* in 1973, "The Cost of Violence," was particularly helpful. Nash's article contained many interviews with both black and white Wilmingtonians probing their knowledge of both the 1898 and 1971 racial violence.

I knew from the secondary sources that although reference to 1898 was made over the past 100 years, the violence was not widely discussed in public. My expectation, informed by the conceptualization of key concepts in Chapter Two, was that 1898 was used by the dominant group at particular moments as a reminder to subordinate groups of their social position. For the purposes of establishing a baseline in the archival materials, I searched for any reference to the 1898 event. While I took every effort to be as thorough as possible in finding public reference to 1898, I did not read every newspaper edition since 1898, or the minutes of all public meetings. I looked for references to 1898 specifically, and examined references to racial tension, race issues, union meetings, and labor issues. Thus, while I feel I followed a rigorous research strategy, using both historical and sociological research techniques, it is likely that I have missed some public references to the event given the one-hundred year period of study.

While examining the archival data, I noted when, where, and by whom the public reference to 1898 was made, and the audience at whom the public reference was directed. My purpose throughout the archival research was to find recurring patterns and motifs over time. Knowing the history of Wilmington, my expectation was that the narrative's function would change, especially given the contestation of white supremacy in the early 1940's and Civil Rights Era. Thus, in my inspection of archival data, I identified when the dominant narrative was contested, or when the dominant narrative was 'summoned' publicly for purposes of reminding locals of power relations. Narratives are context-sensitive (Polkinghorne 1988). Therefore, it is important to be attuned to the speaker, the context in which the narrative takes place, and the audience receiving the story in order to analyze the effect of narrative.

Polkinghorne (1988:161) identifies two strategies for utilizing narratives based on the intent of the research: "1) to describe the narratives already held by individuals and groups or 2) to explain through narrative why something happened." In establishing the baseline to analyze change in narratives over time, I adopt the research strategy of 'descriptive narrative research' in which I use archival data to 'report' the use or reference to 1898 over time. From the archival data, I create a time-line arranging the narratives chronologically since 1898. That time-line provided a descriptive record of change. I then apply the concepts constructed in Chapter Two, and examine the change in narrative to "interpret history guided by concepts" (Skocpol 1984:368). As Skocpol explains, this particular genre of historical sociology uses concepts to interpret history, rather than demonstrating the "repeated applicability of a model" or hypothesis testing. Unlike the historical sociology of Bendix (1966) or Moore (1966) that compares and contrasts several cases, this research focuses on a single case. As Skocpol (1984:368) argues, this genre provides 'meaningful interpretations of history' in two related ways:

> First, careful attention is paid to the culturally embedded intentions of individual or group actors in the given historical settings under investigation. Second, both the topic chosen for historical study and the kinds of arguments developed about it should be culturally or politically "significant" in the present.

Using the concepts constructed in Chapter Two, I examine the ways in which the 1898 narrative has changed over time, its function and role in the development of the dominant ideology of white racism, and the local periods of contestations of the dominant ideology.

As I began collecting and sorting through the archival data, two motifs emerged fairly quickly, and were sustained throughout the archival data collection. The *Cape Fear River choked with bodies* and *Cape Fear running red with blood* themes became part of the coding scheme I devised to sort through the data. I coded for common themes (Bloody Cape Fear/Choked with Bodies), speaker (white/black), function (warning, contestation), and audience (who was the targeted audience to receive narrative).

Contemporary Research—Open Ended Interviews

Building on this first level of descriptive analysis, I then move to the second method of inquiry by adding contemporary informants to my analysis. Since the archival data revealed that narratives on 1898 have been part of local knowledge for over one hundred years, I wanted to tap the narratives that present-day Wilmingtonians possess on this subject. I conducted semi-structured interview that allowed informants to tell their 'narrative' about race relations in Wilmington, North Carolina.

As Miles and Huberman (1994) point out, qualitative samples tend to be 'purposive, rather than random.' I began looking for informants with the closest proximity to the original event, since offspring of those living in 1898 would be part of the initial stages of narrative development surrounding the violence. Individuals who may have moved away from Wilmington for a period of time during their adult lives, yet had returned, were included. In addition, I contacted local senior citizen groups and made inquiries at the 1898 Foundation.[1] As I interviewed those on my informant list, I asked each for more contacts, according to "snowball" sampling techniques. Referrals played an important role in obtaining interviews: after I briefly described the informed consent form to one respondent, an African American woman in her late eighties, she put it down without reading it and said, "Well I guess if Sarah said it is OK, then it's all right."

I sought to build rapport and create social connections and trust with informants (Roberts 1981; Neuman 2000). I encouraged respondents to express themselves in ways they were most comfortable and both showed and felt a genuine concern and interest in the person I was interviewing. Overall, I believe that my status as an educated white female did not pose problems in the interviewing process, but this is not to say that I did not experience a few difficulties. I was denied interviews on a few occasions which most likely had to do with race. This happened twice while telephoning to obtain an interview, even though I explained that I was a friend-of-a-friend, or that they were referred to me by someone they knew. When difficulties did arise, few though they were, my race, more than gender and education, was the source of the friction. One respondent, an African American woman in her late nineties, began our interview warmly, yet when we turned to the topic of 1898 racial violence she began deferring to me as "miss." My race and age became barriers that hindered the interview and produced deference practices of the Jim Crow era from the respondent. Thus although I strove to make connections with informants, my visible characteristics—race, gender and age—at times affected the interview and respondent answers. For some groups, especially older African Americans, my questions covered sensitive issues that some respondents may have found threatening. Questions about sensitive issues, such as race relations in Wilmington, are part of a broader issue of potential respondent bias. Issues of social desirability bias and false claims are reported when observed.

As with the archival data collection, I followed Miles and Huberman's suggestion of keeping the research questions in the forefront of my thoughts, especially during the interview process. As identified in my research questions, I wanted to understand the function of narratives over time and so simply identifying an older population would not suffice. Nor was I interested in simply understanding the elite or dominant narrative as in Paige's research. That is, if the dominant narrative had been contested on occasion, how and in what way had it been contested, and by whom? I knew the answer to this from the archival data, yet would this be confirmed in the contemporary narratives? An assumption I make in this research is that events in the past impact social relations long past the event itself, particularly through narrative and ideology. The concept hegemony represents the battle for control of ideas and consent to the dominant ideas—the cultural is a social site in which hegemonic control is continuously demonstrated and disputed. The assumption is that narrative is a contested terrain whereby subordinate as well as dominant narratives interact. Therefore, examining only the dominant narrative, as Paige does, would omit an important component in understanding hegemonic narrative function. To gauge the impact narratives have on social relations requires sampling from various social categories, not just that of the elite. Thus it is necessary to include in this data set informants from various social categories, or as Janet Hart (1992:635) argues, include "informants who are touched by the experiences being studied." My interview sample is a non-probability sample, which may appear as a limitation. Yet, as discussed above, I have used various strategies to obtain informants from different social age and class locations, and to tap into socially relevant locations for the research problem. It would be very difficult, and perhaps fairly inaccurate, to conduct a probability sample for this research; a list of 65 and older white and African-Americans residents of Wilmington, North Carolina, does not exist, for example. Thus, the definition of the universe is more limited in this research. As Miles and Huberman (1994:27) argue, random sampling in qualitative research is often difficult, "partly because social processes have a logic and coherence that random sampling can reduce to uninterpretable sawdust." My sampling process is theory-driven based on the concepts identified in Chapter Two. I identify major subgroups and seek out informants from each. In a statistical sense my sample is not representative, yet in a purposeful sense, it is.

Using the conceptualization of political generations outlined in Chapter Two, I identified eleven conceivable political generations since the 1898 event; that is, only eleven categories of 18–25 year olds could possibly be alive since 1898. I began looking for informants from each generational category, desiring representation from various class and race positions. I knew from the archival data that many Wilmingtonians, both black and white, were reluctant to talk about the event and what they knew. I relied on contacts made within the 1898 Centennial Foundation. These, in turn, directed me to other community members. Through snowball sampling, my informant list grew.

From the archival data analysis, I knew about the racial unrest surrounding desegregation and The Wilmington Ten. The 1968–1971 events are attributed to the closing of the all-black Williston High School and the end of segregation in Wilmington. I sought out knowledgeable informants on these two events. Williston High School, the all-black high school before desegregation in 1969, has an active alumnae organization which is mentioned frequently in the African-American weekly newspaper, *The Wilmington Journal*. From this, I identified names of alumnae and made contacts for interviews.

I followed Silverman's (2000) advice to begin analyzing data as I gathered it. Having identified the eleven possible political generational informants, I created a table so that I could visually see the initial links between my informants' narratives and the public use of narrative (collected from the archival research) when they were between 18–25 years old. Table 3.1 below describes the temporal location of contemporary informants as they correspond with local public narrative about 1898 violence. I knew from the archival data that there were 'silences' and 'gaps' in the public narratives I had obtained—periods in the history of Wilmington since 1898 wherein I could not find any public mention of 1898 or references to the violence. At other times, however, there were overt references made to 1898. The interviews with informants from each political generation provide information about the following questions: Do the gaps and silences in the public narrative correspond with contemporary informants' narratives? What generational experiences, that is, experiences grounded in historical periods, influence the narratives of contemporary informants? Thus conducting analysis from the beginning, as I collected the data, helped me refine and modify my research as I progressed.

In 2000–2001, I interviewed forty-two current residents of Wilmington, North Carolina. Twenty-two are black residents (52%) and twenty are white residents (48%) ranging in age from eighteen to ninety-nine. Their occupations varied: four college students (two non-traditional); six public school teachers (5 retired from the Wilmington school system); two homemakers; three engineers (1 retired); two retired nurses; one janitor; four program coordinators for non-profit organizations (one retired); one librarian; one office manager; one dental technician; one domestic worker (retired); one pharmaceutical researcher; one radio host; one elected public

Table 3.1 Temporal Location of Informants and Localized Public Narrative/
Event of Political Generations

Age Range 2000/2001	Period in which Informants were 18–25 years old	Localized Public Narrative/Event(s) When Informants Were 18–25 years old
18–25	1994–2001	1994 publication of Phil Gerard's *Cape Fear Rising* 1998 Centennial Commemoration Ceremony
26–33	1986–1993	1989–250th anniversary of City of Wilmington— Play which has a segment on 1898 coup d'etat.
34–41	1978–1985	1984 publication of Prather's *We Have Taken A City*; Prather gives lecture and book signing 1985 in Wilmington. 1980—short article in *Wilmington Morning Star* about 1898 racial violence, entitled *"84 years ago Today."*
42–49	1970–1977	1971—Wilmington Ten. 1976—*Wilmington Morning Star* Bi-Centennial issue coverage of 1898 event. 1977—*Wilmington Journal* 50th anniversary edition runs editorial on 1898 violence.
50–57	1962–1969	1968 riot after death of Martin Luther King, Jr.; Schools desegregated 1969. No public mention of 1898.
58–65	1954–1961	No public mention of 1898.
66–73	1946–1953	Dr. Hubert Eaton launches school equalization campaign in 1951 and is reminded of 1898 by white official. Helen Edmonds' book, which includes several chapters on 1898, is published in 1951; Louis T. Moore responds to Edmonds publication.
74–81	1938–1945	Governor Broughton speaks in July 1943 in Wilmington at launching of the John Merrik and reminds audience of 1898. Camp Davis soldiers start a melee in Brooklyn section of Wilmington. Soldiers are billeted near white school. Local white officials summon 1898 reference in newspaper.
82–89	1930–1937	Harry Hayden's version of 1898 published locally in 1936.
90–97	1922–1929	No public mention of 1898.
98–105	1914–1921	No public mention of 1898. Racial tension in 1919 at shipyard between black and white riveters lasts about three weeks.

official; one political consultant; three university professors; two small-business owners; one fine arts instructor (retired); two counselors (one unemployed); one postal carrier (retired); one freelance writer; one lawyer; and one photographer.

The interviews themselves lasted between 45 minutes and 3 hours. I asked respondents where they would like to conduct the interview, and for the most part we met in their homes, although several were conducted at coffee shops or restaurants. I received their permission to tape record the interviews and obtained their informed consent. The interview instrument was an open-ended interview guide which began by asking informants how long they had lived in Wilmington and for their work experience. In order to assess their ages I asked when they graduated from high school and which high school they attended. Since my goal was to elicit a 'story' from them, I found that asking them to think back to school and work experiences established the background for a story about their lives, framed in the context of race relations in Wilmington. In a few of the early interviews I rushed into asking about 1898 by introducing it too early in the interview questions ("When did you first hear about 1898?"). I revised my interview strategy by simply framing the research in terms of race relations in Wilmington ("Think back to your early recollections of race relations in Wilmington. What are your earliest memories about race issues? Tell me what things were like in Wilmington then.") As informants became comfortable talking about race, I would prompt for 1898 (should it not have come up yet) or Williston High School (for both races) or knowledge about the Wilmington Ten or, depending on age, the 1941–43 racial tension in Wilmington. My desire was to generate a narrative whereby the key issues discussed in Chapter Two—the organizing principle, emplotment and evaluative structure—would surface (Somers 1992:600).

Issues Relating to Validity and Reliability

Qualitative research is often cited by critics as neglecting issues related to validity and reliability. Silverman (2000:177) cites complaints of 'anecdotalism' by these critics, in which it is argued that "brief conversations, snippets from unstructured interviews . . . are used to provide evidence of a particular contention." Methodological triangulation is one way to address validity concerns—in this research analyzing archival data and contemporary interviews allows different ways of viewing the problem to avoid 'anecdotalism.' Silverman also suggests two other ways to achieve objectivity in qualitative research: 'the refutability principle' and using tabulations. The 'refutability principle' is, in essence, Popper's call for 'falsification.' Thus one should "seek to refute assumed relations between phenomena (178)." Like Silverman, Polkinghorne (1988:174) argues that in narrative research the notion of validity differs significantly from the commonplace concept referred to in instrument measurement and tests. Rather, he argues,

> A valid finding in narrative research, however, although it might include conclusions based on formal logic and measurement data, is based on the more general understanding of validity as a well-grounded conclusion. Thus the researcher presents evidence to support the conclusions and shows why alternative conclusions are not as likely, presenting the reasoning by means of which the results have been derived. The argument does not produce certainty; it produces likelihood. In this context, an argument is valid when it is strong and has the capacity to resist challenge or attack.

Polkinghorne (176) contends that narrative research should aim for 'verisimilitude' and that it should use the "ideal of scholarly consensus as the test of verisimilitude rather than the test of logical or mathematical validity." In order to achieve this in my research, I draw analytical conclusions based on the patterns found in the data. I use counterfactuals based on historical arguments to test and critically check the conclusions I draw. I point out where evidence is incongruous or when I am uncertain about findings.

Silverman's (2000) second suggestion for countering claims of anecdotalism is to provide appropriate tabulations of qualitative data. As in quantitative research, one should offer the reader an opportunity to see data: "Simple counting techniques, theoretically derived and ideally based on members' own categories, can offer a means to survey the whole corpus of data ordinarily lost in intensive, qualitative research (Silverman 2000: 104)." Where appropriate, I make efforts to present quantitative data to the reader and to enumerate when possible.

Polkinghorne (1988), Silverman (2000) and Miles and Huberman (1994) all suggest increasing reliability in qualitative research by relying on systemized field notes and well-specified notation systems. As Polkinghorne (1988:177) puts it, "narrative studies do not have formal proofs of reliability, relying instead on the details of their procedures to evoke an acceptance of the trustworthiness of the data."

Strengths and Weaknesses of Methodological Choices

There are several strengths to this research design. Firstly, the combination of historical and contemporary analysis is innovative; the choices made in this research elicit rich, thick data that helps explain the function of narratives over time in a particular community. Secondly, unlike the Paige research on coffee elite, I include narratives from various social locations, and examine public and private narratives to explore the contested terrain of narratives. Also, unlike Paige, I include full stories from the informants I interviewed allowing the reader to hear the ideologies of the dominant narrative as well as the contestations found in counter-narratives. In doing so, the reader is able to examine the interpretations I make of these narratives. Furthermore, I have designed methods of data collection and analysis that enhance the validity and reliability of the findings. Lastly, I consider two other cases—Tulsa, Oklahoma and Elaine, Arkansas, communities with similar racial violence—and generalize beyond the Wilmington case to the importance of narratives in other communities and the role of narrative and ideology in creating fundamental social change.

There are also several limitations to this research. Firstly, my sampling frame for the archival data was limited to references of racial tension in Wilmington. While I sought to be as comprehensive as possible, it is likely that I overlooked instances in the 100-year period when racial tension did erupt. Due to the magnitude of the time-frame, I relied primarily on secondary sources for cues to possible racial uneasiness in the city, and therefore was limited in this regard. Ideally, examining all newspapers since 1898 would have been more thorough and elicited greater confidence in my findings; however the constraints of time and money made this impossible.

Secondly, as in most qualitative research, my interview sample is a non-probability sample, which may appear as a limitation. As discussed earlier in this chapter, I have used various strategies to obtain interviews from informants from different race, age and class locations, and to tap into socially relevant locations for the research problem. In a statistical sense my sample is not representative, yet in a purposeful sense, it is.

Thirdly, a limitation in this research is the possible effect my race, age and education have on different groups of informants. For some groups, especially older African Americans, my questions covered sensitive issues that some respondents may have found threatening. Questions about sensitive issues, such as race relations in Wilmington, are part of a broader issue of potential respondent bias. Issues of social desirability bias and false claims are reported when observed.

Lastly, narrative analysis is a relatively new area for social scientists to embrace. Because of this, it lacks a cohesive methodology, lending itself to criticism that narrative research is 'anything and everything' (Sewell 1992; Mishler 1995; Craib 2000). In this research I emphasize three methodological tools of narrative analysis—employment, evaluative structure and organizing principle. I distinguish between public and private narratives and the functions they serve. In so doing, this research contributes to the methodological refinement of narrative analysis which, as Jacobs (2000:31) notes, is "sorely needed."

Chapter Four
"Men of the Cape Fear"

> The tradition of all the dead generations weighs like a nightmare on the brain of the living. And just when they seem engaged in revolutionizing themselves and things, in creating something that has never yet existed, precisely in such periods of revolutionary crisis they anxiously conjure up the spirits of the past to their service and borrow from them names, battle cries and costumes in order to present the new scene of world history in this time-honoured disguise and this borrowed language.
>
> (Marx 1963:18)

This chapter is largely descriptive. I trace the dominant narrative for a hundred years from its beginning until the construction of a new narrative represented in the centennial commemoration of the event in 1998. Based on findings from archival data, eight key periods are examined in which conspicuous public reference to, or silence about, 1898 is made— the period immediately following the violence up until 1912; World War I; the late 1930s; World War II; the early 1950s; 1968–1971; early 1980s; and 1994. The time-line provided herein describes the way in which the dominant narrative has mutated over time from a coercive recanting of 1898 to the liberalism embodied in the commemorative ceremonies of 1998. My focus is threefold throughout this analysis: 1) the audience receiving the dominant narrative, 2) the actors delivering the narratives, and 3) the function or use of the dominant narrative. The framing of this chapter is guided by the research question: how and in what ways have the dominant narratives been used to maintain a hegemonic ideology and suppress other narratives?

1898–1912

The 'Revolution' of 1898

Interestingly, one of the principal motifs of the white account about the November 10, 1898 violence that resonated in Wilmington and the state of North Carolina for more than 100 years was coined on the steps of the city Opera House seventeen days *before* the actual event to which the narrative refers. On 24 October 1898, during a white supremacy rally that was part of the campaign leading up to the November elections, Alfred Waddell, an ex-confederate colonel, incited his white audience by saying, "We will not live in these intolerable conditions. No society can stand it. We are resolved to change them if we have to choke the current of the Cape Fear River with carcasses."[1]

The image of carcasses choking the Cape Fear was a refrain heard over and over again in reference to the racial violence of 1898. Variants on this theme are "bloody Cape Fear" or "when the streets ran red with blood."

Another principal motif employed in Waddell's speech that day and unlike the longevity of the bloody Cape Fear motif, this one was commonly used only until the 1930s. To stir up support in his white audience Waddell used the rallying cry of 'Men of the Cape Fear.' His reference that afternoon was to a very particular group of men of the Cape Fear—the men of the American Revolution:

> We are the sons of the men who won the first victory of the American Revolution at Moore's Creek, who stormed at midnight the rocky face of Stony Point. We are the brothers of the men who wrote with their swords from Bethel to Bentonville the most heroic chapters in American annals. We ourselves are men who, inspired by these memories, intend to preserve, at the cost of our lives, if necessary, the heritage that is ours.[2]

In her article, "Landmarks of Power: Building a Southern Past in Raleigh and Wilmington, North Carolina, 1885–1915," Catherine Bishir (2000) examines monuments and architecture as symbolic representations of elite Southern Democrats' desire to recast history and "define North Carolina history and public life in accord with their vision of society." She traces the zealousness of elite white men and women of the South from 1885–1915 to adorn public places with remembrances of Confederate and Revolutionary War heroes. Indeed, Colonel Alfred Waddell played a leadership role early on in public speeches urging the state of North Carolina to establish more memorials honoring its heroes from both wars. Bishir argues that the evoking of Revolutionary War heroes along the Cape Fear was a common practice during the white supremacy campaign of 1898. Linking

Revolutionary causes to Confederate causes was also a well-established practice as early as 1895.[3] And so, as in the quote from Marx at the beginning of this chapter, the white supremacy campaign of 1898 borrowed language from the past, cloaking its malicious intentions in legitimate refrains from the Revolutionary War, and borrowed "from them names, battle cries and costumes in order to present the new scene of world history in this time-honoured disguise and this borrowed language."

Throughout the summer and into the fall of 1898, references to patriotism and democracy would combine with references to white supremacy and the protection of white womanhood to elicit support from whites across all class lines for the Democrats' efforts to regain their political foothold. Democrats desperately needed the Populist support that had gone to the Fusion victory in 1894; playing the race card was one way to ensure their victory. Edmonds (1951: 221) explains:

> The Democrats knew that the Populists had no desire to see Negroes hold office, but they accused the Populists of supporting Negro domination because it was the vulnerable spot in the Fusion armor. While it is fundamentally true that the association of the Populist Party with the Negro question hastened its demise, it cannot be overlooked that the party stood for reforms and compelled the Democratic Party to champion reform.

The national Populist platform advocated, "more effective antimonopolistic regulations, government ownership of railroads," (Edmonds 1951:48). At the state level, railroad interests were also critical (Edmonds 1951; McDuffie 1979). For the Democrats, there was an economic incentive to win the 1898 campaign and restore state politics to Democrats' hands to ensure "no legislative attacks on the business, manufacturing and railroad interests (Edmonds 1951:221)." They sought to achieve this through the class/race project of a white supremacy campaign.

The white supremacy campaign, which began early in 1898 to ensure Democratic victory across the state, relied on the fear of Negro domination. The Democrats' rage centered on their loss of control of both state and local politics in 1894, control they had held since 1877. In addition, the successful Republican-Fusionist gubernatorial campaign of 1896 which placed Wilmingtonian Daniel Russell in the governor's seat infuriated Democrats. Russell was known for courting black votes and, although from North Carolina plantation wealth himself, had allegedly worked closely with a former carpetbagger, G. Z. French (Prather 1984:34). The Democrats sought to regain political power and used race rhetoric to service their political agenda.

Of even greater significance to Wilmington Democrats was the amendment of the Wilmington Charter by Governor Russell in 1897 whereby the Governor was given power to appoint one alderman from each of the city's five wards. The Wilmington Board of Audit and Finance, a board constructed by Democrats twenty years earlier to ensure their local power, was now controlled by Republicans.[4] Democrats challenged the governor's action, and although they were unsuccessful, it is important to note that the fiery language they used in court likened the 'right to revolt' to that of the Stamp Act crisis of the Revolutionary War. Prather (1984:45) provides excerpts from Democratic counsel John Bellamy's two hour long speech:

> It was quite in the order of things for Wilmington to be resisting the infamous legislation by which her citizens are deprived of local self-government, for it was the citizens of this city who first resisted the odious British stamp act.

The 'Men of the Cape Fear,' Democrats in particular, now felt an even greater threat to their years of control in Wilmington and the state, arguing they were being dictated to from a power beyond their terrain, similar to British tyranny over the colonies. Republicans from the capital had intervened in their domain, and the loathsome specter of Negro domination loomed ever-present.

Wilmington had great weight in the North Carolina white supremacy campaign: it was the largest city in the state, possessed the chief port, and was the county seat. In addition, the black voting population in Wilmington exceeded that of the whites—the total population was 20,055, with blacks outnumbering whites by 11,324 to 8,731. Prather (1984:31) puts the black voting majority at 1,400—with the black vote supporting the Republican party.

African Americans were visible in many public offices, including justice of the peace, coroner, police officers, two black fire departments, mail clerks and carriers. There were several black lawyers, an architect and many black-owned businesses: tailors, barbers, restaurateurs, as well as the only pawnbroker in the city. Notably, the federally appointed position of Collector of Customs was held by a prominent black citizen, John Dancy. In addition, black males dominated in the area of skilled-crafts labor—brick masons, plasterers, stonemasons—and had long held esteemed reputations among Wilmington's white employers as the best in those trades. White craftsmen grumbled about the preferential treatment these artisans received in the community—a rallying cry Democrats would use to unite whites of all classes in their white supremacy campaign (see Prather 1984; Evans 1966; Edmonds 1951; Hayden 1936).

Despite the success of some African-American Wilmingtonians, most black males were located in low paying service jobs such as cooks, janitors, porters, waiters, while black women served chiefly as domestics (Cody 2000). And although many black males worked as part time, seasonal laborers at the cotton press, massive unemployment prevailed for both blacks and whites (Prather 1984:57). Yet there were enough middle class and professional blacks to create the picture of the 'uppity' black people who did not know their place, leading to the perception of, and belief in, "Negro rule." As discussed in Chapter One, the printing of Manly's editorial in August 1898 in the black-owned *Wilmington Daily Record* on white women and black men set the stage for a seething campaign against black Wilmingtonians. Manly's editorial was a response to a speech printed in the *Wilmington Morning Star* in August 1898. The *Wilmington Morning Star*, an organ of the Democratic Party, resurrected a speech by Rebecca Fulton of Georgia from the previous year which advocated lynching a thousand Negroes a day to deter black men from making sexual advances toward white women. As part of the race-baiting white supremacy campaign, the newspaper neglected to provide the dateline of the year before, and the editor of the black owned Wilmington Daily Record, Alex Manly, thought he was responding to a recent lecture by Mrs. Fulton. Manly's editorial denounced Mrs. Fulton's speech, arguing that white men should keep better watch over their property and that black men were "were sufficiently attractive for white girls of culture and refinement to fall in love with them as is very well known to all."

Newspapers across the state fueled the apparition of "Negro Rule" through editorials and cartoons. For example, the *Raleigh News and Observer* in August 1898 ran a cartoon entitled "How Long Will This Last?" illustrating a dapper spats-clad large foot labeled THE NEGRO stomping over a small figure labeled WHITE MAN. Another, in October 1898, entitled "The New Slavery" pictures a small kneeling white man labeled FUSION OFFICE SEEKER begging to an exaggeratedly large, well-heeled black man. In her article, "The Vampire That Hovers Over North Carolina: Gender, White Supremacy, and the Wilmington Race Riot of 1898," Andrea Kirshenbaum (1998) chronicles state newspapers' portrayal of black males as menaces to white women in the South. Indeed an essential ingredient in the white supremacy campaign, as witnessed in the response to Manly's August editorial, was the issue of gender and 'Southern Womanhood.'[5] In particular, Kirschenbaum notes a September 27th cartoon in *The Raleigh News and Observer* entitled "The Vampire That Hovers Over North Carolina," depicting a vampire with a black man's face labeled

NEGRO RULE reaching out with extended claws toward small, terrified white women and men, while standing firmly on a box labeled FUSION BALLOT BOX. Kirshenbaum (1998:15) finds that cartoons during this period focused on black men exercising power over white women, "often in government settings such as the courthouse or the post office." In addition, cartoons representing white women as "Goddesses of Democracy," clad in the stars and stripes prompting white supremacists to save the white women from the evils of "Negro Domination," appeared frequently in the months prior to the November election. In a period when literacy rates were low for both blacks and whites, the power of cartoons may have been even greater than fiery editorials.

Hayden's (1936:7) account of the Wilmington violence also attests to the dualism, of patriotism and protection of womanhood that the white men of the Cape Fear felt:

> The white citizens of Wilmington and North Carolina became enraged over this unwarranted attack by this 'Smart-Aleck" Manly upon the virtue and character of Southern womanhood, which indeed was in flower in the entire Southland. There was a gallantry and courtliness, too, among the men of this Cape Fear region, as is evidenced by the toast that preceded the banquet of the Wilmington Light Infantry: "The Old North State, the Home of Beauty, Courage, Honor, Industry, Virtue and Independence."

Mixing metaphors of beauty (white womanhood), courage, honor, virtue and independence, all borrowed language from both the Revolutionary War and the Civil War, the white supremacy campaign masqueraded in the guise of 'democracy' via the 'protection of white womanhood' and 'the end of Negro rule.'

Thus the desire of Democrats locally and across the state was to "redeem"[6] their political power through the rallying cry of white supremacy to defeat the Republican, Fusion and Populist coalitions (Prather 1984:56–68). Furnifold Simmons, the chairman of the North Carolina State Democratic Committee, organized the white supremacy campaign by creating 'White Government Unions' and vigilante militias called the Red Shirts and the Rough Riders. These groups held rallies and parades throughout the summer of 1898, intimidating blacks "in broad daylight" (Cody 2000; Reaves 1998; Prather 1984). Simmons enlisted the support of the major newspapers in the state to carry the white supremacy message. These papers, essentially organs of the Democratic Party, included: the *Raleigh News and Observer, Raleigh Morning Post, Wilmington Messenger, Wilmington Morning Star, New Bern Journal,* Winston Journal, and the *Goldsboro Argus*. In August 1898, in the Raleigh News and Observer, Simmons held forth praising the campaign saying,

> Whites are a proud race, which had never known a master, which had
> never bent the neck to the yoke of any other race, but which by the irre-
> sistible power of fusion laws and fusion legislation had been placed
> under the control and dominion of that race which ranks lowest, save
> one, in the human family. The righteous rage of the whites . . . [comes
> from] negro[7] congressmen, negro solicitors, negro revenue officers,
> negro collectors of customs, negroes in charge of white schools, negroes
> holding inquests over the white dead, negroes controlling the finances of
> great cities, negroes in control of sanitation, and police of cities, negro
> constables arresting white women and white men, white convicts
> chained to negro convicts and forced to social equality with them, until
> the proofs rose up, and stood forth like "Pellon on Ossa piled."

Simmons spoke to a caste system that was not being observed; whites, despite class position, were not equal to blacks. Irrespective of a white's condition, whether incarcerated or even dead, whites remained superior to
blacks. The issue of white supremacy dissolved issues surrounding class position among whites, and Simmons capitalized on the coalescing quality of
this rallying cry.

Josephus Daniels, editor of the *Raleigh News and Observer* during this
period and fervent white supremacy advocate, recalled later in his memoirs that
the white supremacy campaign attracted such attention (even more, possibly,
than the Spanish-American War going on simultaneously) that it was:

> sometimes difficult for readers of the *News and Observer* to tell which
> was the bloodier, the war against Spain or the war to drive the Fusionists
> from power (quoted in Bishir 2000:146).

Thus, white elite in Wilmington had little difficulty establishing their
'version' of the events that transpired on 10 November 1898 and dissemi-
nating it both locally and statewide. The support from the press for the local
efforts of Democrats to reestablish their political power was well in place as
the white account of November 10th violence unfolded.

McDuffie (1963) describes ballot stuffing on the part of Democrats on
Election Day, 8 November 1898. Populist ballots were discarded because incorrect paper was used to print the ballots. Red Shirts spent the day threatening and mocking blacks, yet no violence was recorded (Prather 1984; McDuffie
1963). On November 9, 1898, a mass meeting of white male citizens was called
at City Hall in which Alfred Waddell read a document drafted by white elite
entitled "White Declaration of Independence."[8] Harry Hayden's (1936) account of the violence was the first to describe the intentions of a group called
The Secret Nine, white elite Wilmingtonians who organized early in 1898 to
ensure Democratic victory on Election Day and to overthrow elected officials,

whose terms had not expired, after ballots were counted on 9 November 1898. Again borrowing words and imagery from the Revolutionary War, 456 men of the Cape Fear affixed their signature to the document. It begins:

> Believing that the Constitution of the United States contemplated a government to be carried on by an enlightened people; believing that its framers did not anticipate the enfranchisement of an ignorant population of African origin, and believing that the men of the State of North Carolina who joined in forming the Union did not contemplate for their descendants a subjection to an inferior race:

> We the undersigned citizens of the city of Wilmington and county of New Hanover, do hereby declare that we will no longer be ruled, and will never again be ruled by men of African origin. This condition we have in part endured because we felt that the consequences of the succession were such as to deprive us of the fair consideration of many of our countrymen,

> We believe that, after more than thirty years, this is no longer the case. The stand we now pledge ourselves to is forced upon us suddenly by crisis. And our eyes are open to the fact that we must act now or leave our descendants to a fate too gloomy to be borne.

> While we recognize the authority of the United States, and will yield to it if exerted, we would not for a moment believe that it is the purpose of more than 60,000,000 of our own race to subject us permanently to a fate to which no Anglo-Saxon has ever been forced to submit. We, therefore, believing that we represent unequivocally the sentiment of white people of this county and city, hereby for ourselves, and representing them, proclaim . . .

The Declaration of White Independence lists 11 articles. Included herein are articles 7 and 8:

> 7. That we have been, in our desire for harmony and peace, blinded to our best interests and our rights. A climax was reached when the negro paper of this city published an article so vile and slanderous that it would in most communities have resulted in lynching of the editor. We deprecate lynching . . . and yet there is no punishment provided by the laws adequate for this offense. We therefore owe it to the people of this community and of this city, as a protection against such license in the future, that the paper known as the Record cease to be published, and that its editor be banished from this community.

> We demand that he leave this city within twenty-four hours after the issuance of this proclamation, second, that the printing press from which the Record has been issued be packed and shipped from the city without delay, that we be notified within twelve hours of the acceptance of this demand.

> If it is agreed to within twelve hours, we counsel forbearance on the part
> of all white men. If the demand is refused, or if no answer is given within
> the time mentioned, the editor Manly, will be expelled by force.
>
> 8. It is the sense of this meeting- that Mayor S.P. Wright and Chief of Police
> J.R. Melton, having demonstrated their utter incapacity to give the city a de-
> cent government and keep order therein, their continuance is office being a
> constant menace to the peace of this community ought forthwith to resign.

On November 9, 1898, a committee of twenty-five prominent white men,
led by Waddell, was appointed to carry out the resolutions. They met with
a committee representing the black community, comprising thirty-two
prominent black men. At the meeting Waddell read the Declaration, allowed
no rebuttal by the black committee, and adjourned the meeting giving blacks
until 7:30 the next morning, 10 November 1898, to respond.

A group of affluent black men met immediately and drafted a response saying they did not condone the article by Manly, had no author-
ization to act for him, but would "use their influence to have your wishes
carried out." The letter was placed in a mail box, instead of hand delivered, and did not reach Waddell in time.[9] The next morning, November
10, Waddell formed a group comprising the Wilmington Light Infantry,
Red Shirts and Rough Riders, as well as other male citizens, to march to
the offices of the *Record*, whereupon it was burnt down.

A Colt rapid-fire gun had been purchased earlier in the year with the
intention of intimidating blacks and keeping them from voting in November.
It had been paraded through town on several occasions, and on November
10, 1898 George Rountree, a leading white attorney in town and counsel to
the Secret Nine, instructed that it be brought out and used.[10]

The Rough Riders and Red Shirts were described as "ruffians" and
"low class whites." The leader of the Wilmington Red Shirts was Mike
Dowling, an unemployed laborer, who was known as "hotheaded" (Prather
1984: 59 -60, 85). Hayden (1936) described the members of these groups:

> Of course there were some ignorant whites, 'poor-bockers' or 'poor
> white trash' as they were and are still called down South, who did some
> dastardly deed under the cloak of this Rebellion. These poor individu-
> als, in their ignorant and primal way, vented their spleen against inno-
> cent, ignorant and harmless Negroes, possibly thinking that brutality
> was a method of displaying their "White Supremacy" over the blacks.

After the violence on November 10, 1898, Dowling, along with many of the
Red Shirts who were also unemployed white men, were rewarded with jobs
as police officers and fire fighters (Prather 1984:145).

Historians point out that the focus of the Wilmington campaign was to rid Wilmington of its affluent black residents and white Republican and Populist office holders, and in this regard it was successful (Edmonds 1951; Prather 1984). During the day of violence, November 10, 1898, affluent blacks were either escorted out of town or fled for fear of their lives. Hundreds of black men, women and children fled to the woods of the cemetery outside town, where they stayed for several days. Republican and Populist leaders, white and black, fled the city. The mayor, chief of police, and aldermen were forced to resign and also fled Wilmington; Waddell was appointed mayor by the Committee of Twenty Five.

In his book, *We Have Taken A City,* Prather (1984:150) writes about the days immediately following the violence saying:

> The whites of Wilmington had been most hospitable to the military[11] which had come into town to protect them from what now turned out to be a phantom—the Negro menace. . . . When correspondents arrived in town, they were met by a cordial committee, who saw that they, too, were wined and dined.[12] The purpose was clear: they would report the Democratic story as the town officials wanted it reported.

Little time was wasted in securing a version of events favoring those who undertook the coup d'etat. Immediately following the violence, a white account of the event emerged in the press claiming that blacks were responsible and whites had struck back as a means of defense. In the local paper, *The Wilmington Morning Star,* on 11 November, the day after the violence, appeared the following:

> Bloody Conflict with Negroes White Men Forced to Take Up Arms for the Preservation of Law and Order BLACKS PROVOKE TROUBLE Negro Newspaper Plant Destroyed—The Whites Fired Upon by Negroes—The Firing Returned—The Killed and Wounded—State Guard Out.
>
> The testimony of the witnesses before the coroner's jury will prove conclusively that the Negroes were the aggressors in the unfortunate affair and the white men were forced to fire as a matter of protection.

On November 12, from the *Wilmington Messenger:*

> But the tables are turned now forever. Never more shall Sambo and Josh ride rough-shod over the white men who befriended and helped them. Henceforth the rule of the White Race will not only be asserted but with benignancy and mercy.

And November 13 from the *Wilmington Morning Star:*

> Good Order Rules, Business Has Been Resumed and the City has re-
> gained its normal tranquility. 100 policemen to be elected. Coroner's in-
> quest augments evidence of Negro responsibility for Thursday's race
> war, verdict of the jury other developments.

On November 15, 1898, in the Raleigh *News and Observer,* Mr. Kramer, a
Wilmington Alderman, was quoted saying:

> In the riot, the Negro was the aggressor. I believe that the whites were
> doing God's service, as the results for good have been felt in business, in
> politics and in the Church.

By November 26, 1898 Alfred Waddell had provided a story for
nationally circulated *Collier's Weekly* entitled, "The Story of the
Wilmington, N.C. Race Riots by Col. Alfred M. Waddell Leader of the
Reform Movement and now Revolutionary Mayor of Wilmington."
Waddell's article contained the orchestrated account of events rounded
out with a denial of a coup d'etat. The complete article is in appendix
two. Below are excerpts of the dominant version of the appropriation of
local government.

> . . . Then they got seven of the negro leaders, brought them down-
> town, and put them in jail. I had been elected mayor by that time. It
> was certainly the strangest performance in American history, though
> we literally followed the law, as the Fusionists made it themselves.
> There has not been a single illegal act committed in the change of gov-
> ernment. Simply, the old board went out, and the new board came
> in—strictly according to law.

Summoning a paternalistic tone, Waddell assesses black Wilmingtonians
view of the violence and coup d'etat:

> The negroes here have always professed to have faith in me. When I
> made the speech in the Opera House they were astounded. One of the
> leaders said: "My God! When so conservative a man as Colonel
> Waddell talks about filling the river with dead niggers, I want to get
> out of town!"
>
> Since this trouble many negroes have come to me and said they are glad
> I have taken charge. I said, "Never a hair of your heads will be harmed.
> I will dispense justice to you as I would to the first man in the commu-
> nity. I will try to discharge my duty honestly and impartially."

No one knows better than I that this has been a serious matter, but it has, like all such affairs, its humorous side. After the crises had passed, an old negro came complaining to me about his jack-knife which he wanted me to get back for him. It seems it had been taken from him during the fracas. Then another negro came, complaining that some cattle had been penned up, and he wanted them "tu'nd loose."

. . . As to the government we have established, it is a perfectly legal one. The law, passed by the Republican Legislature itself, has been complied with. There was no intimidation used in the establishment of the present city government. The old government had become satisfied of their inefficiency and utterly helpless imbecility, and believed if they did not resign they would be run out of town.

The manipulated rendering of November 10, 1898 events had, in essence, been stamped as 'official' after the *Collier's Weekly* piece. Many references to the 'Revolution' would follow, but few, if any more, references to the changing of hands of local government would be referred to in public again.

The version being published, that blacks were the guilty party inciting the riot and firing upon whites, however, was quietly being questioned outside the public realm. In two letters written by white Wilmingtonian businessman, Brian F. Keith to his friend, Populist Senator Marion Butler, Keith pleads with the Senator to send a newspaper man to find out what really transpired in Wilmington. Below is Keith's first letter to Senator Butler on November 17, 1898:

Senator Butler

Dear Friend

Can you tell me when you think you will be down this way: There are things that the honest people ought to know. Can't you get a newspaper man to quietely [sic] come here and find out things as they are. The sadest [sic] things that has ever happened in this State, but should one publically disaprove [sic] of it he would have to leave at once. They take it some of them do as an honor. It is awful to know the true condition of affairs. I fear our city is doomed, and still the papers keep right on lying. They have to do so to justify their atrocious action. They say how that it was a necesity [sic] as the Republican had got taxes so high they could not do business here. While in fact the board of audit and finance was controlled by democrats, and gone myself, was on the board of alderman and the finances were never better actually, not in several years, and taxes were lower both City and County than when the __?__ were in full control but you see Waddell and Parmele did not have jobs. The poor Negroes have been in the woods like so many stray cattle _____?__ out [in] this bad weather are some of the ___?__ about this wholesale shooting I have heard or know off [sic]. I tell them if God approves of it, all well, if not this town will certainly suffer for the innocent Negroes killed. What I have written keep it to yourself or I certainly will have to leave and probablee [sic] not alive. The miserable Corporation and office hunting by those wicked papers . . .[13]

The 'truth' Keith alluded to is that African-Americans in Wilmington were caught unaware of the mob's intentions on November 10, 1898. Especially given that it occurred two days after an election day in which the Democrats won handily. Wilmington blacks, by and large, stayed away from the voting polls on November 8, 1898, aware of the consequences after the intense months-long white supremacy campaign leading up to the election. Having survived Election Day with no violence, black Wilmingtonians believed the white supremacy storm of the previous six months to be over (Edmonds 1951).

Perhaps the best way to understand the function of the public version of events on November 10, 1898 is to examine the private accounts such as the letters from Keith to Butler. Another letter from Keith to Butler on December 8, 1898 raises some of the same concerns he expressed in the earlier letter:

Dear Senator

If you are not going to have the article clipped for the Chicago paper published, will you please send it to the Times Mercury or the Progressive Farmer, with request to publish it, as the people on the outside ought to know—the true or ? the facts or the ? deeds of the slaughter ? of helpless Negroes for office, or political purpose, while that article does not give the true ? of the bloody premeditated deeds as they really were. Yet it touches upon so many things that were true, that had not been made known before to the world that the article should [original emphasis] be published in our state that those who were fooled by the dirty papers of this town would have the other side of the story or some. If I did not have a wife and children here and what I have ? in and around this place to a great extent, I would given these things to the public what they should know [sic] know and not wait until time shall alone reveal it. The trouble is that the Negro is in the affairs, and of these is any one thing that the people (white) will believe is the reported of the Negroes—so you see they are in a bad shape. For you and myself not being republicans to take hold—or expose the ___?___ of the ___?___ here of the with Waddell, Parmalee, B __?___ and that gang to lead the mob on to the disgrace that will always rest upon this city. I am no negro-man—only I have some respect for justice and if we are not to treat the Negro as a human being let's send him away—we cannot afford to see him murdered in cold blood. For an excuse of the hungry leaders of a mob just for a cloak to cover up the evil doings before the world as was the case in this city. And if you ? Russell to put a stop to

such, and punish the leaders best people then we who have sense enough
to think for ourselves have no longer any business in a place where mob
law can so easily be turned into so called civil law. This gang found the
cities [sic] finances in as fine condition as it has been in years, but they
had to have office even at the sacrifice of helpless negroes lives. I am one
of those who they do not know what to do with, yet ? had a plan to put
me in the C.F. River. So I also learned after the election that had you R
& P come down here you would have shared the same fate of some of
those that were put out of the way. Especially R & P. Let me hear from
_?_ & C at your convenience. Your most respt. friend. B. F Keith[14]

In addition, two letters to President McKinley immediately following the violence, both by black Wilmington women, describe an account like that of Keith's
in which black Wilmingtonians were caught unaware and were suffering:

Please send relief as soon as possible or we perish
Wilmington N.C. Nov 13, 1898
Wm. McKinley-President of the United States of America Hon. Sir,

I a Negro woman of this city, appeal to you from the depths of my heart,
to do something in the Negro behalf. The out side world only knows one
side of the trouble here. There is no paper to tell the truth about the
Negro here in this or any other Southern state. The Negro in this town
had no arms, (except pistols perhaps in some instances) with which to
defend themselves from the attack of lawless whites. On the10th
Thursday morning between eight and nine o'clock, when all Negro men
had gone to their places of work. The white men led by Col. A.M.
Waddell, Jno D. Bellamy & S.H. Fishblate marched from the Light
Infantry Armory on Market Street to seventh down Seventh to Love &
Charity Hall (which was owned by a society of Negro's and where the
Negro daily press was,) and set afire & burnt it up, And firing guns
Winchesters, they also had a Hotchkiss gun & two Colt rapid fire guns.
We the Negro expected nothing of that kind so as they (the whites) had
frightened them from the polls and saying they would be there with their
shot guns, so the few that did vote did so quietly. And we thought after
giving up to them, and they carried the state it was settled. But they or
Jno D. Bellamy told them that in addition to the guns they already had
they could keep back federal interference, And he could have the
Soldiers at Ft Caswell to take up arms against the United States. After
destroying the building they went over in Brooklyn another Negro settlement mostly and began searching every one and if you did not submit, would be shot down on the spot. They searched all the Negro
Churches, and the day (Sunday) we dare not go to our places of wor-
ship. They found no guns or ammunition in any of the places. for there
was none. And to satisfy their blood thirsty appetites would kill unof-
fending Negro men to or on their way from dinner, Some of our most
worthy while Negro men have been made to leave the City. Also some

whites G.J. French, Deputy Sheriff, Chief of police Jno R. Melton, Dr., S.P. Wright Mayor and R.H. Bunting United States Commissioner. We don't know where Mr. Chadbourn the Post Master is, and two or three others white. I call on you the head of the American Nation to help these humble subjects we are loyal we go when duty calls us, And are we to die likes rats in a trap? With no place to seek redress or to go with our grievances? Can we call on any other Nation for help? Why do you forsake the Negro? who is not to blame for being here. This grand and noble nation who flies to the help of suffering humanity of another nation? and leave the secessionists and born Rioters to slay us. Oh that we had never seen the light of the world, When our parents belonged to them, Why the Negro was all right now, when they work and accumulate property they are wrong. The Negroes that have been banished are all property owners to considerable extent, had they been worthless Negroes, we would not care. Will you for God sake in your next message to congress give us some relief. If you send us all to Africa and we will be willing or a number of will gladly go. Is this the land of *the free and the home of the brave? How can the Negro sing, my country tis of thee? For humanity sake help us. For Christ sake do we the Negro can do nothing but* pray. *There seems to be no help for us.* No paper will tell the truth about the Negro. The men of the 1st North Carolina were home on furlough and they took a high hand in the nefarious work also the companies from every little town came in to kill the Negro. There was not any Rioting simply the strong slaying the weak. They speak of special police every white man and boy from 12 years up had a gun or pistol, and the Negro had nothing, his soul he could not say was his own. Oh, to see how we are slaughtered, when our husbands go to work, we do not look for their return. The man who promises the Negro protection now as Mayor is the one who in his speech at the Opera House said the Cape Fear should be strewn with carcasses. Some papers I see say it was right to eject the Negro editor. That is right but why should a whole city full of Negroes suffer for Manly when he was hundred of miles away, And the paper ceased publication. We were glad it was so for our own safety. But they tried to slay us all. To day we are mourners in a strange land with no protection near. God help us. Do something to alleviate our sorrows, if you please. I cannot sign my name and live. But every word of this is true. The laws of our state is no good for the Negro anyhow. Yours in much distress. Wilmington N.C.[15]

And another letter to President McKinley:

Dear Sir, the poor citizens of the colored people of North Carolina are suffering there is over four hundred men, women and children are driven from their home far out into the woods by the democrate [sic] party. Look out for a letter from Wilmington North Carolina and in that letter that it will be the names of the citizens but that letter is not true and if you have ever help the colored people, for God sake help them

now, that old confradate [sic] flag is gloating in Wilmington North
Carolina. The city of Wilmington is under confradate [sic] laws we are
powed [sic] with the rapid fire of gun and they set fire to almost half of
the city. I would give you my name but I am afraid to own my name it
is from a colored citzen [sic]. Wilmington NC[16]

And a third narrative, from a white Wilmington woman, Jane Cronly, contained in the Cronly Family Papers held at Duke University, offers a similar
version to the two given above, and very different from the accounts provided in the white press of those responsible for the November 10 violence.
This unpublished document is titled "Account of the Race Riot:"

For the first time in my life I have been ashamed of my state and of the
Democratic party in North Carolina, and I hope I utter the sentiment of
many other women when I lift up my voice in solemn protest against the
proceedings in Wilmington, North Carolina on last Thursday,
November 10th. It will ever be a day to be remembered in my heart with
indignation and sorrow. At first indignation overwhelmed now sorrow
has taken its place. I waited hoping a stronger voice than mine would be
lifted up in defense of a helpless and much injured race, but such has not
been the case. There was not a shadow of excuse for what occurred after
the election had been carried in favor of the Democratic party, and our
colored people had quietly accepted the fact. The oft repeated cry it was
necessary either is false; utterly, entirely false. _____ [?] property has
ever been in danger from the colored race here. They have been as good
a set of people as could be found anywhere, as witness the way the very
people who have been vilifying and abusing them have entrusted to
them the care of their little children on the street and walked the streets
themselves. I awoke that morning with thankful heart that the election
had passed without the shedding of the blood of either the innocent or
the guilty. I heard the colored people going by to their work talking
cheerfully together as had not been the case for many days. Three hours
later how changed was all this. Men with guns were standing on our
side-walk, yells and cheers were heard in the distance, and a little later
the fire bell began to ring. We learned afterward that the press of the
Record had been destroyed by 1000 white men. The men of the colored
race were in a distant part of the city at their work. The women fled in
terror before the press destroyers, and upon seeing the flames thought
their homes, many of them situated very near, were to be burned. Some
of them managed to evade the white citizens situated upon every block
to keep back colored citizens, who might wish to attack the press destroyers, and told them what they believed to be true.

This unarmed body of men rushing from their work to defend their
wives and children from they knew not what manner of violence, was
pent up, ordered back, and kept at bay by the white citizens stationed
on the blocks who were soon reinforced by the salient press destroyers,

who began shooting off guns and pistols, having avowed as they went along toward the scene that they were "going gunning for niggers." Some blood was drawn by a colored man it is claimed, for I suppose a few armed colored men hearing the uproar, had appeared on the scene, and-then the carnage began. It is pitiful to hear the accounts of reliable eye-witnesses to the harrowing scenes. "We are just shooting to see the niggers run," they cried as the black men began to fall in every direction. A few true-hearted and disinterested men besides also the owners of the compress who had steamers waiting to be loaded with cotton went hither and thither at the risk of being shot among the poor laborers trying to soothe and persuade them to go back and assuring them that their families were in no danger, but it was of no use and when all even possible danger was over for these press destroyers they were conducted to their homes. Some Naval Reserves and a small squad of the Home Guard Light Infantry (the real Cos. being still in the N. Service) had finally appeared on the scene, but if they did any good besides killing a few "niggers" themselves, I haven't heard it, except in one instance. Mr. Buck Buckheimer rode up and down among the rioters (I suppose I can call that class now on the scene), calling out, "Shame, men; stop this. Stop this. Don't you see these dead men?" They kept snapping their pistols at him, but I suppose that he did have some influence. These rioters also shot at Mr. Sprunt's driver and buggy, saying they cared no more for Mr. S's tale than for a. birds. The Light infantry squad has much to answer for. It shot down right and left in a most unlawful way, killing one man who was simply standing at a corner waiting to get back to his work. Another, Mr. Josh Halsey, had gone home, went to bed sick with fright I suppose. A little later a poor colored boy in the neighborhood, goaded by desperation, shot at the L.I. whom I expect he thought were pressing him (and no doubt they were). They then searched every house in the neighborhood. When they reached Halsey's, his poor little child ran in and begged her father to get up and run for the soldiers were coming after him. The poor creature jumped up and ran out of the back door in frantic terror to be shot down like a dog by armed soldiers ostensibly sent to preserve the peace. Two soldiers were seen to have a mail carrier on his knees and one of them was advocating shooting him. The other warned him that it would not do, so after a little [?] threatening, he was allowed to go. The man wore the uniform of the _____ (?). I do not think either was so idiotic as not to beware of doing this. The whole thing was with the object of striking terror to the man's heart, so that he would never vote again. For this was the object of the whole persecution; to make November 10th a day to be remembered by the whole race fall all time. "An object lesson" yes, and one that may perhaps be remembered by both races in the reactionary consequences which it might bring in its wake. The negroes here are an excellent race, and under all the abuse which has been vented upon them for months they have gone quietly on and have been almost obsequiously polite as if to ward off the persecution they seemed involuntarily [to have] felt to be in the air.

In spite of all the goading and persecuting that has been done all summer the negroes have doing nothing that could call down vengeance on
their heads. The whole or nearly the whole Democratic party has broken faith again and again with the race and yet it has patiently submit-
ted; first they were told that if they registered they were to be dismissed
from their situations. In most cases they did register, for the average
negro has a most exalted opinion of the value of his vote. He imagines
that whole constitution will fall to pieces if his vote fails it. So, after reg-
istering, they were discharged and that measure having failed, they were
threatened with dire things if they dared to vote. The secret committee
of twenty-five now began pointing shot guns at helpless Republican
heads and requiring them to write letters announcing their intention to
vote the Democratic ticket in this election from their own honest convic-
tions of course (the pistol point was not mentioned in public, of course).
They then absolutely forbade any Republican speakers to come here.
They sent a committee to Raleigh. No ticket to be nominated. They rode
the mares {?} so successfully that they keep up the enjoyment even to
planning and having carried into execution the killing of negroes, the
driving them out of town into the woods and cemeteries, the arresting
of the leader—that is, all men who had property (who might be pre-
sumed {?} to be leaders, for really they had no leaders) whose lynching
was only prevented by the determined efforts of a few men. They when
the negroes had been informed by a circular the day before written by
Gov. Russell and quoting Dr. Hoge to the effect that they would be allowed to vote for state senator, the only Republican candidate running,
they growled angrily, and about three o'clock on November 8th, election day, the negroes, having been practically disarmed, they started
down with the Gatlin and Hotchkiss guns to mow them down at the
poles [sic], but Mr. Eliott and some other sharp lawyers scurried down
and told them it would be the worse possible policy, that the Republican
leaders would plead intimidation at the polls and so have the whole vote
thrown out, and we would loose [sic] our congressman. Well, the day
passed off without much racket, though that night the Capt. of block N
[?] Rankin rushed in—It was about ten o'clock—and in a very excited
manner called M. out to patrol the sidewalk, for fear the negroes, disap-
pointed in having been cheated out of the election, might set fire to
somebody's property. This fear was probably the outcome of anxiety on
the part of those people, who having abused and maltreated the negroes
were fearful of their just vengeance.

M. took his gun and went out in spite of our protestations. After being
out in the cold and damp for three house, he came in a moment, and four
women took hold of him so vigorously that they made him promise to
come in before very long, threatening to go out with him if he did not.
He knew what a perfect farce it was to be out there in the damp and cold,
watching for poor cowed disarmed negroes frightened to death by the
threats that had been made against them and too glad to huddle in their
homes and keep quietly. So after a time he came home and went to bed.

These five letters provide representations of another narrative stream emerging at the same time the dominant narrative developed that contradicts the orchestrated version offered in the white press immediately following the November 10 violence. The public version was produced to distract attention from the political coup d'etat which took place on November 10, 1898. Baumeister and Hastings (1997:287) find that one significant form of memory distortion centers on 'blaming the enemy' whereupon a group's own wrongdoing are "minimized as mere responses to the enemy. The ultimate form of this allows one to attribute one's own misdeeds to one's enemies." By focusing on the guilt of the Negro, the need to put blacks in their place, and the imperative call of self-defense at the hands of unruly blacks, the transgressions of the white mob became cloaked in an air of legitimacy called self defense.

The version emanating in the white press was one that would be heard for years to come. These letters, two by unidentified black women, one white woman and one white male provide alternative versions of what transpired on November 10, 1898. These alternative narratives also provide evidence of the function that the dominant narrative served. Examining the letters of Keith and Cronly, we learn that sympathetic whites were fearful for their lives should anyone learn of their sympathies. In addition, Kirshenbaum (1998) reports that Cronly also drafted two letters to editors of newspapers, though there is no evidence that they were ever posted—one to the editor of the *Independent* and the other a draft letter to the editor of the *Herald* (Kirshenbaum supposes the *New York Independent* and *New York Herald*). In both drafts, Cronly pleads anonymity:

> I write this to say that you are perfectly right as to the opinion you have formed about the state of affairs here in Wilmington before and during the riot of November 10th. My conscience has reproached me ever since for not writing the truth for publication, but at first like others I feared I might be asked to leave town if I were found out or that I might bring trouble upon my brothers who did much to prevent further lynching here that fatal night.[17]

Like Keith's warning, "should one publically disaprove [sic] of it he would have to leave at once," Cronly too knew that she would have to leave town if it were made public that she sought to tell the 'truth.'

The two letters to McKinley by unidentified black women voice similar fears. They warn the president not to believe the newspapers, "there is no paper to tell the truth about the Negro here in this or any other Southern state." Like Keith and Cronly they describe how blacks in Wilmington were caught unaware of the violence, and were defenseless,

"We the Negro expected nothing of that kind so as [the whites] had fright-ened them from the polls." . . ."there was not any Rioting simply the strong slaying the weak." "We never know their names, as they too realize the need for anonymity," "I cannot sign my name and live" . . ."I would give you my name but I am afraid to own my name it is from a colored citzen."

In the November 14, 1898 edition of the *Wilmington Messenger*, the minister of the local white First Baptist Church is quoted saying, "That a few negroes [sic] were shot was a mere incident. You cannot make an omelet without breaking a few eggs. The primary purpose was not to kill, but to ed-ucate." Accounts tell us that blacks in Wilmington were indeed 'educated' and learned not to counter the dominant narrative being circulated—else their lives would be in jeopardy. The suppressed narratives arising out of November 10 remained anonymous, and were kept underground. Later ac-counts attest to the way in which the black narrative became a subordinated narrative—discussed privately among families yet not publicly brought up by black Wilmingtonians. Narratives collected by June Nash in 1969 demonstrate the way in which the black version of events became subordi-nated. This by a black man:

> We just haven't talked about this affair because we've always been sad-dened by it. The whites and the Negroes had been very friendly and got on together. The unusual relationship of the white and the Negroes here, they had no misunderstanding or anything. They felt that they had been betrayed, that's the idea I had gotten (Nash 1973: 172).

And another, by a black woman in Wilmington recalling the time of the riot, collected by Nash (1973:165):

> They went over there and shot down many colored men because my aunt was on her porch on Fourth Street and she saw these cots pass with men thrown up there like animals, just like dead animals they were tak-ing them out to bury. No she saw that, that they had killed them, mur-dered them, just shot them down. Now you won't find that in history because they don't want that—no! There's not liable to be. But that's true. They didn't allow it to be published.

And as demonstrated in this narrative by a black Wilmington woman, col-lected by Muriel Rose in 1998:

> It's true that Blacks in Wilmington don't talk about these things, even among themselves. But I find it hard to believe that they haven't heard about them. I remember hearing as a child about a woman in my

neighborhood whose son was killed in 1898, and she buried him in her backyard because she feared retaliation. The very next morning, she was on the job as a domestic in the home of white family.

In the days immediately following the violence, white elite orchestrated a version of the events that justified their actions. In addition to serving as a justification for heinous wrongdoing and a means for obscuring an illegal political coup d'etat, the dominant narrative served as a cautionary tale. For blacks, it was a cautionary tale that served as an unmistakable warning that overstepping the new boundaries would result in more violence. Yet it was also a cautionary tale for those whites who were 'traitors'—not only traitors to their race, but traitors to the 'cause' now cloaked in the borrowed language from the American Revolution, with borrowed battle cries of patriotism, justice, and democracy. The tradition of the dead generations cautioned both the black victim and the 'race traitor' who would dare step outside the new boundaries embodied in Jim Crow. A Wilmington resident who had researched the 1898 violence recalled an interview he had with a Wilmington Light Infantry veteran:

> I interviewed a guy who was a surviving vet of the Wilmington Light Infantry, and met him over in the Cape Fear Club room and his response [to 1898] was "Oh yea, that's when we got the liberals and niggers out of Wilmington, and its about time we did it again."

The 'Men of the Cape Fear' continued their patriotic duties after the November 10, 1898 violence. In January 1899, George Rountree, affluent Wilmington attorney and New Hanover County's representative to the North Carolina state legislature, introduced a bill to amend Wilmington's charter, thus returning the city's politics to its pre-Russell/Republican charter. This amendment assured 'legal' Democratic political rule in the city. Rountree's next step was to introduce the 'Grandfather Clause,' already exercised in Mississippi and Louisiana, which effectively disenfranchised black, male North Carolinians. A fellow congressman, Francis Winston, supported the legislation urging fellow congressmen saying, "Every man who now talks of white supremacy must show his faith by his works. Have we so soon forgotten Wilmington?"[18] The suffrage amendment passed in the North Carolina legislature in 1900.

In January 1901, Democrat Charles Aycock replaced Republican Russell as governor. In his inaugural address, Aycock compared Democrats who had waged the "campaign" of 1898 with North Carolina's early heroes of the American Revolution:

> Confident of the support of the ignorant mass of negro voters, the
> Republican party and its ally forgot the strength and determination of
> that people who fought the first fight in Alamance against bad govern-
> ment and wrote the first Declaration of Independence in Mecklenburg.
> They challenged North Carolinians to combat and the world knows the
> result. The campaign of 1898 ended in a victory for good government.
> That was not a contest of passion, but of necessity. When we came to
> power we desired merely the security of life, liberty and property . . . We
> had seen our chief city pass through blood and death in search of safety.
> We did not dislike the negro, but we did love good government.[19]

Aycock devoted an entire section of his inaugural address to the suffrage
amendment equating the recent amendment disenfranchising blacks to the
spirit of the American Revolution:

> . . . So was the war for independence distinctly known as the Revolution,
> and our liberties are founded upon it. Our Amendment may be revolu-
> tionary, but it is a revolution of advancement. It takes no step backward,
> it distinctly looks to the future; it sees the day of universal suffrage, but
> sees that day not in the obscurity of ignorance, but in the light of univer-
> sal education.

For Aycock, the Revolution of 1898 and the Amendment of 1899 were necessary steps toward progress. Aycock, the "education governor" masked the
violence of 1898 and the disenfranchisement of 1899 in the need to educate.
In a speech before the Democratic State Convention in 1904 he said:

> When I was elected Governor it was after the revolution of 1898. It was
> in the same campaign in which we advocated and adopted the
> Amendment to the Constitution. . . . We had made the fight for the
> Amendment in no enmity to the negro, but for the sake of good govern-
> ment, peace and prosperity. When the fight had been won, I felt that the
> time had come when the negro should be taught to realize that while he
> would not be permitted to govern the State, his rights should be held the
> more sacred by reason of his weakness.

As Billings (1979) points out, Aycock promoted universal education,
including blacks, primarily as a means of social control. In Aycock's mind,
emancipation and Reconstruction subverted the paternalism epitomized in
the Old South, and education would restore this paternalistic-type of social control:

> I find in the State men who think that the negro has gone backward
> rather than forward and that education is injurious to him. Have these

men forgotten that the negro was well educated before the War? Do they not recall that he was trained in those things essential for his life work? He has been less educated since the War than before. It is true that he has been sent to school, but his contact with the old planter and with the accomplished and elegant wife of that planter has been broken. This contact was in itself a better education than he can receive from the public schools, but shall we, for this reason, say that he is incapable of training? Ought we not, on the contrary, to study the conditions and realize that the training which he needs has not been given to him since the War in like manner that it was before?

The conservative quality of Aycock's "Progressive Universal Education" can be summed up in his comparison of education to breaking a mule:

> But this is your unbroken mule. We call it 'breaking' them. What is 'breaking' a mule except training him, educating him, bringing out of him what there is in him? Why, when you buy a mule fresh from a drove it takes two white men and one 15th amendment to hitch him to a plow. And when you get him hitched up he plows up more cotton than he does grass; but after you have broken him, trained him, developed him, educated, why the old mule goes right along.

Dwight Billings (1979) argues that the practice of labor control *and* state-sponsored economic development characterized the 'conservative modernization' path in which North Carolina industrialized. These qualities, he argues, were not unlike those held by the planters of the Old South. Aycock's governorship epitomized the 'conservative modernization' policies in North Carolina, as did the "Men of the Cape Fear."

The 'Men of the Cape Fear' were men who would control Wilmington wealth and power for generations, as they had prior to 1898. Hugh MacRae, leader of the Secret Nine, was Director of the National Bank of Wilmington in 1898 and owner and president of the Wilmington Cotton Mills. By 1902 he became head of the Consolidated Railway Light and Power Company—a result of a merger he organized between The Wilmington Gas Light Company, the Wilmington Street Railway Company and the Wilmington Sea Railway Company. In 1907 another reshuffling occurred, again under the guidance of MacRae, creating the Tidewater Power Company which controlled the city and beach railway lines as well as electric and gas systems of Wilmington and New Hanover County. MacRae guided the extension of the rail line to Wrightsville Beach, resulting in development of the island as a tourist destination. At the last station on the trolley line MacRae developed one of the most celebrated landmarks along the east coast: *The Lumina*. By 1904 *The Lumina* was known along the entire eastern seaboard—it was an enormous pavilion with bathing facilities on the first floor; a second floor dance area with orchestra; a movie screen in the ocean where silent films were projected; and an electrically lit exterior at night, giving the building its name. MacRae's fortune in the development of Wrightsville Beach is noteworthy. Fusion and Populist reform including anti-trust laws and regulations of businesses and railroads would surely have dampened his success.

MacRae's real estate developments were not limited to the beach. The seven mile stretch from Wilmington to Wrightsville Beach was largely undeveloped when his railway was extended to the beach. MacRae developed communities along the trolley path, each intended for whites only: Winter Park, Oleander and Audubon (Lee 1984). MacRae was also responsible for expanding trolley lines to the other parts of the city, including Sunset Park where the shipbuilding yards were developed. In 1924 Hugh MacRae donated 101 acres of land in the Winter Park section, to New Hanover County for use as a county park, with the stipulation in the deed that it be a whites-only park (Lee 1984; Block 1998).

Another of MacRae's real estate developments in the early 1900s was the establishment of agricultural communities for white European immigrants. MacRae recruited 300 immigrants mostly from Hungary and the Netherlands, settling them in Castle Hayne of New Hanover County and in surrounding counties (Lee 1984). The success of these agrarian communities centered on bulb production, which developed a large market throughout the US, still operating today.

In Southeastern North Carolina, reference to the Revolution of 1898 and the "Men of the Cape Fear" continued. Bishir (2000:43) follows the 'memorializing' crusade of the North Carolina Society of the Colonial Dames of America who in the early 1900s raised funds to erect monuments to commemorate the heroes of the Cape Fear. Monuments dedicated to Confederate and Revolutionary war heroes were established around the Wilmington area. In a speech at the corner-stone laying ceremony of a Revolutionary War hero in 1906, Mayor Waddell reminded his audience of the "heroes and patriots of the Lower Cape Fear" whose descendants "cling with tenacity to their traditions." A Raleigh newspaper reporter quoted in the *Wilmington Morning Star* notes the frequent reference to the Revolution of 1898:

> [those who] participated in or who flourished at the time of the post-election burning of the negro newspaper office and in the suppression of black supremacy in the city [still] date events from the 'Revolution." That now is heard a good many times here in the course of a day.[20]

Another public reminder of the 'Revolution of 1898' violence occurred in 1912 during Furnifold Simmons'campaign for Senator. Simmons, the leader of the Democratic Party campaign for white supremacy in 1898, was welcomed to Wilmington by supporters, with a banner reading: "Remember the Red Shirts."

The influence of the Wilmington 1898 racial violence was felt outside North Carolina borders as well. In a recent book, Philip Dray (2002:163) cites reference to Wilmington made during the 1906 Atlanta Race Riot:

> Added to and exacerbating this already volatile situation [Atlanta racial tension over successful black business and culture] was a tightly fought Georgia gubernatorial campaign that summer [1906] that pitted Hoke Smith, a former US Secretary of the interior and co-owner of the *Atlanta Journal* against Clark Howell, editor of the *Atlanta Constitution.* Their papers, abetted by John Temple Graves of the *Atlanta Georgian,* had for months been working to top each others' reports of racial and sexual deviancy, describing an epidemic of sexual assaults with the objective of stirring up a white-black confrontation that would frighten black voters away from the polls in the fall election. Smith had publicly declared his willingness to "imitate Wilmington" if necessary, an allusion to the North Carolina riot of 1898 that had driven blacks from power.

WORLD WAR I

As the section above details, public reference to 1898 continued up until 1912. I was surprised, then, when I came across a reference to a racial dispute between black and white shipyard workers in 1919 in William Reaves' book, *Strength Through Struggle,* yet after researching newspapers and local sources did not come across public reference to 1898 during this period. I include this as a nodal point in the development of the dominant narrative chiefly because public reference is conspicuously absent during a time of racial tension in Wilmington. While I can only speculate as to the reasons public reference is absent, it does provide an interesting moment of 'silence' after the 'vocal' period of reminders of 1898 leading up to World War I and is, therefore, worth considering.

From 1918 to 1922 concrete ships were built in Wilmington by the Carolina Shipbuilding Corporation which was leased to the Newport Shipbuilding Corporation in 1920. In April 1918, Wilmington learned it had been selected out of 36 proposed sites by the United States Shipping Board to be one of five sites for the building of concrete vessels. The war contract, which was for the construction of eight vessels managed by the Liberty Shipbuilding Company of Boston, was particularly beneficial to Wilmington's economy and had been the result of a vigorous public relations campaign by the Wilmington Chamber of Commerce. Waterfront land in the southern part of Wilmington along the Cape Fear near Sunset Park was promised by the city and donated by the Kidder family as an enticement for site selection.[21] By September 1918 over 8,000 workers were employed at the shipyard with a weekly payroll of $50,000 (Hopkins 1997).

Reaves (1998:354) cites a public statement in the local Wilmington newspaper by the president of the Carolina Shipbuilding Company, Lorenzo Dilks of Chicago, in January 1919 as saying:

> . . . blacks are good workmen, that they could be easily developed into splendid riveters, and good riveting means good ships.

Reaves contends that white riveters disliked the shipyard's practice of hiring black labor and a row developed between the two groups leading to the arrest of four black men and injury of one white man on January 19, 1919. The *Wilmington Morning Star* followed the clash over the course of the following weeks. On January 31, 1919 the newspapers' headline read:

> Separate Cars for White and Colored—Carolina Officials Take Matters Into Own Hands—Workmen of Company Held Meeting Last Night to Protest Against the Retention of Negroes—Situation Not Alarming

Interestingly no local officials spoke to the matter in the newspaper, and absent, too, was any reference to 1898 during the disagreement between white and black workers. The newspaper reported further on the dispute:

> Conditions at the yard were normal yesterday, with the exception of the absence of a number of negro workmen who did not show up yesterday morning. There was no demonstration of any sort, and work ment [sic] along smoothly. About 200 employees of the corporation held a meeting at the court house last night to protest against the retention of negro workmen in certain departments, particularly the carpenter shop and the blacksmith shop. Committees representing several of the crafts were appointed to meet again tonight to determine some form of protest to the officials of the company.

> . . . Protest was made against the retention in certain departments of alleged unskilled negro labor on a parity with white men. There was also protest against the trolley system that crowds white and black indiscriminately into the same cars, and against the lack of sufficient cars to handle the crowd going and coming from the plant morning and night. . . . To the effect that the Tidewater Power company did not contemplate running separate cars for the two races was read amid howls of ridicule and abuse. Several demanded that the Carolina company force the traction company to provide more cars. This demand met with prolonged applause.

And on February 2, 1919 the *Wilmington Morning Star* reported:

> Altogether the matter has caused more talk and speculation in the city than it has in the yard. People generally have been seriously concerned about the possibility of trouble spreading, but one walking through the yard or the administrative offices of the company might go for a whole day and not hear the matter mentioned. It will be a relief to the people of the city to know that the possibility of trouble has about disappeared.

The omission of a public reference to 1898 is worth considering, especially given the frequency with which it had been summoned in the years leading up to this event. Given the newspaper coverage of the clash between workers, which continued close to three weeks, and the expressed 'serious concern' by people in the 'city,' the absence of a reference to 1898 stands out. Furthermore, the director of the Tidewater Power Company which ran the trolleys that the shipyard workers were angry about was Hugh MacRae, leader of the Secret Nine in 1898.

Hopkins (1997) notes that local labor was quickly exhausted and by October 1918, skilled labor had to be imported from Massachusetts, Georgia, and Charlotte. On January 21, 1919 the *Wilmington Morning Star* reported:

> The Liberty company is suffering from a serious labor shortage, according to Mr. Ferguson, who describes the Wilmington district as a "lean section." It is necessary to bring all the skilled carpenters and steel reinforcing men who are familiar with this character or construction from other sections of the country.

Real estate agents profited with the influx of labor; however, by late 1918, Hopkins reports a housing shortage in the area. Hopkins (1997:121) also notes that the local Rotary Club "initiated a campaign to forestall any price gouging and to keep non-Wilmington businesses from moving into the city." To add to the problems of labor shortage, Spanish influenza swept through the area and according to a features article in a 1972 edition of the *Wilmington Morning Star* the influenza epidemic halted ship construction for a brief period.

In the fall of 1918 plans were underway to develop another shipbuilding site at the other end of Wilmington city limits on the northeast branch of the Cape Fear. However, it was decided that Wilmington 'support facilities' had reached their limit and a new site was sought in New Bern, north of Wilmington (Hopkins (1997:123).

I was struck by the mood of the newspaper coverage of the violence between black and white riveters in January 1919. Near each article about the confrontation was a piece about the prospect of an additional concrete yard being built in Wilmington, or the courting of new shipbuilding-related business into the area, or the hope of additional shipbuilding contracts. One article running below the news of the shipyard racial tension in the *Wilmington Morning Star* on February 1, 1919 ran the caption "No Limit to What We Can Do At Wilmington" and read:

> There is no limit to what we can do at Wilmington when we get busy and go at it. Noting that we are now doing things not dreamed of in Wilmington four years ago, the New Bern Sun-Journal says, "Over at Wilmington Tuesday a shipbuilding company operating that place began pouring concrete for the first stone ship to be built in North Carolina. This marked a new epoch in the history of Tar Heelia." This state has been backward in some things in recent years, but we can do almost anything here than can be done in any other state in the Union and in the next few years North Carolina will make the rest of the world sit up and take notice. The adaptabilities and opportunities are here for doing what our valued New Bern contemporary says–"make the world sit up and take notice." Lots of things can be done in Wilmington that we haven't even thought of yet. It is simply a matter of initiative, alertness and capital. We have shown how we can get behind constructive movements and the thing to do is to get behind more of them.

Local businesses were profiting from the new shipbuilding burst and were looking for ways to continue the success, as well as to maintain an environment conducive to new business surrounding shipbuilding. Not until the summer months did the newspaper mention returning soldiers.

Absent was the patriotic rhetoric from the Men of the Cape Fear so common a few years before. Local businessmen and officials did not play the 1898 race card because they needed black labor. In 1898 local elite consolidated power by eliminating Republican-black-Fusion influence, but by 1917 the dominant race narrative works against them. Elites, MacRae in particular, passively manage the race tension by deploying modernization rhetoric and suppressing the 1898 rhetoric: in 1917, two narratives are deployed selectively.

LATE 1930S

Another public reminder of 'the Revolution of 1898' appeared in late 1936, when Harry Hayden's account of the November 10, 1898 violence was made available for $1.00 in a self-published pamphlet entitled "The Story of the Wilmington Rebellion." Apparently the account was well received with reviews featured in *The Journal of Southern History; The Charlotte News;*

The Richmond Times-Dispatch; and *The London Book-Dealer's Weekly.* The *Wilmington Morning Star* ran two articles on Hayden's publication, one on December 10, 1936, and the second January 7, 1937, both highlighting the positive and expansive reception of Hayden's book noting that orders for the booklet have been "received from such distant places as England, California, Massachusetts, Illinois, New York, Georgia, Louisiana, and request for copies have also been made by consolidated schools in various parts of the country." Hayden's account retold the original white version of the violence, yet was the first to disclose a secret group of elite, white men in Wilmington who had met early in 1898 to plan the white supremacy campaign and orchestrate a coup d'etat (Prather 1984; Godwin 2000). The Secret Nine were described by Hayden in favorable terms, as protectors of white neighborhoods and guided by a noble purpose.

Hayden must have received feedback from his fellow Wilmingtonians as indicated in this Letter to the Editor:

To the Editor of The Star:

By reason of the fact that a few Wilmingtonians have vocally criticized my "Story of the Wilmington Rebellion" on the grounds that it is not altogether comprehensive of the rioting phase of this revolution. I am begging a line or two of type from you.

First, I am appreciative of the criticism voiced by my critics. Secondly, I did not attempt to write a detailed story of the "Wilmington Riot" as there have been hundreds of riots and they do not look good in black and white (in print).

Thirdly, the rioting was only one phase in the Wilmington Rebellion which was organized and directed by a group of nine prominent and influential Wilmingtonians, whose main motivation was the establishment of clean, orderly government in this city, the state and the south.

There are a thousand and one ramifications connected with the Wilmington Riot that did not interest me in the slightest, for the reason that the immediate cause and the lasting result impressed me far more than the lurid details of the strife at the moment.

History of the World War, like that of the "Wilmington Revolution" will not record so much as to "Who Killed Cock Robin?" but it will stress who got him to kill and who prevented him from fighting himself to death.

Harry Hayden, December 23, 1936 [22]

I found no other mention in the newspaper about Hayden's work, other than the ones listed above. It appears the criticism Hayden refers to in the Letter to the Editor above may have had to do simply with details Hayden omitted in his account, rather than criticism of the manner in which his account supported the dominant version. A copy of Hayden's pamphlet from the North Carolina Collection at the University of North Carolina at Chapel Hill, handwritten corrections signed by J.A. Taylor, a member of the Secret Nine who participated in the violence, provides details and additions to Hayden's text, thus the 'thousand and one ramifications' Hayden did not provide. In reading through these 'corrections,' Taylor does not dispute what Hayden wrote, but rather provides the names of those involved and the tasks they carried out during the violence. Taylor's four signed 'enhancements' to Hayden's pamphlet actually added legitimacy to Hayden's work, as Taylor was an influential leader during the "revolution" and afterwards.

While the mingled references to heroes of the Confederacy and the Revolutionary War continued into the late thirties, this motif did mutate as the United States moved closer to the Second World War. The organizing principle of the dominant narrative remained that of a cautionary tale. Yet, in the 1940s-1950s, it shifted from patriotism and democracy as exemplified in the spirit of white supremacy, to the views of 'progressivism' represented in the development of the Old North State as a center of forward thinking southerners no longer mired in the notions of the 'Old South' (Godwin:2000). Chafe (1980;1981; 1998) calls it the "progressive mystique" citing historians' designation of Charles Aycock as the "progressive governor" and "education governor" and V.O. Key's 1949 heralding of North Carolina as an "inspiring exception to Southern racism" (Chafe 1998:280). As Chafe argues (1998:280), North Carolina's progressive mystique, "involves a set of ground rules that support the notion of North Carolina as a more civilized, enlightened, and tolerant place than the rest of the old Confederacy."

The dominant narrative about 1898 violence resurfaced in Wilmington in the 1940s and 1950s as a cautionary tale, once again, reminding black audiences that while 'progress' was the objective, blacks should not necessarily expect it on their terms.

Reaves (1998:268–272) mentions two Jim Crow trolley violations between the 1920s and 1940s, yet I found no public use of the dominant narrative in this period. I turn now to two examples of the cautionary tale summoned in the 1940s.

WORLD WAR II

Two public references to 1898 occurred during this time frame, one in 1941 and the other in 1943, both serving as 'cautionary tales.' The war years brought a period of tremendous change to Wilmington. The local population grew from 33,000 in 1940 to 120,000 in 1943. The shipbuilding enterprises that slumbered in the early 1920s were furiously revived during the Second World War. From 1941 until 1946 the shipbuilding industry boosted the local economy, building 243 vessels, including Liberty ships, and employing at its peak in 1943 roughly 25,000 women and men, with an annual payroll of over $50 million. People from surrounding towns and from other parts of the region converged on Wilmington to take advantage of the available jobs.[23] As Scott (1979:19) describes, "The city became a latter day version of the Alaska Gold Rush as rural southern farmers flocked to employment opportunities at the North Carolina Shipbuilding Company."

The bid to win the war contracts and develop shipbuilding in Wilmington involved a bitter dispute with Morehead City, just up the coast from Wilmington. Wilmington businessmen had organized a group called 'The New Hanover Defense Council' to recruit shipbuilding to the area. Two of those serving on the Committee were Bruce Cameron, businessman and mayor of Wilmington, and Hugh McRae. Louis T. Moore, Director of the Wilmington Chamber of Commerce, was also instrumental in lobbying for the Wilmington site choice. Scott (1979) outlines the rivalry between the two bidding cities, citing numerous last-minute strategy and plotting sessions. Despite the active support of Governor Broughton for the Morehead City site, Wilmington won the bid. Interestingly, Josephus Daniels, the former owner of *News and Observer* and one of the leaders of the state-wide white supremacy campaign, was brought in at the last minute to help in making the decision (Scott 1979). Though I have not read anything definitive on why the bid went to the Wilmington site, Daniels' interest in Wilmington had been longstanding. Daniels was instrumental and supportive of Wilmington elite during the 1898 white supremacy campaign. In addition, Daniels' name surfaced during the 1919 Wilmington shipyard bid. Daniels had served as Secretary of the Navy from 1913–1921 with Franklin Roosevelt as his Assistant Secretary of the Navy; he was later appointed Ambassador of Mexico by Roosevelt in the 1930s, resigning in 1941 to return to North Carolina with his ailing wife. One can only speculate that his long ties with the Wilmington business community lent support for the shipbuilding project.

Prior to the World War II contracts for shipbuilding, the Atlantic Coast Line Railroad had been Wilmington's biggest employer, and indeed saw Wilmington through the lean years of the depression. By September 1943, over $3 million in contracts for shipbuilding and dry docks had been awarded to the North Carolina Shipbuilding Company and the V.P. Loftis Company. These two firms accounted for four-fifths of manufacturing employment in

New Hanover County.[24] Scott (1979) puts the percentage of black workers at the North Carolina Shipbuilding Company (NCSB) at 36 percent, roughly 6,000 who were trained as riveters, drillers, shipwrights, angle-smiths, and riggers. Most of the work crews at the shipyard followed an integrated pattern of work found at the Chesapeake Bay shipyards, and this practice was brought to the Wilmington yard (Scott 1979:74). This is a note-worthy contrast to other shipyards in the South at which black crews worked on one vessel while white crews worked on another vessel (Scott 1979:74). One respondent I interviewed described his work experience at the shipyard in the 1940s:

> Shipyard—only thing about blacks is you had no welder. No black welders. Shippers were black and white, cutting steel. We had black and white in my department. And most had, it was more integrated than any thing else.

Another influx to the Wilmington population was Camp Davis open-ing in 1941, stationing 20,000 troops, 6000 of whom were black soldiers. Camp Davis was located thirty miles north of Wilmington in Holly Ridge,[25] and servicemen frequented Wilmington during their off-time, especially at the U.S.O. clubs built during those years, one for white soldiers and another for black soldiers.

Transportation was a very serious problem during this time. Shipyard workers and married Camp Davis soldiers were housed in Wilmington and struggled with segregated bus services to and from work and base. Hurtis Coleman who lived in segregated quarters at Camp Davis recounted in 1991 that segregated buses had only 15 seats allowed for black passengers in the back of the bus, making soldiers late for duty as there often was not enough room for the number of men traveling back and forth to Camp Davis. Coleman said that in 1941, frustrated black soldiers overturned buses at the corner of Grace and Second streets in Wilmington to protest the limited seat-ing.[26] The bus company, the Tidewater Power Company owned by Hugh MacRae, added an additional 'black-only' bus, with added excursions to Camp Davis to address the complaints.[27]

Accounts of a 'riot' involving black servicemen are discussed in Dosher (2000) and Reaves (1998). The *Wilmington Morning Star* reported on the 'melee' two days after the event took place, and as Dosher points out used large, bold-faced type generally reserved for World War II news coverage. The newspaper coverage on 19 August 1941, reported that drunken black soldiers in uniform from Camp Davis damaged a drinking house in the Brooklyn section of Wilmington (a black section of town), and proceeded to "knock boys off bicycles and beating [sic] every civilian in sight." Police estimated there were between three and four hundred blacks who were "uncontrollable" on the scene. The story further reported that with the assistance of police officers, the soldiers were sent back to Camp Davis, leaving nine men (five soldiers and four civilians) hospitalized with serious injuries. Dosher (2000) traces the development of the story in the press pointing out that running aside the reports of the riot were other, unrelated stories about blacks in Wilmington, all with violent overtones, all covered on the same page. He argues that the portrayal of the day's events in the newspaper gave readers a view of blacks as violent and lawless, "In sum, the reports amounted to a time-honored tactic of branding blacks lawless and of using the press to put them in their so-called place (2000:15)."

To further disquiet Wilmington whites, on the same day, August 18, 1941, the U.S. Army made arrangements to house 500 black soldiers who were to serve as stevedores at an Army supply depot in Wilmington. They were billeted on federal property adjacent to a predominantly white neighborhood school. The City Manager told the *Wilmington Morning Star* that

> "We were given no notification of any kind and did not even know until told by newsmen. . . . We are already having trouble with negro troops from Camp Davis and I am afraid if this kind of thing continues there is going to be even more."

Dosher points out that adjacent to the article quoting the City Manager was an article about a black soldier who attacked a white girl. The headline read: "Police Abandon Attacker Hunt, 15-Year-Old Fights Off Negro On Lonely Road Near Camp Davis." On the following page I found an article with the headline "N.Y. Negroes Die In Mad Stampede." The sensational article read:

> . . . about 10,000 pleasure-seeking negroes were stampeded by rumors that their $1.25 Hudson river excursion tickets were bogus. The care-free crowd clad in their colorful "Sunday best" and in high good humor, was transformed within minutes into a mauling, milling maelstrom of fighting humanity as word spread that some held counterfeit tickets for the ship that could carry fewer than one-third their number.

In his 1943 publication *Race and Rumors of Race,* Howard Odum labels rumors circulating in the South at this time that portrayed blacks as unrestrained. According to Odum, there was a "universal rumor appraisal that Negroes could not become soldiers, that they would not obey, that they would run before the battle, and that they would shoot their officers. . . .

that when the Negro soldier returned he would be dangerous both in his aspirations and in his training as a fighter (Odum 1943:54)." Odum's 'cata-
logue of rumors' recapture, he says, the "tensions of the past"—variations
on the old theme of black men seizing white women circulated widely
throughout Virginia, North Carolina, South Carolina and Georgia. Two
prevailing North Carolina rumors circulating during the early war years
were that: "Negro men were all planning to have white wives when all the
white men have gone to war as the white women will be left for the Negro
men;" and "Every Negro man will have a white girl when the white boys go
off to war." The Wilmington paper seemed to be echoing these rumors.

What fueled these rumors? In her book, *The Color of the Law*, Gail
O'Brien (1999) argues that World War II created feelings of greater efficacy,
entitlement and esteem in black Americans resulting in a changed voice and
demeanor, and in greater frustration in the way in which black Americans
felt they were being treated. Odum's work cites rumors about Eleanor
Clubs—clubs which allegedly developed by blacks in towns where Eleanor
Roosevelt had spoken. Rumors claimed that Eleanor Roosevelt "goes
around telling the Negroes they are as good as anyone else (Odum
1943:81)." The Clubs were said to make "Negroes discontented, making
them question their status (Odum 1943:73)." One rumor in North Carolina
at the time attested to black organization against unfair labor practices, " . . .
all the colored maids at a hotel joined Eleanor Clubs and walked out in a
body one day because their pay and hours did not suit." Another North
Carolina rumor about 'uppity blacks' circulated during this time (Odum
1943:74):

> Why all the Negroes are getting so "uppity" they won't do a thing. I hear
> the cooks have organized Eleanor Clubs and their motto is: A White
> woman in every kitchen by Christmas.

A variation on another prominent rumor recounted throughout the South
eventually appearing in comic strips went like this:

> A white woman asked a Negro woman to do her laundry for her. The
> Negro woman replied, "All right, you come and wash for me one week
> and I'll do yours the next."

Tales of black women walking in the front door of their white employer's
homes and calling their employers by their first name reflected the way
whites perceived the new sense of efficacy and entitlement blacks felt due to
the war for democracy.

The racial trouble in Wilmington in August 1941 may reflect some of the issues raised by Odum and O'Brien. Whites in Wilmington began publicly to express their concern over the melee and the billeting of black soldiers near a white school. In addition, an event that had been planned prior to the Brooklyn riot, Negro Soldier Day, was advertised in the newspaper on August 17, to be held the following Sunday. Whites in Wilmington were feeling very uneasy. On August 19, 1941, the *Wilmington Morning Star* quoted the white register of deeds for New Hanover County, Adrian Rhodes, saying:

> We haven't forgotten the race riots of 1898, when there was so much trouble between whites and negroes. I am afraid there eventually will be some serious trouble here if something isn't done to prevent disorders that have occurred here recently.

Should the black soldiers, or 'outsiders,' be unaware of the history of race relations in Wilmington, this cautionary tale provided a quick lesson, as well as a reminder to local blacks. A local white attorney, Cyrus D. Hogue, told the *Wilmington Morning Star* on August 20, 1941, that:

> Several of our outstanding negro citizens have told me they are greatly perturbed over the situation. They fear that the activities of the soldiers will adversely affect the decent law-abiding citizens of their race.

The black community organized to ease the mounting tensions in the city. "Negro Soldier Day" went off as planned, with each soldier being 'signed off' to a family, church or civic group who served as sponsors for the day, most of which were located in Brooklyn where the melee occurred less than two weeks prior. Meals in homes and churches took place, along with a church service and community baseball game, followed by musical entertainment at Williston Industrial School. More than 3,000 soldiers attended the day's activities. The *Wilmington Morning Star* heralded the success of the day. Reaves (1998:369) argues that "efforts like this one stemmed the tide of disorderly conduct and problems between civilians and servicemen. Thereafter, servicemen behaved themselves and were welcome in the city."

The influx of 'outsiders' during the war years may have made local white elite in Wilmington feel as if it were necessary to summon the 1898 cautionary tale for black soldiers and especially for local blacks who could potentially be influenced and encouraged by outsiders; thus explaining Hogue's warning that "our blacks" know what happens when racial caste lines are crossed.

Two years later, in the summer of 1943, North Carolina Governor Joseph Broughton gave a speech at the shipyard at the launching of the Liberty Ship *John Merrick*. John Merrick, born a slave in Sampson County, North Carolina, became the first president of North Carolina Mutual Life Insurance Company, which at his death in 1919 was one of the wealthiest companies in North Carolina. Broughton's speech praised the success of North Carolina's "foremost Negro" and the progress North Carolina had made in the advancement of its black citizens. On the launching podium with the governor that day was John Merrick's daughter, who christened the vessel, and her three companions, also black women from Durham. The wives of twelve black shipyard workers, who assisted in making preparations for the launching of the *S.S. John Merrick* represented the black employees of the Wilmington shipyard. An all-black thirty-five piece band from the U.S. Navy Pre-Flight School at the University of North Carolina provided the music. In addition, Broughton was accompanied on stage by black leaders C. C. Spaulding of the North Carolina Mutual Life Insurance Company and Dr. James E Shepard, president of North Carolina College for Negroes.[28]

Attendance at the launchings was by invitation only, and size of the launching crowds varied considerably. Photographs of the first launching at the shipyard of the Liberty ship *Zebulon Vance*, also led by Governor Broughton just two years earlier, drew a remarkably large crowd with several hundred people attending (Broughton refers to thousands attending the launching in his subsequent speech). The governor may have been expecting a similar crowd to hear his speech, though later photographs in the publication *Shipbuilding News* show crowds at a 'typical' launching in which fewer than a hundred people were in attendance. I have not been able to determine how many people attended the *Merrick* launching, and the newspaper article the following day does not provide an estimation of the crowd size.

The governor's speech raised concerns about racial strife, stressing the harmonious race relations in the state of North Carolina. Broughton borrowed from a speech Merrick once made to illustrate the point of positive race relations:

> . . . In the same speech, mindful of the fact that there were radical Negro leaders in his day even as there are today, more intent up on stirring up racial strife than in building constructively, Merrick said:

> "Now don't the writers of the race jump on the writer and try to solve my problem. Mine is solved. I solved mine by learning to be courteous to those that courtesy was due, working and trying to save and properly appropriate what I made."

The governor then reminded his audience of November 10, 1898:

> Forty-five years ago, in the city of Wilmington, where this launching is being held, there occurred the most serious race riot in the history of North Carolina. Blood flowed freely in the streets of this city, feelings ran riot and elemental emotions and bitterness were stirred. We have come a long way since that event. There has been no race riot in North Carolina since that time. There has been only one act of lynching in this State in over twenty years. A record of racial harmony has been made in this State unsurpassed and perhaps unequaled in any state of the American Union.

> . . . We are not unmindful of the fact that delicate situations as between the races exist in certain places in North Carolina, even as they do in other sections, north and south. Certain inflammatory newspapers and journals, white and Negro, are dangerously fanning the flame of racial antagonism in America today. There are individuals and groups in certain quarters, including the National Capital, who are seeking to use the war emergency to advance theories and philosophies which, if carried to their ultimate conclusion, would result only in a mongrel race (a condition abhorrent alike to right-thinking citizens and leaders of both races.

> We are striving in North Carolina to give the Negro equal protection under the law, equal educational advantages, the full benefits of public health, agricultural advancement, decent housing conditions and full and free economic opportunity. This is our honest and determined purpose; and it is being carried out. This is the assured path toward racial harmony and progress, not only in North Carolina but in all America.

> In the launching of this ship bearing the honored name, John Merrick, it is fervently hoped that the life and character of this great man may be brought freshly to the minds of both races in North Carolina and indeed in America; that in the light of his wholesome philosophy and successful career we may find a path of harmony, success, victory and peace through mutual respect and honest cooperation.

Though the governor summoned the cautionary tale of 1898 it is interesting that the news coverage in the *Wilmington Morning Star* the following day did not report this part of the speech. In a lengthy article entitled "Broughton Points Way To Future of Negroes" the newspaper highlighted the following excerpts:

> We are striving in North Carolina to give the Negro equal educational advantages," . . . (in entirety as above)

The article lists efforts

... in behalf of Negro welfare; many of which represent works achieved
during his administration: 1. nine months schools for Negroes, as well
as whites, with free transportation and textbooks; 2. supplementing
salaries of Negro teachers by more than $1,000,000; 3. improvements
in the North Carolina college for Negroes and elevation of the institution to accredited "A" standing, etc.[29]

There is much ground for speculation as to why the governor chose to remind his audience of the 1898 violence. Broughton had a very real purpose
that day, regardless of the fact that the reference to 1898 was not picked up
by the newspaper. Given that he had not referred to 1898 in his launching
on the same spot a year and a half prior, it seems the governor had something on his mind. Was it simply because he was launching a ship named
after a black man? Or were there other factors?

Tyson (1998), Godwin (2000) and Dosher (2000) suggest the governor's remarks had to do with concomitant racial tension in other parts of the
state like Erwin and Durham. While this probably did fuel his concern, the
Wilmington shipyard itself was a far greater worry. The North Carolina
Shipbuilding Company at Wilmington was decidedly anti-union, and had
created a company union, Cape Fear Shipbuilding Association (CFA), in response to AFL/CIO attempts at organization in their yard. According to
Scott (1979:76) the North Carolina Shipbuilding Company (NCSB) tried to
bar AFL/CIO members resulting in a citation for unfair labor practices with
the National Labor Relations Board (NLRB). In late December 1941 the
Congress of Industrial Organizations (CIO) on behalf of the Industrial
Union of Marine Shipbuilding Workers of America (IUMSWA) notified the
North Carolina Shipbuilding Company that IUMSWA claimed majority rep-
resentation at the yard. Scott (1979) traces the development of the labor dis-
putes at the Wilmington yard, citing an IUMSWA publication, the *Shipyard
Worker,* which outlines wage discrepancies between workers at NCSB in
Wilmington and union wages at IUMSWA yards:

> "Men in North Carolina yard lose up to $42 weekly. Anglesmith NCSB
> rate $47.60, IUMSWA rate $81.60" ... and painters received fifty-eight
> cents an hour at NCSB, while CIO yards paid $1.20 according to the
> *Shipyard Worker.*

In September 1942 IMUSWA filed formal unfair labor practice charges
against North Carolina Shipbuilding Company, under the Wagner Act (Scott
1979:78). The trial began October 15, 1942, and lasted until November 3,
1942. IUMSWA accused NCSB of dismissing seven employees because they
were CIO members and that ...

> [NCSB] . . . had by their officers, agents and employees [sic] formed, dominated and interfered with the operation of and administration of, and contributed financial and other support to labor organizations among their employees known as the . . . Cape Fear Shipbuilders Association (Scott 1979:79).

The National Labor Review Board examiner listed seven violations of the Wagner Act at NCSB including

> . . . NCSB official had urged members to join the company Cape Fear Union, had threatened to discharge members of the CIO. The company had in addition made "disparaging remarks" about the CIO union and had grilled employees on their CIO activities. Employees were also promised better working conditions if they withdrew from the CIO union and prospective employees were told that CIO men had been fired in the past. It was alleged that prior union activity was a cause for non-employment (Scott 1979:79).

During the testimonies in the Fall of 1942, further stories of intimidation and coercion on the part of North Carolina Shipbuilding management towards CIO members surfaced. Witnesses testified they had been instructed to act as 'spies' for NCSB and to report on CIO activity in the yard. One witness said that Bruce Cameron, mayor and director of NCSB, told him to "do all he could do to keep the union out of the shipyard (Scott 1979:81)."

The trial resulted in NCSB pulling out its influence in the Cape Fear Union, which in essence dismantled the union altogether, only to be recreated under the name "United Shipbuilders of America." The NLRB report called for the rehiring of the CIO men who had been fired, and cessation of discrimination against the IUMSWA.

Labor problems continued at the yard, though. The Liberty shipbuilding contracts peaked in 1943, and as Scott (1979) points out, the switch to C-2 shipbuilding brought dismissals at the yard. Again IUMSWA and CIO claimed unfair dismissals of union workers. The summer of 1943 (the summer the governor launched the *Merrick)* was marked by NCSB stalling tactics in response to an IUMSWA call for a recognition election. The day after the governor spoke, July 12, 1943, the NLRB ruled that an election should be held to determine if collective bargaining representation should be through the CIO, AFL or USA, or no union representation. The September 3, 1943 election results, in which 11,210 workers out of an eligible 14,800 voted, 6628 voted for no union. IUMSWA petitioned NLRB, filing an objection on the election procedures, saying that NCSB employees were

> . . . subjected to physical violence and threats of violence by other em-
> ployees of the Company who had . . . been given free rein by the com-
> pany . . . on behalf of the Cape Fear and United Shipbuilders. He
> [IUMSWA representative] stated that the mayor of Wilmington, "one
> Cameron had promised that every person participating in activities to
> keep the CIO out of the yard . . . would be well taken care of."

By June 1944 IUMSWA filed an unfair labor practice charge with the NLRB
and by early January 1945 the CIO had entered into one of the longest unfair labor practice hearings in the history of the NLRB with a total of 668
witnesses (Scott 1979). Trial testimony pointed to more NCSB intimidation
towards CIO members. The organizer for the Cape Fear Union, Richard
Shew, testified that Bruce Cameron told him to "get rid of all CIO men even
if it meant getting them put in the draft."[30] Shew also stated that he was employed as a machinist but that most of his work was spent as organizer for
the Cape Fear Union and that he reported directly to Bruce Cameron. Other
testimony confirmed unfair labor practices towards CIO members, which
included coercion to leave town, as well as violence (beatings) against CIO
members. Testimony also pointed to USA (the former "Cape Fear Union")
organizers playing the 'race card' in recruitment practices. As cited in Scott
(1979:111)

> James Bass stated that a USA organizer told him, "I want you to join the
> USA. If the CIO comes in, you will have a colored boss, and white peo-
> ple will be forced to work with colored people." Bass was terminated
> shortly after he refused to join the USA. Bass was called by assistant
> foreman Pully "nothing but a CIO lover" prior to his discharge.

The labor dispute continued at the yard until 1946 when NCSB agreed to a
back pay settlement, yet the company never admitted culpability in its unfair labor practices.

To whom was Broughton directing the cautionary tale that afternoon
at the launching of the *Merrick?* I think there are at least two ways to read
Broughton's warning. First, the launching of a ship named after an affluent
African American prompted Broughton to remind African Americans of
their place, or the limits to their success, despite the increased feelings of efficacy and entitlement during this period. Secondly, the labor issues at the
shipyard and the suppression of union activity had to be on Broughton's
mind. Cape Fear Union organizers, the union sponsored by the shipyard
owners, used race as means to pull support away from the CIO which
brought unfair labor practices charges against the shipyard. If race or reminder's of racial violence could be used to intimidate blacks, why not to

intimidate whites who join forces with blacks in labor sympathy? I interviewed an African-American man in his eighties who explained:

> Shipyard. Only thing about blacks is you had no welder. No black welders. Shippers were black and white, cutting steel. We had black and white in my department. And most had, it was more integrated than anything else. Blacks never did complain about that job they got busy making their money. They tried to get unions there, in the middle of it. The shipyard paid good money, and Wilmington always wanted to keep wages down. No you talk about Right to Work Law, that's just to keep wages down. You do all the work but you get less wages. And so Wilmington has always been against organized labor.

At the same time Broughton was giving his speech, a black woman, Mamie Williamson, was arrested for a Jim Crow bus violation, in which she refused to give up her seat in the front of a bus. While other incidents of Jim Crow violations were reported during the War years, Mamie Williamson's arrest stands out as it stimulated interest outside Wilmington.[31] A letter from Duke University Professor H. Shelton Smith to the governor shortly after the Williamson arrest asked Governor Broughton to investigate the case:

> My dear Governor Broughton:
>
> Doubtless you are fully apprised of the alleged brutal beating of Mrs. Annie [sic] Williamson in Wilmington on July 11th. Such evidence was submitted to the local Recorder's Court is reported as showing that Mrs. Williamson was acting within her legal right when she took a seat near the front of the bus, since all seats back of her were being occupied by colored passengers; nevertheless, she was held guilty by the Court.
>
> Is it not within your power as Governor to have that case carefully investigated? This episode is being heralded as a flagrant case of human injustice. Is this report true or false? If the agents of the law were acting extralegally in that episode, they should be dealt with accordingly and swiftly. On the other hand, if they were not guilty from the point of view of law, they should be exonerated from false charges.
>
> But even if the authorities did act under the law in ousting the woman from the particular seat, what right did they have (if the facts be correctly reported) to mete out to her brutal treatment? In any event I sincerely hope that in the interest of equal justice and of truth you will have the case thoroughly investigated and the true facts published.
>
> Sincerely yours
> H. Shelton Smith
> Professor of Christian Ethics and
> Director of Graduate Studies in Religion

The Governor wrote the mayor of Wilmington asking him to look into the case. Actually, the governor sent two letters, and the mayor, Bruce Cameron, responded close to two weeks later indicating he had been out of town, and then ill and was recuperating at the beach when he wrote. Cameron,[32] a wealthy businessman and landowner, as well as Director of the North Carolina Shipbuilding Company and member of the New Hanover Defense Council which recruited the shipbuilding contract, provided the Governor with documentation from the Chief of Police which "will prove to you conclusively that this woman was in the wrong." The police report said that Mrs. Williamson resisted, delayed and hindered arrest for Jim Crow violations and it defended the action of the policemen who arrested her, claiming that Mrs. Williamson "lost her bridgework during a scuffle." The police chief explains in a letter to Mr. Cameron that the arresting officer, "has denied striking her with his fist or unmercifully beating her. He states that he only used such force as was necessary to subdue the prisoner and keep her in his custody."

In the course of an interview with an African American woman in her eighties I asked if she remembered the incident. She responded, "Sure did. They beat her up unmercifully. Sure I remember it."

Cameron offers this commentary on race relations in Wilmington at the time:

> It seems the Negroes are ready and willing at all times to go en masse to the Court House to try a case and the Negro newspapers are just as ready to write up a story of the trial in any way they see fit, almost always, entirely different from the evidence given in the Court.
>
> We have had tremendous difficulty with the Jim Crow law as the bus driver has to turn around and drive to the City Hall when there is a case of violation and most times, just before arriving at the jail, the offender jumps up and moves back and then has witness to prove the bus driver wrong.

Cameron then tells the governor:

> I do not like the tone of the editorial of the Durham paper and I hope you will tell them as long as you are Governor the colored people will have to behave themselves.[33]

The letter is signed by Cameron's secretary and is accompanied by the report from the Chief of Police, the Complaint Report, the Judgment Order, and a copy of the Statutes on Jim Crow violations.

The 1940s were marked by the tremendous change brought to Wilmington by the war and shipbuilding. The influx of newcomers, the rumors of race, along with the increased social space for blacks and greater efficacy and feeling of entitlement prompted white Wilmingtonians to summon the cautionary tale of 1898. Most importantly labor disputes at the shipbuilding yard threatened the traditional power structure in Wilmington, requiring the governor to summon the cautionary tale—this time for whites as well as blacks. Combined with Odum's findings on the rumors of miscegenation, a great fear of Broughton's which he addresses not only in the speech above but in subsequent letters and addresses,[34] as well as the 1941 racial consternation the Camp Davis soldiers elicited, the climate of change in Wilmington most probably precipitated the governor's evoking of the cautionary tale.

1951

There are two public references to 1898 during 1951, both serving as 'cautionary tales.' The first occurred in response to a campaign to equalize black and white schools in Wilmington. The second in response to an academic publication that advanced a different version of the events in 1898, in essence a challenge to the dominant narrative.

The population of Wilmington ebbed from its war time high to 45,043 by 1950. African Americans comprised 36 percent of the city's population. The median family income in Wilmington was $2,241.00; the median income for non-white families in 1950 was $1,080.00, whereby 44 percent of non-white families' income fell below $1000.00, and 80 percent fell below $2,000.00.[35] Godwin (2000) characterizes the 1950s in Wilmington as a time of growing awareness of civil rights among black citizens. The school equalization campaign described below generated widespread support in the black community and provided the seeds for later civil rights organization.

In late 1950, two Wilmington physicians, Dr. Hubert Eaton and Dr. D.C. Roane, both black and neither native to Wilmington, launched a campaign to equalize white and black schools in New Hanover County. With the help of legal counsel outside Wilmington, they requested from the Board of Education permission to inspect black and white schools in the county to "investigate whether or not the colored school children are being afforded an education inferior to that being provided for white children (Eaton 1984:42)." The response to the request, signed by superintendent of schools and chairman of the board of education, read:

> We have never had presented to the Board of Education of this county any complaint from the colored citizens of this community as to discrimination between the colored and white schools in respect of the matters

mentioned in your letter. Until such a complaint is made by local interested parties to the Board of Emulation we feel that an investigation by
attorneys from another state representing anonymous clients . . . would
be disruptive of the friendly relationship which has existed for many
years between the colored and white people of his community and
would serve no useful purpose . . . We are confident that we can show
substantial equality of treatment of colored and white pupils in the
school system of this county.

In his 1984 autobiography, Eaton says

The reference to "friendly relations" between colored and white people
was without doubt veiled intimidation based on the race riot of 1898,
which resulted in the murder of some colored citizens and the banish-
ment of others from the city; still others were frightened out of town. . . .
The terrorism applied by Wilmington whites in the ensuing turmoil
frightened the colored community into pitiful docility. It was not sur-
prising, therefore, that our public challenge to the establishment, the
first such action in over a half century, caused concern to the board of
education.

Eaton and Roane then established the Wilmington Committee on
Negro Affairs, a small group in which they presided as co-chairs. Eaton says,

Our most difficult task was the development of an adequate list of petitioners and potential plaintiffs. Most colored citizens who worked in
homes in the white community or in white-owned businesses feared they
would lose their jobs as reprisal for any efforts they might make toward
racial justice. Those older citizens who remembered the race riot of
1898 also feared for their safety, as did many younger members of the
colored community who had heard tales of the riot from their parents
and grandparents. Years of telling may have magnified the event.

On March 6, 1951, the New Hanover County school board agreed
to meet with the petitioners and according to Eaton about twenty-five
black citizens attended. Godwin (2000:65) sets the white attendance at
one hundred. In his autobiography, Eaton (1984:44) recalls the school
board meeting:

As Negro citizens slowly filled the meeting room to face the all-white
board of education, I instinctively perceived an atmosphere of
hypocrisy. There was an open show of amicability and an overabun-
dance of politeness, but this could not erase from the minds of those
present the fact that this was the first public confrontation between
white and Negro since the infamous race riot of 1898.

Citing minutes from the Wilmington City Council, Godwin (2000:65) provides a quote from the school board's attorney, Cyrus Hogue, in which the attorney indicated that a lawsuit on behalf of blacks might unsettle Wilmington's "fifty three years of good race relations."[36] In his autobiography Eaton wrote:

> Near the close of the meeting the school board attorney, Mr. Hogue, alluded to the race riots of 1898. However innocuous his intention, his statement was inescapably interpreted as an effort to intimidate—to warn that it could happen again.

The board denied permission to inspect schools, and Eaton's group filed a suit against the New Hanover County Board of Education on March 12, 1951. The school equalizing campaign resulted in a three million dollar bond issue the following year of which close to one million dollars went to improvements in Wilmington black schools, the other two million to white school improvements. More importantly, Godwin (2000) argues, the school equalization campaign marked the onset, if small, of collective action by black community members in Wilmington toward a general civil rights campaign.

One of the final public references to the 'Revolution of 1898' also occurred in 1951 in response to the University of Chapel Hill's publication of Helen Edmonds' *The Negro and Fusion Politics in North Carolina*. The publisher's press release ran in the *Wilmington Morning Star* on May 27, 1951:

> The "white supremacy" political campaign of 1898, with its resulting reign of terror and bloodshed in Wilmington, is given full and objective treatment in "the Negro and Fusion Politics in North Carolina" published by the University of North Carolina press yesterday.
>
> Written by Dr. Helen G. Edmonds, professor of history at North Carolina college, this work is a re-evaluation of the period of fusion politics, 1894–1901. The author tells how the era of bitterness reaches its climax in a bloody race riot in Wilmington, where according to eye-witnesses, throughout the day of December 10, 1898 "streets were dotted with dead bodies . . . rioters went from house to house looking for Negroes and killing them, and poured volleys into fleeing Negroes like sportsmen firing at rabbits."
>
> According to the author several white men were wounded and about 30 Negroes killed on that day.

Local historian Louis T. Moore, Chairman of the New Hanover Historical Commission, and former Director of the Wilmington Chamber of Commerce, was outraged by the publication of the book. Moore was born and raised in Wilmington and was thirteen at the time of the 1898 violence. He responded to the Edmond's publication with a summer-long campaign to discredit the contents of the book. His first letter, dated May 30, 1951, was to the President of the University of North Carolina. It begins:

> Dear Dr. Gray
>
> One is inclined to speculate and wonder just what activated the management of the University of North Carolina Press in accepting for publication the book. "The Negro and Fusion Politics in North Carolina," written by a Dr. Helen Edmonds. This woman is doing racial relationships no possible good in this state by reviving and discussing conditions which developed ill will, bitterness and conflict more than a half century ago.
>
> Just why it is not definitely stated in the review by George Scheer, sent to state papers last Sunday, that North Carolina College at Durham, of which the author is said to be a faculty member, is a Negro institution and not a part of the University of North Carolina proper, is hard to comprehend.
>
> The assumption is that this Dr. Edmonds is a Negress. It is said she is a graduate of Morgan College, at Baltimore, a Negro institution, and that she is a faculty member of the state supported North Carolina college for the colored race, at Durham. If she is of the Negro race, certainly that is nothing to her discredit. Whether she is colored or white, however, doesn't excuse her references to the Wilmington event of 1898. It was distinctly a REVOLUTION [emphasis original] and not a race riot as she terms it. Her general statements are inflammatory, not in accord with real facts, distorted and sensational. They certainly are of a caliber calculated to disturb the present pleasant and agreeable racial relations which exist in North Carolina.
>
> Since this Dr. Edmonds has produced an inexcusable and disturbing first chapter as regards the happenings here, then a second chapter by one interested in the preservation of good feelings between the races certainly may be in order.
>
> To judge from the review of the book sent out by Mr. Scheer, the totally unjustified and misleading study? disregards some very pertinent facts significantly, this may have been calculated and planned deliberately, since the author teaches in a Negro college and evidently may have been disinclined to outline full facts which led to the Wilmington disturbance of Nov. 10, 1898, and not Dec. 10, as the well informed writer is quoted to have said, at least in one paper.

Mr. Moore continues his letter with eleven 'pertinent facts' that were not included in Edmonds' book. I include the letter in its entirety as it provides an insight into the preeminence of the dominant narrative fifty-three years after its birth. Mr. Moore resumes:

> Just why did she not outline and include some very pertinent facts, among which the following may be noted:
>
> 1. Prior to and during 1898, North Carolina, New Hanover County and Wilmington, particularly, were under the distasteful domination and control of a combination represented by a misguided Negro majority, which was guided and ruled by unprincipled and rascally whites from other sections of the country.
>
> 2. The city and county governments here, and the police force were under full control of the combination just mentioned. White men of good character were arrested by negro policeman for little or no justified reason. They were hauled into local courts presided over by ignorant and power-drunk negro magistrates, and there adjudged, just as a despicable spirit directed. God save the mark for being forced to dignify such legal slaughter pens with the word "court."
>
> 3. Under the baneful influence of the "lily white" renegade, a portion of the negro populace went to the extreme of pushing white ladies in to gutters, and slapped abusing young white children when no white adults were near.
>
> 4. Four months before the Revolution in Wilmington a negro editor of a local weekly paper, A. I. Manly by name, wrote and published a filthy, lying and defamatory editorial impugning the honor and purity of the white women of North Carolina and of the south.
>
> 5. The white men of Wilmington served notice on the negro race that Manly must be banished forthwith.
>
> 6. That instead of delivering an answer in person, to the ultimatum decreeing banishment of the negro editor in 24 hours, an indifferent negro decided the place the reply in the mails. This contemptuous delay was what actually precipitated the Revolution.
>
> 7. That the first shots in the Revolution were fired by negroes and the first one desperately wounded was a white man.
>
> 8. That instead of a wildly exaggerated number of 30 negroes killed as glibly recited by the author of the book, the death list did not exceed eight or nine, based on coroner's investigation and reports.
>
> 9. That the following day the white men of Wilmington assumed charge of the city government, the former alderman composed of negroes and "lily whites" resigning as directed. Then these white renegades were marched through the streets to the railroad station, placed on a train and ordered never to return.

10. Following departure of the renegades, who were largely responsible for the Revolution, the white men of Wilmington sent squads in the suburbs to tell many of the frightened negroes they could return to their homes and would be given full protection.

11. That when several hundred negro stevedores, who were ignorant of what was happening, gathered at a down town street corner and not knowing what the trouble really was all about, a white commander threatened to jail several white men under his command. They were demanding that orders be given to fire upon the negroes. The commander replied by telling them no such order would be given and if they did not take their proper places in line within one minute they would be incarcerated.

The foregoing outline represents just a few of many points which can be advanced in reply to the useless, senseless and unjustified book produced by this female author. The general effect of her production will be only to mislead and disturb pleasant existing racial relations.

It has been a half century ago that white men properly got control of their government state, county and municipal, paid for with their taxes. Prior thereto government here especially had been a shameful disgrace. It had existed, and had been a shameful disgrace as influenced and operated under the domination for some men whose skins were white but whose hearts were black or that the sins which actuated and prompted them to mislead the negro race.

Possibly this female writer will not be able to comprehend the infinite harm which may result from publication of her book. In like manner she undoubtedly will lack willingness to realize that the attitude of whites here to the negro race is well illustrated by a recent incident. Several weeks ago three young white boys saved the life of a little negro boy at Greenfield Lake. Through their Boy Scouts training they resuscitated him after he had been taken from the bottom of the lake, apparently dead after ten minutes submersion.

Or maybe she and other who think as she does, just cannot comprehend the attitude of several prominent white men in Wilmington just now in helping Rev. D. L. Grady, a prominent and esteemed negro minister, to arrange details for the formal dedication of a recreational camp for colored children of this area. The date for this dedication is June 10. These same white men have invited Dr. T.C. Johnson, Commissioner of Paroles for North Carolina, to deliver the principal address. He has accepted the invitation. This joint dedicatory service between Grady, his daughter, an intelligent and cultured colored school teacher, other leading colored citizens, and supported unreservedly by interested and cooperative white citizens, will launch a very fine institution. It will render intelligent and needed service to young colored children, supported with moral and influential support of leaders of the white race.

So much for this feeble effort, in answer to many indigent requests from people here, to give a necessary reply to this book dealing with "Fusion." It will undoubtedly lead to "Con-Fusion" and misunderstanding between the white and negro races.

Many here think the University Press has rendered an unjustified and inexcusable disservice to this section of North Carolina particularly, in practically endorsing, through publication, a book undoubtedly conceived in racial rancor, and produced without adherence to full fact and complete truth.

Alumni and supporters of the University of North Carolina rejoice in the temperate, conciliatory and cooperative statements and objectives you outlined in your address accepting the Presidency of the Institution.

While it may require many years to eradicate objectionable trends which have manifested themselves in and about the University during the past quarter of a century, you are entitled to, and should receive the untinted support and confidence of every right thinking man in North Carolina who would like to see under your competent, conscientious and sacrificing guidance, a restoration of the thoughts, ideals and aspirations of a half century ago.

Please pardon this lengthy missive. It has been sent following suggestions and urging of many people here who feel that the book referred to above does this area a gross injustice.

> With cordial good wishes,
> Sincerely yours,
> Louis T. Moore, Chairman,
> New Hanover Historical Commission

Copy to

Editors, Wilmington Star-Raleigh News & Observer-Charlotte Observer-Greensboro Daily News—State Department Archives and History—President North Carolina College, Durham; Reverend G. I. Grady

We learn several things from Moore's ardent letter: firstly, that the initial white version, or dominant narrative endured for fifty-three years; secondly, that by 1951 white Wilmingtonians were loath to have a version of the past imposed on them by someone outside their ranks especially given that Edmonds' version tested the legitimacy of the dominant narrative; and clearly, the fact that Edmonds was black *and* female raised even greater indignation at the publication of a contradictory version of the dominant narrative. Study, for example, Moore's language in reference to Edmonds. The third paragraph is devoted to her inferior qualifications: "She is a Negress"; a graduate of a Negro institution; a faculty member at a Negro institution;

and later a "female writer." Yet, more telling perhaps is Moore's language for other blacks, particularly those in *his* community. Moore's usage of Negro or more typically lower-cased 'negro' shifts to the less-severe and more polite term 'colored,' " . . . Reverend Grady, his daughter, an intelligent and cultured colored school teacher, other leading colored citizens." This paternalistic sentiment is not unlike the 1941 reminder from Cyrus Hogue that 'our blacks' are disquieted by 'outside' blacks who do not understand the way relations between whites and blacks are carried out in Wilmington; the assumption is that local blacks understand the way things are, and 'outsiders' only cause trouble. Moore provides 'evidence' to support his view that local blacks 'understand' these relations. In a subsequent letter written by Moore, this time to Lambert Davis, the Director of the University of North Carolina Press, three weeks after the letter to Dr. Gray above, Moore writes:

> . . . . Already there has come one harmful result from the publicity she has resurrected from its burial place of a half century and more. That is a spirit of apprehension and fear among the colored people here. The white element has hoped that such would forever remain interred and forgotten. This is evidenced by an editorial within the past two weeks carried in the local Negro weekly. Its gist is, in answer to troubled queries whether new dissension is brewing, that racial harmony and good will still prevail here. The editorial stresses that in the effort to keep history straight, representatives of the white race merely adhered to a duty, not failing to endeavor to preserve harmonious and understanding spirit between the races here. It was emphasized that such a condition has existed since the overthrow of the baneful days of Fusion, when evilly inclined white men from the North mislead [sic] and misguided the colored race through political chicanery and deception. So, here it is at least, one unpleasant and unnecessary development, which we apprehended might come to pass, when we sent our letter to Dr. Gray.
>
> Of course, Mr. Davis, your Board of Governors, members of the Press staff, and those qualified to judge the merits of the particular book under discussion, and you, have no conception or idea whatever as to the dreadful conditions which prevailed here in 1898. This was prior to, and following issuance of the despicable and defamatory editorial by the negro, A. L. Manly. This infamous production diabolically attacked the virtue and character of the white women of North Carolina and the South. Hold in mind this would have applied to the mothers and wives of your Board, staff, and of yourself as well, if they had been living here at the time. Nor are any of you in position in this day of 1951 to understand the forced travail, torment and suffering the white people here were forced to undergo under Fusion rule. And for all things the then Governor of North Carolina, Dan Russell lived here, and was one of the

unprincipled white leaders responsible for the eventual Revolution, which occurred.

. . . So these are slight samples of what happened here in the days of Fusion. In intervening years both white and colored people here have tried to forget. Now, recollections have been both resurrected and revived by this book. We must emphasize that we still consider it ill-timed, ill-advised, indefensible, defamatory, and calumniating, insofar as the quoted references to Wilmington, carried in the State press reviews, are concerned. Like Tennyson's brook, which goes on forever, the influence and effects of this book, misrepresentative of, and untruthful against Wilmington, will continue to spread and extend themselves, with no opportunity to present the factual, truthful other side of the case.

All of which, however, and unfortunately will generate nothing in defense of Wilmington, as the volume circulates. We repeat we can see neither reason nor excuse for publication of such a book, a half century after incidents related therein, some of which are untruthful, have been buried and forgotten in the minds of both races here. Again, we wonder what possible good could have been expected to result from it, in connection with approval of the Board of Governors, or other representatives of the University Press.

Borrowing slogans and battle cries from the past, Moore appealed to the sexualized rhetoric that Democrats used in 1898 to stake his allegation, " . . . diabolically attacked the virtue and character of white women. . . . Hold in mind this would have applied to the mothers and wives of your Board, staff, and of yourself as well . . ." And like the tradition of the dead generations before him, Moore pulled out his trump card—the race card, " . . . the torment and suffering the white people here were forced to undergo" [because they were dominated by blacks]. The success of the dominant narrative up to that point had been in the way it had mutated and transformed. Its organizing principle was that of safeguarding liberty via the myth of the 'Revolution.' White Wilmingtonians had been able to call upon this narrative as a cautionary tale, yet with the public release of an alternate version—a counter-narrative—the myth of the "revolution," constructed to conceal the undemocratic moment, had been exposed. Moore's commitment to the portrayal of 1898 as a "Revolution" expressed the intensity of the challenge to the dominant narrative. The war years in Wilmington expanded, to some degree, the economic and social space of its black citizens and, as O'Brien argues, their feelings of efficacy and entitlement. Edmonds' public counter-narrative, along with recent organization by blacks in the community toward school equalization, contested the narrative dominance of the "revolution" and "progress" motifs and the ideological distortions they masked.

One respondent I interviewed, a black middle-class woman who knew Dr. Edmonds told me:

> I do remember that Dr. Helen G. Edmonds, a professor from North Carolina Central—she was writing on Fusion politics. When she went to the public library, I heard this straight from her, they told her any material regarding 1898 was under lock and key and they were not supposed to move it out of there until they got the OK from some of the city fathers. And I don't think she ever got the material. She had to go to New York, she had to research elsewhere to get the material. Because then it was hush-hush, we don't want you to know about this period of Wilmington's life—existence. I heard her say that.

On June 1, 1951, the *Wilmington Morning Star* ran an article outlining Moore's grievances, and in so doing provided another opportunity to provide a tolling of the dominant narrative:

> Louis T. Moore, chairman of the New Hanover County Historical Commission, yesterday mailed a letter to University of North Carolina President Gordon Gray protesting the version of the Wilmington race disturbance of 1898 published in a book by a woman professor at North Carolina College, Durham.
>
> Moore said many Wilmingtonians feel that the University Press, which published the work by Dr. Helen Edmonds, has "rendered an unjustifiable and inexcusable disservice to this section." He also pointed out what he termed a number of misstatements of historical facts by the woman historian.
>
> Moore listed 10 points of protest against the book, "The Negro and Fusion Politics in North Carolina." He said the book would lead to "con-Fusion" and misunderstanding between the white and Negro races.
>
> The county historian maintained that the disturbances, which occurred on November 10, 1898, was [sic] a "revolution" and not a "race riot," as Dr. Edmonds wrote.
>
> Copies of the letter were mailed to newspapers here and in Raleigh, Charlotte, and Greensboro, the State Department of Archives and History, the president of North Carolina College in Durham, and the Rev. D.L. Grady, leading Negro minister here.

Moore's fevered public letters tell us about other incensed citizens who felt threatened by a public counter-narrative that challenged their dominant version that heretofore had not been publicly contested. A letter in the Louis T. Moore Collection at the New Hanover Public Library dated June 2, 1951 supports Moore in his protest against the Edmonds' publication:

Dear Louis

Thank you very much. We have read this carefully together and are with you in condemning this writer—or anyone who throws hindrances in the way of the sincere work we are trying to make towards race harmony.

Yours cordially,
Susan E. Hall
820 Princess Street Wilmington North Carolina

As Moore points out, the only black newspaper in Wilmington responded with an editorial entitled "No Cause For Alarm:"

Many persons have asked this newspaper editor if he attached any undo significance to the two articles on the Riot of 1898 which appeared within two days in the Wilmington Morning Star to which we replied, Emphatically No! And we repeat it here! Wilmington enjoys good race relations and we predict a continuance and improvement of the same.

In review, it appears that a woman writer at Chapel Hill wrote a book on "the Negro and Fusion Politics n [sic] North Carolina." Of course she mentioned Wilmington, which at that time found Negroes holding public office. This is not the initial book on the subject; nor may it be the last. For many years, young white students from North Carolina colleges, in writing theses, rave [have] approached us for information on the Riot. We never were able to supply such information, because we did not live here during the Riot. And we have refused to have any literature on the event housed where we conduct out business because we have no desire to be reminded of this unfortunate occurrence. Louis T. Moore, chairman of the New Hanover Historical Commission, and a friend of this newspaper's states in the second article in the Morning Star, that the author's treatment of the incidents here were "inflammatory." Accordingly, he sought to outline what he termed the "true" story on the Riot.

It is Mr. Moore's duty as historian of our county to "keep the record straight," and because he did, we see no justification of some quarters viewing his action as one of intimidation of the present Wilmington Negro.

Books are written daily as history; and we cannot oppress the views of the authors. But we can, as Mr. Moore did, point out inaccuracies. The release from Chapel Hill was routine and appeared in the entire state press. Its source was not local. Mr. Moore simply answered it.

As we stated, race relations, we view them, are excellent, and we see no reason why they should not continue so. Wilmington is moving on to greater heights. We all want to forget the Riot, which is history. But the country [sic] historian is on safe ground when he does his duty in seeking to prevent the future smearing of our city.

> The JOURNAL is particularly proud of its history in advancing the
> cause of harmonious race relations. We say, with pardonable pride, that
> we have been cited many times for the intelligent, yet forceful manner in
> which we conduct this organ. That it is a proud heritage is attested by
> the fact that the foundation of this newspaper, Robert S. Jervay, has been
> honored locally in that one of the public building has been named in his
> honor, and this primarily for his part played, through this newspaper's
> predecessor, the Cape Fear Journal, in strengthening and increasing bet-
> ter race relations. He did not operate from a soapbox, but in many in-
> stances, some unknown to most folk he smoothed the troubled waters
> in inter-race relations through private conferences with many of the
> leading white citizens of his day. And County Historian Moore can bear
> us out here.
>
> The present day management of the JOURNAL shall continue to es-
> pouse the cause of the American Negro. We shall do every thing with in
> our power to see that justice is done to one-tenth of our total American
> population. But in our promotion of the onward march of our race, we
> shall recognize that of equal importance in the continuation of our slo-
> gan: An Apostle of Inter-racial Goodwill.

Jervay's editorial tells us quite a bit. Firstly we learn that Moore's remarks did cause a commotion in the black community as did the publication of Edmond's book for the white community. The question of whether
or not Moore's "true" account of 1898 served as a cautionary tale may be
answered by Jervay's rejoinder, " . . . we see no justification of some quarters viewing his action as one of intimidation of the present Wilmington
Negro." Whether Jervay saw Moore's retelling of the dominant narrative as
a threat is probably less important than the fact that some blacks in
Wilmington did see it as a means of intimidation. Secondly, it is not clear
that Jervay is supporting Moore, though there seems to be some level of ob-
ligation in his editorial. Jervay writes about Moore, " . . . accordingly, he
sought to outline what he termed the 'true' story on the Riot"—can we ex-
tract from this that there is more than one version of the "true" story—that
Moore's was one version, "what he termed the 'true' story," and perhaps
there are others? Jervay scolds Moore, it seems, when he says " . . . books
are written daily as history; and we cannot oppress the views of the authors" given that Moore sought to have UNC Press rescind the book, or at
least admit it was inaccurate.

Eaton, Jervay and Roane were politically strategizing around this time,
and by January 1952, Eaton had decided to run for Board of Education with
Jervay as publicity chairman and Roane as campaign manager. Eaton recalls
in his autobiography:

The first problem was, again, the ghost of 1898 race riot, with its per-vasive negative influence on colored citizens. Many colored Wilmingtonians had been children during the riot, and a half century later they had fearful memories of it. They had been conditioned and disenfranchised by the repression that followed. In a county with a col-ored population of 23,000 out of a total of 65,000, only 1,800 Negroes were registered to vote. My first task was to persuade other colored cit-izens that the tenor of politics had changed in the past 50 years, and it was now possible to vote without fear of reprisal.

Godwin's (2000:94) analysis of this period finds that Eaton and Jervay be-came increasingly active politically throughout the 1950s focusing on black voter registration. Eaton would run for elected office several times in the 1950s, and Jervay attempted to win a city council seat in 1956—neither suc-cessful. The *Wilmington Journal* was burned down during the Wilmington Ten events in 1971, and no copies of the paper are available today, other than the occasional copy found in attics and donated to the public library; thus there is no way to gauge the tenor of the paper during this time. Godwin's (2000:94) research provides snippets of the *Wilmington Journal's* mission, leading him to conclude that Jervay and Eaton represented an "op-timistic sense of the future" through increased voter registration. In 1954 Jervay's editorial in the *Journal* read:

New Hanover County has a long and honorable record in giving the franchise to the Negro. The shame is ours that we have not taken advan-tage of this heritage. We do not have to fight to vote, but we have had to fight our own people to get them to vote. Many people in Europe would do almost anything to vote. Here, the ballot is ours for the asking.

Eaton, Sloane and Jervay's work marked the beginning of civil rights organ-ization in Wilmington and demands for black citizenship rights, and thus prompted the use of the cautionary tale. Helen Edmonds' book contested the dominant narrative and made public another version of the 1898 event. This period marks the last public reference I found to the dominant narrative. The ideology of Liberalism embodied in values like equality and freedom and represented in the Civil Rights Movement usurped the legitimacy of the dominant narrative, which had dominated Wilmington political conscious-ness since 1898.

1968–1972

This section examines the events surrounding racial violence in Wilmington from 1968 to 1973. Three secondary sources provide excellent background and context for this period in Wilmington's history: Larry Thomas' (1980) master's thesis on the Wilmington Ten; a book by John Godwin (2000) on civil rights protest in Wilmington, North Carolina; and a 1978 article in the *New York Times Magazine* by Wayne King. I also examine local newspaper coverage of the violence. I supplement these with excerpts from interviews I collected from people who lived in Wilmington during this period.

The population of New Hanover County in 1970 was 82,996, an increase of approximately 10,000 since the 1960 Census. African Americans accounted for 23 percent of the County's population. The city of Wilmington proper, however, had a population of 46,169 of whom African Americans comprised 34 percent. Twenty percent of families in Wilmington had incomes below the poverty level. Forty-three percent of African American families in Wilmington had incomes less than the poverty level.

Of the African American males over 25 years of age in Wilmington in 1970, only 23 percent were high school graduates, whereas 28 percent of African-American females over 25 years of age had matriculated from high school. Of the African-American males over 16 in Wilmington, 67 percent were in the labor force; and of the African American females over 16, 46 percent were in the labor force in 1970. The leading occupations for African Americans in 1970 were operatives, service workers, and private household workers (women mostly). Less than 1 percent of African Americans over 16 years of age were in professional occupations.

The material conditions of African Americans in Wilmington in 1969 were palpably deficient. Yet Williston High School had long been a source of pride in the black community and in many ways represented great achievement for the black community in spite of material deprivation. The decision to close "The Best School Under the Sun," as the Williston motto claimed, was made just prior to the beginning of the 1968–69 school year. According to Godwin's (2000:212–258) research, confusion reigned as black students were funneled into the two white high schools. Improper enrollment and scheduling difficulties for black students marked the beginning of the new school year. A retired black administrator with the schools explained:

> The black students never wanted to leave Williston. White students did not want them over at Hoggard. Nothing had been planned over the summer to take care of a student who had won a class presidency at Williston. What was going to happen to that student when there was a senior class president, or sophomore class president? Nothing had been worked out. They had felt rejected and the white students felt trampled upon. And this is the kind of situation we had.

Few of the Williston staff and faculty made the transition to the white schools. Black students comprised about one third of the newly integrated student body, yet lacked mentors and institutional programs to reflect their interests. The closing of Williston became a key point of contention in the black community, in which a resentful air still surrounds.

The transition to integrated schools was particularly difficult in Wilmington. The first year was marked by high absenteeism and violent confrontations between white and black students. Thomas (1980) notes that throughout the summer of 1969, black students voiced their frustration and dissatisfaction with the new arrangements, calling for organized protest in the upcoming school year. In May 1970 violence between black and white students resulted in suspensions–mostly black, according to Godwin (2000:235) and Thomas (1980:35), and after a series of suspensions and more violent run-ins, black high-school students organized a boycott of classes. According to Thomas (1980:38), Christmas school vacation of 1970 was a welcomed period for the parents of black students, many of whom were against the boycott. Many parents hoped the holiday would provide a period of time for emotions to temper. Upon return in January, however, a sit-in was held on school grounds to observe Martin Luther King Jr.'s birthday, given the school board's refusal to provide a school forum remembering King. The students who participated were suspended. Another violent exchange between white and black students occurred a week later in which a black student, Barbara Swain, was cut with a bottle in an altercation with a white male student. More violence followed after Ms. Swain was suspended but the white student was not (Thomas 1980: 39).

Thomas (1980) interviewed Reverend Eugene Templeton, the young white minister of the all-black Gregory Congregational Church, in 1978 about his participation in the Wilmington Ten events. Templeton explains:

> On the afternoon of the Swain incident, a group of students decided to start an alternative school. They went over to the 4th Street Neighborhood Center, but the anti-poverty program directors decided they could not use that building. So, they went to several black ministers in the community, who told them that they thought the idea was ridiculous. Finally, they asked me could they set it up at my church. They said that people were really angry about what was happening. They wanted to set up an alternative school until the board of education would acquiesce to some of their demands. That made a lot of sense to me.

The group of black students at Gregory Congregational Church grew exponentially over the next week and Reverend Templeton contacted Reverend

Leon White of the North Carolina-Virginia Commission for Racial Justice
of the United Church of Christ for support. On February 1, 1971, Ben
Chavis, a staff-member for the Commission for Racial Justice, arrived in
Wilmington to provide leadership for the boycott.

The older black Wilmingtonians who had been active in the 1950s
school equalization campaign remained in the background and did not support the boycott. One participant in the boycott recalled:

> In retrospect, Chavis' arrival was positive. Because before he came we
> were unorganized. Besides, the local so-called 'black leadership' wasn't
> doing anything, except criticizing the boycott. Chavis unified us.[37]

The February 5, 1971, edition of the *Wilmington Morning Star* quotes
Leon White, director of the North Carolina-Virginia Commission for Racial
Justice during his visit to Wilmington:

> "We are here to look into areas where black people are looking for self-
> determination," White said. . . . In describing Wilmington, White said
> there appears to be a vacuum of leadership in the black community, and
> he was here simply to try to pull that leadership together.

On February 2, 1971, Chavis and a group of black high school students issued an announcement declaring a black student class boycott and
petitioning the school board to meet eight demands centering on reinstate-
ment of suspended black students, and greater development of Afro-
American culture on the high school campuses and in the curriculum
(Thomas 1980:40; Godwin 2000: 237; *transcript of WECT telecast*). The
symbolic references to 1898 are worth noting here. Eight demands were
made, echoing the eight demands whites made to blacks in 1898 in the
White Declaration of Independence. A deadline of noon the following day
to have the demands met, or else "we as black students will take further action" struck comparable chords to the ultimatum whites gave blacks on the
night of November 9, 1898 before the bloodletting of November 10 the next
morning. While no direct public reference to 1898 was made by either
blacks or whites during this time, one can speculate that leadership for the
black boycotters was well informed of the events in 1898. I asked a respondent if he recalled people talking about 1898 during this time:

> I came back from college, and spent every summer here. We knew what
> was going on, when they wanted to close Williston we wanted to raise
> hell. And some of us did. It was a done deal. The so-called black leaders
> sold out, basically. I say that and I believe it. They sold out. Some of them

I look at now, and I say, "don't say nothing to me." But it will always be there. They really did! *Do you recall 1898 being mentioned during this time?* 1898 was rarely mentioned during this time, rarely mentioned. Except now, there were families I knew who were directly involved and their grandparents had to run and hide, and things like that. Certain families told me how their parents had to hide, and these people were older now, and I said, I don't believe it, and they said, yea, you know. That was during this time. But for the most part it just stayed in the background.

By February 4, 1971, Chavis and armed followers had ensconced themselves in Gregory Congregational Church and had put up a barricade outside the church to prevent white snipers from firing on them, placing large concrete pipes in front of the church to block traffic (King 1978:70). Rock throwing and armed confrontations between blacks and whites ensued, and eight cases of arson were reported.

The *Wilmington Morning Star* reported that on February 5, 1971, Chavis led a group of between 300 and 400 young black citizens on a march from Gregory Congregational Church to City Hall (about a twelve-block walk) demanding better police protection for blacks in all-black neighborhoods from hostile whites, including policemen.

An article in the *Wilmington Morning Star* on February 7, 1971, headlined, "Police abort white backlash" described the arrest of three white males who were attempting to (invade the black portion of Wilmington" charging them with "going about armed to the terror of the populace." Also discussed in the article was a meeting held by white men with an attendance of about thirty-five to forty in which a participant was quoted as saying, "It's getting so the white people in this town don't have a chance the way the school board and Chief Williamson are giving in to these blacks." Another participant said:

I've got a son at Sunset Park. Things are in pretty bad shape there. Nobody can get an education with all these interruptions and bomb threats. What we need in this town are some dead agitators. They should be shot and left out in the street as a reminder for three days and then bury them. I've got my gun. If two or three more of these men will go with me, I'm ready to get some things straightened out.

A white woman I interviewed recalled the time:

I remember something my father told me. It must have been in the 1970s. Interestingly, my father had come from a good family, and was a northerner, but he had been in the south a while and as an adult, a young adult, I realized my father was somewhat prejudiced. Easy to fall into

categorize people. During the 1970s when we were having the riots and
everything, I remember my father saying, that some of the "boys" had
taken some uppity [pause] nigger, I guess, although I don't know if I ever
heard him say that word, black man, negro, I'll have to think about
what he might have said, and took him out in the woods and taught him
a lesson, or something like that, for these things they were doing, and he
seemed to approve of it, and my father was not a redneck, but it seems
like he sort of—I could just imagine a room full of men of that age
around talking about what.

The cases of arson were directed at businesses owned by whites located in
primarily black neighborhoods. Mike's Grocery, located behind Gregory
Congregational, was firebombed on February 6, 1971. Firefighters and police officers arriving on the scene were shot at by sniper-fire. One white police officer was wounded as he shot at and killed a young black man, Gib
Corbett. The following morning, a white man armed with a pistol was shot
and killed in front of the Gregory Congregational Church. On February 8,
1971, National Guardsmen took over Gregory Church after Chavis and followers fled the night before.

The violence in Wilmington continued until February 9, 1971, marked
by more sniper fire, curfews, more cases of arson, and bombings. The newspaper coverage during this period captures the mood of the city, yet one is
struck by the juxtaposition of front page headlines heralding the excitement
of the Apollo 14 lunar voyage along-side the grim violence engulfing the city
of Wilmington: the new frontier of space and the excitement of the unknown
against the old, familiar terrain of racial violence.

The case against the "Wilmington Ten" developed three months later
and centered on the burning of Mike's Grocery. According to King
(1978:74), a seventeen-year-old black high school student who dropped out
of school after the violence, Allen Hall, was arrested in May 1971 for as-
saulting a teacher and high school students during the protests. Under ques-
tioning he admitted taking part in the arson and shooting at Mike's Grocery.
In an effort to reduce his sentence he identified ten accomplices in the
February 6 arson and shooting: nine black males and one white female who
became known internationally as 'The Wilmington Ten.' King (1978) interviewed a young black man in the late 1970s who told him he participated in
the February 6, 1971 burning of Mike's Grocery, but was never accused of
being there. King believes the story the young man told him was credible and
provides pieces of the interview in his article. The informant told King that

> [Allen] Hall just picked from the top of his head . . . He could have had
> the Wilmington 50. He could have picked a lot of people . . . Let me tell

you what happened. They blamed Chavis for burning Mike's Grocery. Yeah, Hall started the fire. It was under orders. Chavis was there but he wasn't *actually* there, you know? He just gave out directions and the orders were carried out. There were just seven of us. We firebombed about six or seven places on Castle Street. Then we set Mike's Grocery on fire. From Mike's Grocery you could crawl under houses all the way to the church. And under these two houses there were about six of us, and we had 12-gauge pump shotguns, you know? And when the firemen came, we just started shooting at them. They had to call the cops, you know? We were just firing away, and they were firing back at us. I got hit on my back with a goddamn pellet. Our guns were going 'boom, boom' and their guns were going 'BOOM, BOOM, BOOM!' Hey! We had this riot going, man! I don't believe we hit any of them, but we were just letting them know to get out of there and let Mike's burn down. And after we shot at them, we just crawled on back and gave out the code name— 'rabbit, rabbit, rabbit'—to get back in the church.

King's (1978) article describes the trial against the 'Wilmington Ten' and the duplicity of the key witnesses for the prosecution. After the five-week trial, Chavis and the other nine were each sentenced to twenty-nine years in prison. Five years after the trial, Allen Hall, who had completed his reduced sentence and was released on parole, announced that his testimony had been a lie. Two key witness in the trial said they had lied—one in exchange for a gift of a mini-bike for his testimony in court. Another trial was set for May 1977. Yet after the State Bureau of Investigation made another probe into the case, and concluded that the original trial was fair but that the sentences were too long. This was a month after London-based Amnesty International put the 'Wilmington Ten' on their "prisoners of conscience" list. In January 1978, Governor Jim Hunt commuted their sentences, and they were released on parole.

Michael Myerson's 1978 book *Nothing Could Be Finer* includes an interview with Chavis in which he recalls the student activism in Wilmington in February 1971:

I was really shocked to see people battling like that. At that point, I just didn't understand the depths of feelings involved. I didn't know much about the history of Wilmington. I had heard something about 1898 but I didn't know it was as deeply ingrained as it apparently was. You had some folks that actually thought that just because the Black students marched and because they were having some meetings, that they were going to pay back the white people for what happened in 1898. And so to keep the Blacks from paying them back, they were going to wipe out the Black community again. And even with all this shooting the mayor refused to set a curfew. People could still go downtown, buy

a gun and ammunition, come shooting into the community, and go
back downtown again.

June Nash's interviews with black and white Wilmingtonians shortly
after the February 1971 violence provide insight into the community during this time. Nash interviewed Wilmington natives familiar with the 1898
violence as well as later generations of Wilmingtonians active in the school
boycotts. This interview was with a young black woman speaking about
the defeatist attitudes older blacks in Wilmington had, which she attributed to 1898:

> I have a feeling that the riot did exactly what it was intended to do. It
> suppressed the Negro, and it was doing it afterward. I remember an
> uncle I had—and I remember him saying to me—(I don't remember
> whether I was working for the union; I was always walking round say-
> ing "Thus and so is true")—"Well I'll tell you one thing, it'll never hap-
> pen in this town." He was always saying, "The Negro will never do
> anything in this town. The white people will never let him do anything
> for themselves." But I noticed this defeatist attitude, and the violence of
> it. Even the mere suggestion that you were going to do something was
> irritating to him, I think. I don't know whether they felt that even the
> suggestion of it was a criticism of their valor [laughed] or what, I don't
> know what.
>
> I remember saying to him one day (I was not given to answering him dis-
> respectfully, not ever to the adults; you were brought up never to do
> that, believe me) but I remember telling him one day, "Your generation
> was the 'riot generation,'" or something like that. And I remember that
> he was so furious with me, and I've often wondered if I touched a nerve.

In several of my interviews I was told about the '1898 mentality' like the
'riot generation' referred to above. One respondent, a black middle-class
woman described her arrival to Wilmington in the early 1950s:

> When I came to Wilmington–I always felt when I came to Wilmington
> that something was wrong. Whites and blacks weren't communicating
> with each other. And the blacks seemed to be almost scared of their
> shadows. Well I did not have the 1898 mentality. And let me tell you
> what that is: if you are born in Wilmington, remain here, get a job here,
> don't go anywhere else, don't get exposed—you may have the 1898
> mentality. If you graduate from any school, go away and work in some
> other part of the United States and you return, you have lost that 1898
> mentality. When I came here, I didn't have it. I couldn't, I was ebullient
> and personable and was going to change the world. And the blacks
> looked at me like, "What is your problem." I didn't realize how they felt.

An African American woman I interviewed who lived through the 1971 violence described the period:

> Yes I was right here in 1971. We were really afraid. When the shooting was going on. I happened to go down 6th; I was on Castle going down 6th Street to go to Chestnut, that's where our church was. And there were men there down on the ground with guns. And they stopped us. "We'll let you go by this time." But the girl driving that car, she's dead now, she's passed, she was scared and I was too! We were both sitting up in the front. They were really acting very ugly. People were afraid. And seems like around on 7th Street, oh it was terrible, I can't even hardly get it together. I don't know but we were afraid. Now those who carried on like that, they were out there, younger ones, but the older ones were afraid to get out to go anywhere, turn on the lights at night, anything. I think that was started by some young people, some young man.

It is interesting that no public reference to 1898 was made during this time. It is clear, however, that privately discussions about 1898 were being held (Thomas 1980). One respondent I interviewed, an African-American woman who lived during the events in 1971 told me:

> Those old experienced teachers who talked in hush-hush tones talked about 1898 during the 1971 riot. Now there was one young man who talked about 1898 Wilmington in 1971.

This period marked a difficult time for Wilmingtonians. Godwin (2000) describes the rise of the Ku Klux Klan during this time, as well as another white supremacy group, the Rights of White People (ROWP). A white male I interviewed said his father had driven into Wilmington for the first time during the events of the Wilmington Ten, a newly recruited employee for a local firm who was in the process of moving to Wilmington. Not realizing he was driving into a city engulfed in a race riot he was taken aback. The respondent explained:

> My father drove over the bridge into Carolina Beach and saw this huge banner that said "Welcome to Carolina Beach, Home of the KKK." He was terrified and thought to himself, "what have I gotten myself into?"

The cautionary tale of the dominant narrative was no longer a means to control blacks; the meta-narrative of the Civil Rights usurped the influence it once held. White supremacy groups like the KKK were allowed greater social space during this time and local white supremacists reached "hero" status as they fought against black militants (see Godwin 2000).

While the dominant narrative is not summoned publicly, we still hear echoes of 1898 during this period.

1982 AND 1985

While the Edmond's publication in 1951 marked one of the most profound contentions of the dominant narrative up to that time, the publication of Leon Prather's *We Have Taken A City* in 1984 probably equaled the controversy the Edmond's publication provoked. Unlike the 1950's in which the Edmond's piece was released, the late 1970's–1980s marked a time of remarkable 'silence' in public discourse about 1898. Indeed virtually the last public mention I uncovered was in 1951. One exception, however, was a November 10, 1982, article in the *Wilmington Morning Star* entitled, "84 Years Ago Today . . . 'Riot of 1898' halted black political power." The article provides fragments of the dominant narrative, stating that blacks precipitated the violence and armed white supremacists had to restore calm. Yet it also names local influential Wilmingtonians who were involved, specifically Alfred Waddell, Hugh McRae, Walker Taylor and George Rountree. I found no letter-to-the editor responses to the piece.

Prather's publication in 1985 aroused the community and displeased many whites in Wilmington. Prather gave a lecture at the Cape Fear Museum[38] followed by a book signing in July 1985. His publication and presence in the city prompted an entire page of coverage in the *Wilmington Morning Star*. In an article entitled "Writer Exposes Wilmington 'Coup d'etat,'" Prather's findings were covered in-depth.[39]

Beverly Tetterton, public librarian for New Hanover County's local history, recalls the disquiet the Prather book caused in Wilmington:

> So, I guess it was 1984 whenever *WE HAVE TAKEN A CITY* came out, and I had been corresponding with Dr. Prather, for little bits and pieces you know that he needed, you know a name of a street, and had been trying to answer questions for him like from the City Directory, or things like that, so I knew who he was and I kinda knew that he was doing this book, but I didn't really have an idea how it would have such an impact, and I guess I was pretty naive. And when it first came out, of course we got copies immediately, and a lot of people, I would say, I don't know exactly, but I would say 100% white came into the library and wanted to see that book. And I don't think they wanted to buy a copy, but they wanted to read it. And some of them were people whose families were involved in it, and that were descended from a member of the Secret Nine. And so there was quite a bit of do about it. I think it was the first time, I don't know about Helen Edmonds because I wasn't around then, but I think that it was . . . [pause] it became the letter-of-the-law to the black

community. Mainly because a black man had written it. A black man with a Ph.D. has written this. And I don't think that they would have trusted a white historian, not at that time anyway. There was a lot of controversy. He was invited to speak here. He spoke at the Museum, 'cause I went over there to hear him. You would have to talk to Harry Warren, but I think the museum got some flack from some segments of the community for having him. With the Prather book it was more . . . it was just more alarm that somebody had gone and done this and this was in print. Every book that we bought and put on circulating shelf was stolen.

The period since "The Wilmington Ten" up to the Prather publication had been marked by a period of public 'silence' relating to 1898. Tetterton joined the New Hanover County library staff in 1980 and recalls the 'silence' surrounding the 1898 event and the instructions given to her by a senior librarian:

> When I joined the library, you've got to understand, this is the period of grand dames of the library—the librarian who had trained me and who had been here since the 1950s said to me: Beverly, I've got something to show you. And she pulled out the Colliers. The original copy of Colliers. And she said I've got this under lock and key. And I said "Why?" And she said, you know it just brings heart ache to people and it is just something we don't want to make available to people because it will probably just . . ."make a stink" those are probably the words she used [chuckled]. So I kept it and conserved it, and then after she left I put it into the regular collection and have always brought it out anytime any one asks for it. Although I have had to put it behind locked doors because anything that has to do with 1898 or Wilmington Ten seems to disappear from our collection.

I had heard many stories about the lock and key policy at the library from various informants in the community. Cynthia Brown, an African-American woman, recalls her experience in 1973 as a high school senior wanting to research the 1898 event. Ms. Brown grew up hearing the stories about the violence from her grandmother, and went to the New Hanover County Library to learn more about it. She describes the response from the librarian,

> "The information that we have about that era is down in our vault, and it's not available to the public and what do you need this for?"[40]

A white woman I interviewed recalled a similar experience in the late 1970s.

> *White respondent:* I was doing research about black Wilmington and went to the Library when it was on Market Street. I told the librarian, Katherine Howell, I was researching a book on Wilmington and had few

> black community documents. She turned and whispered to me "we keep
> those under lock and key and only show them to certain people—it
> might stir up things." Can you imagine, a public library and there is no
> access to a "secret archive?"

The two public reminders of the coup d'etat and racial violence, first in 1982
and then in 1985, broke the silence that had submerged public discussions
on race in Wilmington since the 1971 Wilmington Ten violence. In 1989 a
play written and performed to commemorate the 250th anniversary of the
city of Wilmington contained a brief segment on the 1898 violence. The next
public reference to 1898 violence in 1994 also created controversy in the
Wilmington community.

1994

The publication of Philip Gerard's *Cape Fear Rising* provoked an angry response from white Wilmington. Gerard's historical fiction about the racial violence and coup d'etat used names of actual participators in the violence. The
Wilmington Sunday Star devoted several lengthy articles to the publication in
its February 13, 1994 edition, including a book review by the managing editor; an extended article which interviewed Gerard as well as descendants of
the Secret Nine; and an editorial piece written by Gerard himself.

    An article in the *Atlanta Constitution* on March 6, 1994 covered the
response Wilmingtonians made to the release of Gerard's book,

> According to Ben Steelman, who reads the letters to the editor at the
> *Wilmington Star-News,* black people seem to like the book, but whites
> tend to regard it as "troublemaking and carpetbagging" by an author
> who came to teach at the University of North Carolina in Wilmington
> less than five years ago.

Letters to the editor about the book were printed just after the February 13
coverage and were pretty evenly distributed over a two-week period whereupon a pressing school bond referendum took over the public's attention.
On February 19, 1994, a letter read:

> Regarding the four-page coverage of *Cape Fear Rising:* It's not the
> "awful event played out on the pages of a novel," but rather the author's
> blend of "equal parts history and imagination"—stuff he made up—
> using local surnames, which disturbs me.

> When researching his fiction, did Philip Gerard consult any members of
> the Wilmington families whose names he has so freely published to ask
> their version of what happened—or might his be a biased account?

Perhaps he hopes to sell film rights and shine a camera light directly into the real-life homes on his fictionalized characters' descendants? After equating these 1890s local city officials with Robert E. Lee, Mr. Gerard defends his use of actual names for fictional characters by stating, "To change their names would have . . . turned the novel into a guessing game of pseudonyms." Instead, he has presented a guessing game of what is truth and what is not.

It seems unfair to use university funds to help publish what amounts to half-truths about families of a community in which he not only lives, but teaches. As a creative writing director at UNCW, Mr. Gerard should know that published work stand alone: Its author may no longer stand over each reader's shoulder, explaining what it is written as it is. Therefore, his after-the-fact statement that his intention was not to offend seems pale.

Following a sentence fragment describing his research, he concludes: "the more I read, the more confused I became." Well written.

On the same page,

What's this about a university professor writing a novel about the 1898 Wilmington race riots? He labels his book fiction and then proceeds to use real names of some of the people that he says were heavily involved—even to the point of thinking up stuff for them to say. This is not a very nice thing to do! I think we should all just ignore this book.

On February 21,

I have yet to read Cape Fear Rising but if it is as thorough as Sunday Star News says then Philip Gerard's book could be a catalyst to the healing of strained race relations in this community.

On February 22,

In response to the writings pertaining to the 1898 revolt, I commend Philip Gerard for tackling this old wound and the Sunday Star-News for giving it front-page coverage.

I am a descendant of Isham Quick, one of the many leading black entrepreneurs here in Wilmington who was affected by the revolt.

Years ago, before I moved to Europe, the local museum had a wonderful exhibit concerning the revolt . . . The museum had given me a page from a book titled *Race Riots* which was a documentary of several riots in the South.

My grandfather's name appeared with 99 others . . . (who) called themselves the "Colored 100," consisting of 100 black entrepreneurs of this city who had written a document requesting government protection. They were aware of the revolt but did not know when it would take place.

How ironic: Today, Wilmington is practically run by a Committee of 100, less the "colored" faces. I often tell people how proud I am to be a citizen of Wilmington and how powerful the black influence here used to be.

It hurts me deeply to see our city commemorate a bigot and massacrer like (the first) Hugh MacRae with a park . . . (yet) nowhere in this city is a marker or monument to commemorate my great-grandfather and the 99 other leading citizens of this community who tried to prevent this travesty. What happened to their business or property? No one has ever asked for reparation, but I do think it is time for a landmark of honorable memory for these brave men.

On February 25,

The recent furor surrounding the release of Cape Fear Rising has focused on the moral and intellectual integrity of historical fiction. As a resident who attended area schools, I think another important aspect of this controversy is the obscurity which surrounded the event.

Local education should take advantage of the rich history of our region so that our children will not be required to rely upon historical fiction to form their ideas and opinion. In a similar vein, it is not too early or too late to begin classroom discussion on the Wilmington 10 and the racial tension of twenty years ago.

On February 28,

Ninety-six years after the event—after nearly ten decades of lies agreed up on and a conspiracy of silence extraordinary—an age-old cause of fear along the Cape Fear is at risk of abating thanks to Philip Gerard's blockbuster, myth-destroying book, *Cape Fear Rising.*

Mr. Gerard's book is a reminder that the past is not only prologue, but that the past is never as past as some of us would have it so, and that no one can ever be certain that what is done in the dark will never come to light . . .

Since your fulsome treatment, this writer has heard some interesting reasons for dismissing the book . . . but little respect for the murdered descendants or the murdered themselves, and no respect for those who have grieved for them nearly a century.

Where is our vaunted Judeo-Christian concern, compassion, humanity? Where is our alleged passion for justice, even justice delayed? Or is it still, in 1994, difficult to respect and revere black life, just as it was in 1898?

Yet even the worst of times have their value; we can expose that festering sore of our collective local past to critical scrutiny, and learn: or *Cape Fear Rising* can, if we allow it to, help us lay to rest our dead—and our dread.

Cape Fear Rising could help us declare an armistice with each other across the great racial divide, and try to bear one another, even if we cannot bear each other's crosses.

Perhaps more than any other challenge to the dominant narrative, Gerard's publication created a sensation in the community. An African-American woman I interviewed spoke about the disquiet the Gerard book generated in the community, telling me to find the newspaper article on the day Gerard's book was published because Wilmingtonians were in an uproar:

Alex Manly's niece wanted to sue Phil Gerard, because they did not like they way he portrayed their uncle. Hugh McRae and all of the others did not like the way his grandfather was portrayed, and the Kenan's certainly didn't. I don't know why Phil Gerard would not write a book; if it was going to be historical fiction, then use a pseudonym. It was stupid. It was STUPID! Something that sensitive and controversial . . . They could have picked them out if they wanted to, but it was unfair to the people who carried their names. And that put a bad taste in many white leaders' mouths.

Beverly Tetterton of the Local History room at New Hanover County Library said that scores of people came in asking for the book. She recounts what the library experienced after the publication of Gerard's book:

And then it [reaction to Prather's book] kind of died down again except for an occasional thing when Dr. McGivern would bring it up, until *Cape Fear Rising*. And that really had a much bigger impact I think that any other thing. I don't know why. If it is because the town has changed. I do feel that people who have moved here—they are just fascinated by it. They just could not get enough of it. They wanted to read about it and they wanted to study it. Maybe they wanted something on Old Wilmington.

And of course the African American community and in the white community. And the newspaper did a much bigger, huge article, and I think they got a lot of flack from it too. Dot and I finally just took everything we had about it, which is considerable, because there has been a lot written on it—then they wanted to know about Hugh MacRae—and we just put them all across the front desk. There was that much traffic. And we got tired of saying the same thing over, so we just said why don't you take a look at these. And that's when we heard the most preposterous things. Like a woman told us that her grandaddy had come across the river that day and that the blood was just, from the blacks killed, was just flowing down Market Street and into the Cape Fear River.

Then an African American woman just got real hysterical and that her great-grandfather had owned a bank and the white people had taken the bank away from her and her family. And then we heard from people whose families were in the book. And they were very upset because their ancestors had been portrayed fictionally in a very bad way that was not true.

For days we just sat there and listened to these stories. You know everything from "we saved at least 25 black people because my father had a store over on 4th Street and he put them all in the basement and he was scared for his life" to . . . "my family said that they came into the house and killed three and we buried them in the back yard." Quite often the stories would start like, "my grandmother told me that." These books awakened the community.

Conclusion

This chapter provides a descriptive continuum of the use of the dominant narrative about racial violence in Wilmington, North Carolina over the course of a century. Using archival data, I examine public reference to the 1898 violence and analyze how and in what ways the dominant narrative has been used to maintain a hegemonic ideology and suppress other narratives.

All narratives contain an ideological project . . .

Immediately following the November 10, 1898, racial violence, white Wilmington elite fostered the ideology of white domination through motivated distortion of the event and the creation of a dominant narrative. The white elite used self-deceptive techniques of selective omission, blaming the enemy, fabrication, exaggeration and embellishment to create a positive image of itself (Baumeister and Hastings 1997:278). The organizing principle of the dominant narrative, as embodied in the "White Declaration of Independence," was the natural supremacy of whites over blacks. The overt white racist narrative that developed obscured the class interests of the ruling white elite. By focusing on race superiority, Wilmington white elite rid itself of its greatest enemy—Fusion politics—which was against privatization of utilities and transportation, arenas where the leaders of the 1898 violence profited greatly. The dominant narrative was an ideological project that hid the underlying contradictions of history by both concealing the political coup d'etat and suppressing alternative versions of the event (Jameson 1981).

Remember 1898 . . .

The archival data shows that the dominant narrative was used widely up until World War I. A severe local labor shortage and the need for black labor created a conspicuously silent period that included 1919 when racial tension developed at the Wilmington shipyard but no use of the 1898 dominant narrative was made to quell the unrest.

During World War II shipbuilding years, a period of increased economic growth, local dominant whites once again summoned the cautionary tale to *Remember 1898*. The dominant narrative was used to caution blacks who may have felt greater levels of efficacy and entitlement due to their contributions to the war effort fighting for freedom and democracy (O'Brien 1999). Increased black citizenship rights, appeals for fair labor practices, and a rapidly growing population prompted local white leadership to manipulate and deploy the dominant narrative.

In 1951, a local civil rights organization pushed to equalize schools and a University of North Carolina at Chapel Hill press publication by Helen Edmonds publicly countered the authenticity of the dominant narrative, provoking an outcry by dominant local whites to *Remember 1898*. In the 1970s, the ideology of white racism in Wilmington was sustained through white supremacy organizations, yet not via public reference to the dominant narrative about 1898. The meta-narrative of Liberalism—represented by the right to freedom, equality, and individualism—and symbolized in the Civil Rights Movement, was slowly becoming part of the mainstream political values of the nation and effectively silenced the overt public reminders of 1898. The notion of white superiority and right to rule was no longer acceptable. Silence about 1898 continued, but then an important publication in 1984 by Prather, *We Have Taken A City*, contested the dominant version of the 1898 events. Gerard's *Cape Fear Rising* in 1994 along with the 1898 centennial commemoration of the event provided a venue for public discourse about subordinated narratives surrounding 1898. A new narrative arose from the centennial commemoration of the event, to which I turn now.

Chapter Five
A New Narrative
1998 Centennial Commemoration

In this section I examine the development of a new narrative about the 1898 racial violence based on a centennial commemoration of the event. I rely on an executive summary written by the director of the *1898 Centennial Foundation, Inc.* that traces the formation of the foundation and its efforts in commemorating the centennial of the 1898 event (Anthony 1999). An article by historian Melton McLaurin, Executive Council member of the *1898 Foundation,* provides supplemental material for this section (2000). The question guiding this section is: What are the mechanisms by which narratives combine elements of the dominant ideology with subordinate narratives to produce new narratives which, for the most part, sustain rather than challenge ruling hegemony?

CENTENNIAL COMMEMORATION

The 1898 Centennial Foundation, Inc. was formed in 1997. Membership was composed of two community groups that had originally met independently to plan commemorative activities. The two groups aligned and organized as a non-profit, tax-exempt corporation:

> Our mission is to develop and coordinate a broad-based community effort in appropriate remembrance of the Wilmington coup and violence of 1898. It is our hope that this remembrance will be the beginning of a continuing effort to improve race relations in Wilmington and help bring about a spirit of justice and tolerance for all residents of the community (Anthony 1999:9)

The *Foundation* endeavored to create a broad-based coalition of diverse community members by adopting a black-white co-chair policy for each of its committees and by actively recruiting local support from diverse organizations in the community. The composition of the Executive Council changed over the course of the two years. Table 5.1 below provides a breakdown of all Executive Council members:

Table 5.1 1898 Centennial Foundation Executive Council Membership
from 1997–1998 by Race and Sex

	Male	Female	TOTAL
White	7	12	19
	(22%)	(36%)	(58%)
Black	8	6	14
	(24)%	(18%)	(42%)
TOTAL	15	18	33
	(46%)	(54%)	(100%)

Data collected from Executive Summary by Bolton Anthony and 1898 Foundation
Newsletters "Reports on Activities"

A small majority of the Executive Council members were white and female.
Many of the members were retired. As has been noted in the literature on organizations and voluntary associations, people engage in volunteer activities
based on the time demands of the participant (March and Olsen 1976; Perrow
1986). Thus retirees and/or those who are not employed outside the home
may have more time to devote to volunteering (March and Olsen 1976).

Based on descriptions in the *Foundation*'s newsletters and the
Executive Summary, it appears all members of the *Foundation*'s Executive
Council were professionals, virtually all college educated, and many holding
graduate degrees. The Executive Council comprised numerous university
faculty and, along with other professional organization affiliations, provided a strong network in the community (Anthony 1999).

Early support from the Chancellor of the University of North Carolina
at Wilmington, combined with support from community organizations, provided an aura of 'legitimacy' for the organization. As one African American
male *Foundation* organizer explained:

> Initially it was like someone start thinking it's 1996, and 1998 is coming
> up soon and is there going to be anything said and done to commemo-
> rate 1898? And so we started meeting out here at the university and con-
> necting with community people and that kind of thing, and early on there
> was real reticence about, in some quarters, about commemorating 1898.
> There were some people in the community who were afraid that it was
> going to stir up animosities and some people were actually afraid there
> was going to be some sort of riot or civil disorder coming out of the com-
> memoration or something like that, and many people were reticent about
> that and kind of standoffish about it. It's interesting that the City and

County governments kinda got on board, because initially they were not overwhelmed about the idea of commemorating 1898. And later, when they came to believe that it was not going to cause any kind of violence or whatever, they began to step on board. But they were reticent about it. And although we had some of the first meetings at the university, I actually think there were some quarters that were kind of reticent about it, and they got on board later but not initially. It was like somebody who said to me, who was in the 1898 committee, said "This thing is going to happen, this commemoration is going to happen. People outside of Wilmington are going to know that this is going on." How does the Wilmington community want to be seen? Of people who want to try to embrace the idea of reconciliation, or those who want to distance and run away from this particular thing. And I think that when people, when I mean people I mean those in the power structure, for lack of a better word, those people became convinced that there was not going to be violence, which I didn't think there was going to be anyway, which I thought was a groundless fear, when they became convinced of that and that this was going to go about in a way that they felt they could sign onto, then they began to fall in line. Now of course there were various segments of the community, for different reasons, for various different reasons, never bought into the 1898 commemoration ceremony.

Both McLaurin (2000) and Anthony (1999) describe the onerous task the *1898 Foundation* faced in organizing commemoration activities in the community given the widespread lore and dominant narrative about the 1898 event (discussed in Chapter Four). Obtaining support from descendants of the organizers of the violence proved difficult (Anthony 1999:23). George Rountree III, local attorney and descendant of the lawyer who abetted the organization of the coup d'etat in 1898, agreed to participate in a lecture at St. Stephens A.M.E. Church in the Brooklyn section of Wilmington where much of the violence took place in 1898. McLaurin (2000:50) describes the "near-capacity crowd with a slight African American majority" who listened to Rountree's speech in which he praised his grandfather as a good man and valuable community leader, yet offered no apology for his participation in the violence. Anthony (1999:23) notes that the *1898 Centennial Foundation* had met with Rountree in early 1997 requesting he and City Council member Katherine Moore, a descendant of Armond Scott, an African American attorney who fled Wilmington in 1898, serve as co-chairs for one of the Foundation's committees, yet both declined. The Foundation did receive financial support from Hugh MacRae II, the grandson of the Secret Nine leader Hugh MacRae, who made a $10,000 contribution to the organization in 1998 (Anthony 1999:39).[1]

Anthony (1999) and McLaurin (2000) note other difficulties faced by the *1898 Foundation*. Anthony (1999:39) explains:

The issues of staffing and compensation were such difficult ones for the Foundation because it was concerned with a possible perception in the Black community that white people were making all the money off the commemoration. Mayor pro tem Katherine Moore, the only Black member of the City Council had raised this issue in May 1997 when the Foundation presented its funding request to Council at the Budget Hearing; Moore had wanted reassurance that Blacks would benefit directly from any money that flowed into the Foundation.

And McLaurin (2000:46) writes:

Some prominent whites publicly objected to any effort to commemorate the events of 1898, while others privately expressed the concern that such efforts would worsen race relations. . . . Whites seemed most threatened by black concerns that the issue of economic justice be addressed, especially by calls for reparations, and by the depiction of their family members as immoral and unfeeling racists. Some objected strenuously to the concept of a memorial to the victims, one prominent white Wilmingtonian going so far as to boast that he would be the first to tear down any monument that was erected. . . . Rumors that commission [Foundation[2]] staff members were pocketing thousands of grant dollars surfaced in the African American community, a charge echoed within the traditional white elite.

Another problem for the *Foundation* was the lack of support from the *Wilmington Journal,* the weekly African American newspaper which voiced its disdain for the *1898 Centennial Foundation* in early 1998. In the November 19, 1998 edition, *The Wilmington Journal* ran a lengthy editorial entitled "Commemorate 1898????" explaining why the *Journal* supported neither the commemoration nor the *Foundation.* Part of the two-page editorial explained:

We believe that only part of the story has been told. The first step of atonement cannot take place, until an all out effort is made to determine all who were killed on that bloody night, all who fled the city, by force or by will because of fear, and all who lost their businesses and other property.

If it was too difficult for the 1898 Commemoration Foundation to research and bring back to our community a complete list of African Americans who suffered a the hands of those bruts [sic] then let the African American community tell all of the story. Provide us with the grant money, etc. and we can put together our own team of researchers who can determine who was killed, who fled the city and who lost businesses and property. We have yet to figure out how a monument is going to bear names of those who suffered, if no attempt is made to find out who they were.

The single most personal insult throughout this two year fiasco was having a television reporter from the state capital come to my office to find the location of the newspaper office that burned during the massacre because the executive director of the 1898 Commemoration Foundation did not know exactly where the building had stood. This should be an insult to all of the Blacks who volunteered their time and all people and taxpayers who footed any of the bills. Of course, there are other sites that would be appropriate for this tour, but we feel you now have a good picture of 1898 and should understand how you have perpetuated the "persecution of the lowly."

The *Journal*'s emphasis on 'atonement' contrasted greatly to the *Foundation*'s emphasis on 'reconciliation.' A white male respondent explained:

I think the Journal's attitude was, "This is something to make the white community to salve their conscience, what is it, what's the point, nothing of value is going to come of this, we're not going to have an honest discussion of what occurred, and it is not going to solve any of the underlying problems that exist here." And they didn't have much faith that it would.

The *Foundation* requested financial support from both the City of Wilmington and New Hanover County, receiving $15,000 from the City over a two-year period and nothing from the County (Anthony 1999:9). Funding from the Z. Smith Reynolds Foundation, North Carolina Humanities Council, North Carolina Department of Cultural Resources, Unitarian Universalist Funding Program, Mary Duke Biddle Foundation, and the North Carolina Arts Council, enabled the *Foundation* to create a vital program over the course of the year including academic lecture series, interracial dialogue sessions, performances, a website, plans for a memorial park, and a forty-two page publication outlining the Foundation's activities over the year.[3] The commemoration activities culminated in a well-attended symposium[4] at the University of North Carolina at Wilmington in October 1998 with Dr. John Hope Franklin as keynote speaker, receiving local, state and national coverage.

An African-American male who participated in the commemoration planning for the *Foundation* illustrates:

Considering how things were in the beginning, it was, I just thought it was amazing that the committee was able to bring this thing off and to have it be as successful as it was. It was quite successful. The events were very well attended, they spawned all the dialogue groups across town talking about race and those types of things, uh, I thought it was a tremendous success. And of course, it is going to culminate with the park that is going to be built at the foot of the, I guess it's the Martin Luther King Expressway, now, so.

THE CREATION OF A NEW NARRATIVE

Steinmetz (1992), Linde (1986) and Somers (1992) focus on the organizing principle of narratives and the evaluative structure narratives contain. For Linde (1986:187) the evaluative structure passes normative judgment about, "the way things are, the way things ought to be." Through garnering support from the City of Wilmington, New Hanover County, various funding institutions throughout the State of North Carolina, and the highest echelon of the University of North Carolina at Wilmington, the *1898 Foundation* accrued legitimacy as a voice for a new narrative emerging from the commemoration activities. I examine three organizing, evaluative principles embodied in the work of the *1898 Centennial Foundation* which frame the new narrative: a plea for reconciliation that absolves those living today for the deeds of their ancestors; an "official history" of the 1898 racial violence commissioned by the *Foundation*; and the *Foundation's* position on reparations.

"NO ONE LIVING TODAY . . ."

Early on, the *Foundation* adopted the aphorism: "Tell the Story; Heal the Wound; Honor the Memory; and Restore the Hope" as a reflection of their goals for the organization, appending it to most public notices about events the organization sponsored (Anthony 1999:6). Another adage, also appearing on most printed material by the Foundation, including their website, framed the new narrative about 1898:

> No one living in Wilmington today was a participant in the events of 1898. Consequently, none among us bears any personal responsibility for what happened. But all among us—no matter our race or history, whether we have arrived here only recently or come from families that have called Wilmington home for generations—all among us are responsible for 1998. On each of us falls the personal responsibility to make our community one where economic justice and racial harmony flourish. Surely this is a challenge we are willing to accept.

McLaurin (2000: 49) explains that the *Foundation* insisted on using this narrative as a means to encourage widespread involvement in the commemoration activities. Another *Foundation* member explained:

The group was getting a negative reputation. Both the whites and some blacks were arguing among themselves. The whole group was getting a reputation as activists and something else. If it not inclusive and representative of the leaders of this community and then another group may take it and you may be sorry that we didn't do what we should have done. The City sent three and the County sent three representatives. In some instances it was difficult because of Phil Gerard's book to turn them around. I said, "No, we are not related to Phil Gerard's book. Here is a proactive group to commemorate something we know has to be commemorated now," and with that logic [trails off]. There was a group out there trying to take it on. There were rumors that Farrakhan was coming. And we had to quell these rumors. Now I did hear a white tell me that there were whites who were purchasing guns. They were getting prepared. They didn't know what was going to happen. These are the kinds of things I prayed about. We decided to tell the story, be factual, but not pointing fingers. The broader the base, the better the involvement. Why do you want to be exclusive?

An African-American male founding member of the *Foundation* explained:

So the ideals that came out of the 1898 foundation: honor the memory; restore the hope; heal the wounds; tell the story; all those things; those are all feel good things. But they do make you feel good. But it doesn't do anything to address the real issues. You gotta talk about economics. Economic issues. You can feel good about yourself for a little while, but if you wake up and you're still in poverty and you still wondering where your bills are being paid. And you're still underemployed. And you don't have an education, so you're in the same fix. And you see that's one of the things that a lot of blacks said about the 1898 [1998 commemoration] initially. It was an event that made a lot of white people feel good and after it was over they went about their business, know that we finally addressed this issue, we finally talked about it, but we haven't done anything to change the dynamics of race in the community.

For many, the slogan exonerated whites of the wrongdoing of 1898. The *Wilmington Journal* publicly voiced its disdain for the organization and its blueprint to commemorate through absolving those responsible. Privately, members of the community voiced their disagreement with the organization and its message. A white male I interviewed gave his position on the "no one living today" slogan the *Foundation* adopted:

Right—"they are not alive today, but we're spending the money they made for us" [laughter]! Which, by the way, was the elephant in the room, which is why nobody wanted to touch this: the blacks have always maintained that huge amounts of money changed hands—that blacks had a lot of property down on Masonboro Sound. We do know that black families lost property! The big bugaboo—Sue Cody says not a lot of property changed hands, but that's still the big question to settle.

An African-American female expounded:

My sense is, and this is my take, is that the people who were in charge of 1898 were, in fact they had that little slogan, for white people to be comfortable or acceptable of what they were doing, you cannot be held responsible for what your folks did, but you can be from here on out. And other black people were saying, "Yes they can be held accountable for it." That, I think, was the split. And people decided they either wanted to learn about it regardless of what all that motto was. Uh, others said, "I don't want to hear nothing about it, it's a bunch of crock and you trying to make these white folks feel comfortable. We are looking for restitution." So that was that in the community, and probably still is.

An African-American male argued:

The whole concept of 1898 [referring to the 1898 Foundation] to me, there were too many people involved in 1898 [Foundation] that had ulterior motives, and that's my personal opinion. It was self serving for a lot of 'em. And I, I really don't see that it's done *any* good, to be honest with you. There's been no healing process; it's actually made more divisions. As far as I'm concerned, you know. You can't believe that commemoration did anything! [heated] Not if you're honest, not if you're honest. Look around! We used to have all these meetings with the MacRae families, the Rountrees, and we are supposed to get together and talk about things. What's the purpose of it? What's the solution? If you don't have a solution, you're just making it worse. You're part of the problem. And my thing, I can see getting together, talking about it, acknowledging it, but—don't use it to try for your benefit, as far as I'm concerned. And I've seen a lot of it. A lot of it. No use for it. [How did you get involved?] Well I came in, how did I get involved, some friends of mine were working and they said "come on." And I did some of the circle groups, I was a facilitator. [Pause] Most people *don't support* the 1898 commemoration, if you get me, why *should* you support it? If you start here, let's have a plan, let's not start here and go everywhere as we think on our feet. You start with a plan and you bring it to a conclusion. That's the way I think. If you start off, you don't know where you're going, you'll never get there! It was just a feel good about yourself thing. I don't think enough, I know they broke it down in several facets, economic and all that, but there's *no economic development!* Not gonna be! The people who have, still have. So what's the point, you know? I tried to be objective; sometimes it's easier than others.

An African-American male *Foundation* member commented:

> We had a session with George Rountree, and a lot of blacks came to that session that hadn't been to others, but they were still outnumbered by whites because they were there to support George. And it even goes to show you that even a fool gets somebody to support him. George made some statements that still—he talked about Dred Scott v. Sanford, 1837 [sic] and he used the justification of the riot, the Dred Scott decision, and that the mindset of the people was that black people wanted to cause economic turmoil in Wilmington. I talked to George afterwards. I said, "I can't understand it; Dred Scott v. Sanford was in 1837 [sic], but by the time the 1898 riots took place we had the 13th, 14th, and 15th amendments, the law had changed, even though Scott had been the law of the land in that time, by the 1860s and 1870s the law had changed. So therefore, if you look at it, whites overtly violated the law and people's civil rights. How can you justify that? How can you justify indiscriminate killing?" I can't think for what his thought process was, but I got the impression that OK I'm not condemning, and it was never my view or anyone else's intention to get him to condemn the actions of his grandfather. You know the only thing I expected Rountree or Hugh MacRae or any of those folks? To say, not to condemn their grandfather or great-grandfather, but to say that the incident itself was wrong. It was wrong. It was wrong. I can't put the blame on anyone in particular, but the whole incident was wrong. And no one has said that. And so consequently what's happened is, we have had this event taken place, we've had all the festivities, the activities and things, but we still haven't sorted out the problem, because we still haven't addressed the root problem.

"OFFICIAL HISTORY"

Believing that a concise account of the November 10, 1898, racial violence was needed, the *Foundation* contracted a history professor at the University of North Carolina at Wilmington to write an 'official history' (Anthony 1999:14). Anthony (1999:14) describes the internal concerns over the new 'official' version:

> It created some controversy in its own right. The professional historians on the Executive Council found it as neutral as could possibly be expected. Two of their colleagues in the Department of Philosophy and Religion, however, expressed serious concerns; and some of the "lay" members of the Council found the article overly provocative.

Below is the two page 'official' history provided by the *Foundation* available on their website, and printed in several of their organizational mailings:[5]

THE 1898 COUP AND VIOLENCE

Several years ago Wilmington journalist Bennet Steelman wrote an essay called "Black, White and Gray: The Wilmington Race Riot in Fact and Legend." The title was apt, for the causes and effects of the November 1898 coup and violence are subject to multiple and conflicting interpretations. Over the course of the last century, this particular incident has been mentioned in dozens of scholarly studies, ranging from unpublished research papers, masters' theses, and doctoral dissertations, to articles, novels, textbooks, biographies, and full-length historical monographs. Some of these accounts are colored by the racial attitudes of their authors, others by the passing of time.

Recognizing the need for a brief, useful, and accessible account, the 1898 Centennial Foundation commissioned the following summary. As everyone who has ever written about this controversial topic knows, however, the real story will never be distilled into a single, undisputed narrative. The real truth lies "somewhere in the gray area between these variant accounts."

The Civil War took its toll on the port city, but Wilmington made a quick recovery. During Reconstruction, the local economy shifted away from naval stores and rice to cotton, lumber, peanuts, and fertilizer. Although ships continued to dock along the Cape Fear River, Wilmington solidified its role as a regional railroad center, and the city's commercial and industrial districts expanded accordingly.

Attracted by this economic revitalization, hundreds of people came here looking for wage work. These newcomers included poor white tenant farmers, newly freed slaves from nearby plantations, and immigrants from Europe, especially Ireland. Despite the general air of prosperity, economic opportunity was not available to everyone, and there were new political and social problems as well.

In particular, Wilmington had become a kind of "mecca" for African Americans. Unlike other cities in North Carolina, Wilmington had always had a small, black middle class of entrepreneurs, skilled craftsmen, and professionals. Although the majority of black citizens were unskilled laborers with low-paying jobs, the size of this "Talented Tenth" seemed to expand in the 1880s.

By 1897, blacks owned 13.6% of the 918 businesses listed in the city directory. Lawyers, teachers, ministers, and doctors supplied additional services. The high visibility of these 150 or so individuals supported the perception that blacks were advancing faster than–and at the expense of–wage earning whites. When the United States entered a deep economic depression in 1893, white resentment turned into open hostility.

Increasing black political participation added to these economic tensions. African Americans gained the right to vote in 1866, when Congress passed the 14th Amendment. Whereas white Southerners tended to vote Democratic, blacks favored the party of Lincoln. Because blacks comprised more than 50% of the city's population, their superior numbers contributed to the rise of the Republican Party in the Cape Fear region.

By 1877, the Democrats had successfully recaptured control of the state legislature, New Hanover County, and the city of Wilmington. Blacks and Republicans did not regain their political influence until the 1890s, when many Southern farmers blamed the economic downturn on their Democratic governments and defected to the Populists, an independent third party based on agrarian reform. Sensing the change, Republicans quickly allied themselves with the Populist Party. The resulting "Fusion" coalition swept to power in 1894 and 1896.

As a reward for their party loyalty, certain prominent black Republicans received political appointments and municipal jobs. By 1897, there were 40 black justices of the peace in New Hanover County, along with the county treasurer, recorder of deeds, coroner, and assistant sheriff. Wilmington had three black aldermen, two all-black fire companies, and numerous black policemen, mail carriers, and health inspectors. When compared to the offices and jobs held by whites, none of these positions were particularly powerful and there were not very many of them.

Nevertheless whites felt increasingly threatened. Some resented the number of blacks in high-paying jobs. Others focused on the social implications of rising black economic and political power. As one Wilmingtonian later reported, "The Negroes became more and more intoxicated in their newly acquired freedom. Instead of enjoying their rights privately, many of them insisted on publicly demonstrating their foolish belief that the uncultured African was the social equal to the cultured whites."

To blacks, assertive behavior was an important sign of their changed status. To whites, it was disrespectful, insolent, and even "uppity." Believing that their entire world had been turned upside down, Southern whites wanted to set it right again. When the Democrats waged their statewide "white supremacy" campaign in 1898, they finally got an opportunity to "redeem" their fair city from "Negro Domination."

Racial tensions increased throughout the fall of 1898. In Wilmington, white supremacist organizations and Democratic Party leaders staged rallies and parades, held public meetings, and circulated racist propaganda. To add fuel to the fire, Democratic newspapers insisted that black men posed a sexual threat to white women. Their lurid articles and cartoons not only played upon white fears of rape and assault, but they raised the specter of miscegenation, or race mixing, as well. Although deliberate sensationalism certainly sold a lot of papers, it also had the power to inflame public opinion and influence voters. Emotions ran even higher when Alex Manly, editor of *The Daily Record*, the city's only black newspaper, contended that some of the alleged "rapes" were actually consensual relationships.

Despite several weeks of interracial skirmishing, the day of the election, November 8, was actually quiet. The few blacks who did vote returned immediately to their homes, and the whites voted overwhelmingly in support of the Democrats. In Raleigh, party leaders congratulated themselves on a job well done, but in Wilmington, the real business of "redemption" was just beginning.

Recognizing that the newly elected Democrats could not actually take office until the spring, nine prominent businessmen took decisive steps to effect an immediate transfer of power in Wilmington. At 11 am on November 9, they held a public meeting at the courthouse, where the city's white citizens enthusiastically adopted a series of resolutions called the "White Man's Declaration of Independence." Among other things, this document resolved that black office holding was unnatural, that the preferential hiring of blacks had to end, that the city's Fusionist administration must resign, that *The Daily Record* must cease publication, and that Alex Manly must be banished.

Later that afternoon, a committee of 25 prominent white citizens presented the Declaration to select representatives of the black community, and ordered them to submit a written response within twelve hours. The black men had little choice in the matter, but they drafted a carefully worded reply and placed it in the mail. The letter failed to arrive in time. In retaliation, a mob of angry, armed white men destroyed *The Daily Record* office, put a bounty on Manly's head, and instigated the so-called riot of November 10, 1898.

The episode was not really a riot in the true sense of the word. Some of the violence was indeed random, but much of it was controlled and almost all of it was directed by whites against black targets. It was one of the worst racially- and politically-motivated episodes in American history. Homes and churches were damaged, businesses were destroyed, and lives were forever altered.

In the midst of the turmoil, another mob of white citizens surrounded the city hall, where prominent local Democrats forced the Republican mayor and aldermen to resign and then appointed themselves as replacements. This event may be the only coup d'etat in the United States. Interestingly, the violence was over in less than eight hours, and almost all of the damage was confined to a single neighborhood. By nightfall, the Wilmington Messenger reported that "an uneasy calm had descended over the city." In reality, the resolution of the drama continued for several more days.

The two-page 'official' history provides the economic, social and political context in which the November 10, 1898 violence, focusing on the development of Fusion politics in the area and the perception that blacks were prospering in Wilmington. The new narrative about 1898 mentions the group of secret nine prominent businessmen who organized the coup d'etat, yet does not provide their names. The new 'official history' describes the violence as white-organized aggression against blacks, thus challenging the dominant narrative in which whites were portrayed as "protectors" against black rioters.

Yet noticeably absent from the new version of the 1898 event is any mention of deaths resulting in the violence. The only reference to the toll of the violence in the *Foundation's* official version is in terms of property damage.

The issue of the number of blacks killed on November 10, 1898 is a contentious one (Cody 2000; Prather 1984; Edmonds 1951). The dominant version created immediately after the violence put the death toll between nine and twelve. Participant Waddell (1908) asserts twenty; Hayden's (1936) account says ninety. Historian Edmonds (1951) estimates twenty-five. Prather (1984:134) provides accounts of hundreds dead and citing the editor of the *Wilmington Messenger* on November 11, 1898, "How many blacks were killed will never be known." In its 'official version' *The Foundation* chose neither to address whether or not deaths occurred, nor reflect on the loss of black lives as a result of the mob violence.

The stories about the loss of life in 1898 are widespread and longstanding. An African American woman interviewed by Nash in 1968 describes:

> They went over there and shot down many colored men because my aunt was on her porch on Fourth Street and she saw these cots pass with men thrown up there like animals, just like dead animals they were taking them out to bury. Now she saw that, that they had killed them, murdered them, just shot them down. Now you won't find that in history because they don't want that—no! There's not liable to be. But that's true. They didn't allow it to be published.

A white female newcomer to Wilmington described to me the lore she heard about the death count:

> I've heard from one member of the black community who said at first she wasn't sure, but then she got some definitive information that it was what some of the accounts had said. That it was bloody, there were lots of people floating in the river, that it was much more of a massacre than we have ever been told it was. Yet we hear from others that it was nine or ten, or we don't know how many, that people fled into the woods.

An African-American woman I interviewed explained:

> You know that's what the people say, that's why the Cape Fear is pol-
> luted—because of the toxins of the bodies that are on the bottom of
> the river.

An African-American male I interviewed recited the stories he heard about
the loss of black lives growing up:

> The old stories say that you could see blood, actually in the Cape Fear
> River. That there were bodies there. Bodies strewn about . . . It was far
> greater than nine or twelve. From my perspective, as well as I can re-
> member, and the old folks, you know many of them weren't very well
> educated, but they just say something like 'a whole heap of them' or
> hundreds and hundreds and hundreds, and you know that it probably
> wasn't 4 or 5 hundred, but when they say hundreds and hundreds and
> hundreds, you know it's more than 12, and more than a hundred. So
> that's the way I take it. You have to understand the dialect and the lingo
> of folks in that era. When they say hundreds and hundreds and hun-
> dreds, that generally meant more than a hundred. Didn't mean count the
> times I say hundred. I mean based on what I've heard and all I would
> have to put it in the hundreds.

An African American female *Foundation* member, who stressed the importance of 'telling the story truthfully, but not pointing fingers,' asked
that I turn off the tape recorder when she explained a story she had heard
about the number of deaths in 1898. Her voice changed and she spoke in-
tently saying:

> I *know* it was a massacre. I *know* it. I was told a story by a woman who
> was talking to an old white man downtown who said "Why don't you
> talk about the ghost of Wilmington?" And the woman said "what
> ghost?" The man said that his father had told him that there were
> enough bodies in the Cape Fear to build a bridge from one side to an-
> other. I was at a luncheon and told this to a white wealthy Old-
> Wilmington friend of mine who said, "Why Mildred, that's what we
> were told all my life!"

There will never be a consensus on the loss of African American lives
on November 10, 1898. Yet the 'official history' produced by *The
Foundation* chose neither to address whether or not deaths occurred, nor reflect on the loss of black lives as a result of the mob violence. By neglecting
to address the loss of life, the culpability of whites on November 10, 1898,
is tempered.

REPARATIONS

The issue of reparations was a subject the *1898 Foundation* was forced to reckon with early on. According to Anthony (1999) the *Foundation* struggled internally with the issues of reparations and in a footnote explains the attitude concerning reparations among *Foundation* members:

> The issue was a derisive one with the Executive Council itself; and her strong disagreement with the position of the Foundation ultimately took probably permanently alienated Inez Eason, who had participated from very early in the process and was a vocal advocate of reparations . . . (Anthony 1999:51 footnote 67).

In October 1997 the *Foundation* formulated a "Statement on Reparations":

> It has been documented that during the Wilmington Coup and violence of 1898, in addition to the loss of life, many African-Americans had their livelihoods and property unjustly taken away. The acknowledgment of harsh realities such as these is a crucial aspect of the healing, which we hope will come out of the commemoration of that event. It is our position, however, that the actual seeing of reparations or other redress for individual acts of confiscation is something best left to the descendants of those whose property was taken. Our task with the 1898 Foundation will be the larger task of bringing to the light of day what transpired, commemorating the event, helping to create an atmosphere conducive to equal opportunity and empowerment and in so doing bringing about reconciliation. A key component of that reconciliation is gaining economic development for the African-American community as a whole because the black community as a whole, not just the direct descendants of victims, has been adversely affected and its economic growth stunted by the events of 1898 (Anthony 1999:51).

The statement on reparations was essentially an internal document. Members of the *Foundation* described the way in which the issue of reparations became a 'muted' voice.

An African-American female respondent explained:

> I was very hopeful about the 1998 commemoration planning. But soon I learned that everything was for show only. They just wanted to keep the status quo of the people. No one was to apologize, no one was to blame, everything was just for show. The 1998 events divided the community.

> In particular, no one wanted to talk about reparations. If I brought up reparations in a meeting, it just brought shame. No one would discuss it. There was this same arrogance that you see with any white group— if you complain the "*intellectuals*" leave you alone. Having the events at

UNCW didn't help the community. Half the buildings at UNCW are named after people who participated in 1898! The pain was in the center of town. That's where the healing was needed, not at UNCW. If they had held meetings downtown, more regular citizens would have attended. Gregory Auditorium holds 900 people! Why not have something there in the black community? Blacks are not part of UNCW. Everyone knows that.

One professional white male respondent commented on the issues of reparations:

Everbody has been very careful to mute it [reparations]. Most of the discussions, I went to a lot of the meetings, were like "who will get this or that?" and they pretty much got hushed up. The way you can do reparations for a community, do something that signals what you are doing. A Scholarship fund—the City of Wilmington could send ten black residents to study somewhere.

For McLaurin (2000:49) the calls for reparations came from 'inner-city residents':

Although it rejected calls from some segments of the African American community, especially younger, inner-city residents, to demand reparations from the white elite, the foundation developed a program to promote economic justice.

Yet many of the African-American professionals I interviewed expressed contempt for the way the *Foundation* dismissed the issue of reparations. An African American businessman explained the issue of reparations:

"Let's not talk about the past let's talk about the future." Kinda like 14 acres and a mule. Clearly the reparations voice was silenced. As soon as it was voiced there was the air of alarm and militancy that was spoken and alluded to all around the town: "Are they going to start asking for something now?" Well, the fact is that there should have been on that commission [1898 Foundation] a real effort to: one, acknowledge that that is a viable option. Two, they should have commissioned a group of neutral parties with legal capability, research capability, and sociological knowledge to look back as far as they could into the notions that property and wealth was extorted and taken. But you see it wasn't until the '50s that the Register of Deeds had any real recording methods or system, but there were families who could trace, through voice and letters, their assets and personal assets back a century or more. And they [the Foundation] didn't want to open that up. Because there were certain families that clearly took property. Took it, stole it. And their heirs,

many of them who were afraid to come back and make claim, in fear
that they might get killed or destroyed, same thing, if you dead you destroyed. So there's a lot of fear involved here.

A professional African-American male explained:

> The reparations . . . well, nobody would talk about it! I look at it two
> ways, as a black person: yea, give me some. But as a realist, what are
> you going to give me? Are you going to give it to everybody? How is
> that going to make things better? There are people out there on drugs,
> are you gonna give it to them? So how can you be fair about it? It is a
> tough question. There were some hard factions: hard factions over
> here, hard factions over there. They [the Foundation] didn't want to
> give and the others didn't want to give. So I guess, it turned out, and
> that's the way it was. But this group [the Foundation] it was either "my
> way or the highway." All or nothing. So obviously 'the nothing' made
> this group feel good anyway, 'cause they actually got what they
> wanted. See what I'm saying? And this other group was too stupid to
> realize what was going on! You know what's so funny about this, most
> of the people involved in this were white middle-class females. Think
> about it: who had time, who needed a project or something to do, hey,
> come on. That's what happened! That's what happened! Where were
> their husbands? You know? The ones who really control the money?
> "No problem. You go ahead baby, you do this one. But that's where
> the line stops." And I saw through all of that. The community is not
> going to be healed. They don't care. They really don't care. I'm being
> realistic. You have to change people's hearts. There is still institution-
> alized racism. They just cover it with coats, and coats, and you don't
> know what's going on. The sad part is a lot of people have given up.
> They've given up. It's either this or that, no compromise. We don't
> even have leaders capable of change. Nothing has changed. Put a coat
> of paint on it, whitewash it, that's it.

CONCLUSION

McLaurin (2000:55) concludes his essay on the 1998 commemoration activities saying:

> The commemorative events of 1998 clearly indicate that in Wilmington,
> as in much of the South, the mythic past, though still powerful, is no
> longer what it was.

Or is it? How different is the new narrative from the dominant narrative?
The *1898 Foundation* developed legitimacy among official organizations
and institutions, thus enabling the 'new narrative' to develop recognition as

a legitimate interpretation of the 1898 violence, yet to what extent does the new narrative represent something 'new'?

The question posed at the beginning of this chapter examines the way in which narratives combine elements of the dominant ideology with subordinate narratives to produce new narratives that sustain rather than challenge ruling hegemony. Table 5.2 below represents the organizing principles of the dominant narrative and 'new' narrative.

In this chapter I examined the way the new narrative combined elements of the dominant ideology with the subordinate narrative to produce a new narrative that sustains rather than challenges ruling hegemony. The organizing principle of the narrative of reconciliation embodies the meta-narrative of liberalism. Key to liberalism is individualism and equality of opportunity. Addressing reparations implies that equality of opportunity does not exist; that is, someone who requires payment for past grievances must have been wronged in a way that requires redress.

Though the new narrative attempts to 'tell the story,' it provides an 'official history' which neither names those responsible nor addresses the number of deaths of blacks by whites. In not assigning blame ("no one living today") the belief in individualism and meritocracy—that privilege is not passed-on but earned is sustained.

The new narrative incorporates elements of previously subordinated narratives claiming that whites were aggressors against blacks yet like the dominant narrative, the new narrative deflects white culpability through the organizing principle of 'reconciliation' and an official history that is silent on the number of deaths whites perpetrated. The irony of the new narrative is that in calling for inclusiveness and reconciliation, it has effectively silenced claims for reparations. The new narrative distorts the class interests

Table 5.2 Organizing Evaluation Principles of Dominant Narrative and New Narrative

DOMINANT NARRATIVE	NEW NARRATIVE
1. Deflects white culpability	"No one living today . . ." 'Official history' is silent on black death toll
2. Suppressed alternate versions of violence	Suppresses voice of 'Reparations'
3. Justifies white aggression against blacks	Incorporates elements of subordinate narrative "whites" are aggressors against "blacks"

of the group, middle-class whites and blacks, responsible for the development of the new version of 1898 events. These interests, I argue, reflect the ideology of color-blind liberalism (Cochran 1999), a type of liberalism that argues the color of one's skin should make no difference in the way one is treated. This is a newer form of liberalism that argues the victories of the Civil Rights Movement have effectively broken down the barriers that once prevented blacks from having the freedom of opportunity, and the responsibility for success of everyone, regardless of skin-color is on the individual. This ideology has widespread support in the nation among whites of all social classes as well as a growing number of middle class blacks who have indeed made gains from the political and social dismantling of discriminatory practices. Color-blind liberalism, therefore, does not look back to past injustices. Rather it focuses on moving forward "together."[6]

Chapter Six
Contemporary Narratives and Political Generations

"You got to look at the period of time you come in and the living conditions of your time and the way things are. And that thing is ingrained
in you. And it's ingrained in me. I learned to live with it, and adjust myself to it." (80 year-old African American male)

In this chapter I examine when and how respondents learned about 1898
using the political generations delineated in Chapter Three and outlined
below in Table 6.1. The interviews with informants from each political generation provide information about the following research questions: Do the
gaps and silences identified in the baseline public dominant narrative correspond with contemporary informants' narratives? What generational experiences, that is, experiences grounded in historical periods influence the
narratives of contemporary informants? I wanted to know specifically, if
and when informants in each political generation learned about 1898; if informants are familiar with the 1998 Commemoration activities, and
whether or not they support the 'new narrative.' I also wanted to know if
whites differ from blacks in how and when they learned about 1898.

In order to preserve anonymity, I use fictitious names for people,
streets and businesses, etc., that in any way may reveal the identity of respondents. The stories these informants tell are commanding, and so, for
the most part, I provide lengthy quotes so the reader can get a sense of the
richness of the data. While I provide a brief analysis after each narrative,
I save detailed discussion of the findings of these personal narratives for
the end of the chapter. The key informants I interviewed offer powerful
stories about race and respect and the tremendous impact of narratives of
terror on communities.

Table 6.1 Political Generations[a] by Race

Age at time of interview 2000–2001	Period in which informants 18–25 years old	N =	B	W	Localized Public Narrative/Event when informants were 18–25 years old
18–25	1994–2001	2	1	1	1994 publication of *Cape Fear Rising;* 1998 Centennial Commemoration Ceremony
26–33	1986–1993	4	2	2	1989—250th Anniversary of Wilmington play that mentions 1898
34–41	1978–1985	2	1	1	1984 publication *We Have Taken A City;* Prather gives lecture and book signing in Wilmington; 1980 *Wilmington Morning Star* article on 1898.
42–49	1970–1977	5	2	3	1971—Wilmington Ten; 1976 *Wilmington Morning Star* bi-centennial issue covers 1898 event; 1977 *Wilmington Journal* 50th anniversary edition runs editorial.
50–57	1962–1969	5	2	3	No public reference to 1898. 1968 riot after death of Martin Luther King Jr.; Schools desegregated, 1969.
58–65	1954–1961	7	5	2	No public reference to 1898
66–73	1946–1953	3	2	1	1951—Dr. Hubert Eaton's school equalization campaign. Eaton is reminded of 1898 by white officials. Edmonds' book is published and Louis T. Moore responds.
74–81	1938–1945	3	2	1	1943—Governor Broughton reminds Wilmington audience of 1898. Black Camp Davis soldiers start melee in Brooklyn. Local white official refers to 1898 in newspaper.
82–89	1930–1937	1	1	0	Hayden's account of 1898 published in 1936.
90–97	1922–1929	1	0	1	No public mention of 1898.
98–105	1914–1921	1	1	0	No public mention of 1898. Racial tension in 1919 at shipyard between black and white riveters lasting about 3 weeks.
	TOTAL	34	19	15	

a Political generations are calculated based on first political generation of 18–25 year olds in 1898.

B=Black / W= White

"I THINK ALL THOSE THINGS, ALL THOSE BAD THINGS, I THINK YOU SHOULD JUST FORGET THEM."

The political generations up to and including World War II–1914–1921; 1922–1929; 1930–1937; and 1938–1945—provide a uniform narrative of the way in which they learned about 1898 and their feelings about commemorating the event. All but one learned about 1898 as a child and from a close relative. No respondents in these political generations participated in the 1898 centennial commemoration activities and none supported the new narrative about 1898, mostly because each believe it is better to forget about 1898.

The oldest respondent I spoke to, the person with closest proximity to the 1898 racial violence was an African-American woman in the political generation 98–105. She was born a few years after the 1898 violence and except for four years she spent away at college, she lived in Wilmington her entire life, as did her parents. We spoke a while about her schooling and work experience. I probed about her knowledge of 1898:

> Well I don't know much about it. I'm hearing more about that now and— my parents never talked about that. It was always love and kindness that's all. I don't know much about 18—but they say that blacks had even offices and places here, I don't know any thing about it. Not when I was growing up; I hear more about it now, 'cause they are looking into it now. I hear more of it now. But I don't give it a thought. I couldn't tell you. I know they say they ran the black folk out, some had to leave and give up the jobs, and some had to go to Jump N Run, that's where it got its name, I don't know that much. I don't think I can help you. My parents, she didn't talk about it. My parents worked, they had to work to send me to school, and they worked. And they worked for some of the, they used to tell me, the blue blood in Wilmington. The Harris's, the Long's, let me see, 2nd and Long, the Reaves, some of the big money, and they stood out. The Harris's, the Long's, the Smith's, that's who she worked around. And they were all nice to her. I used to go with her. I can remember as a little girl, going and playing in the back yard, and I can remember Harry Smith, who was a very noted artist in Wilmington, he's dead and gone now, used to take a little bar piece of soap, and say, now I'm going to cut this up and make it look like you, or he would get a pencil and draw it, and it would look like you, I remember that from a child. And I had to have been 10 or 11, 12. My mother didn't leave me, she carried me with her, and the folk I don't know they all, they would even tell me, "Listen don't go out on the sidewalk you might get hurt, you better stay back here where your mother can see you." I can remember Miss Lorna Smith lived the corner of 2nd and Long, right on the corner, right across the church, Baptist, I believe it's Baptist. I don't know too much about it. I hear more about it around my church and in the papers that I read and all. Yes, it's being talked about more now. One thing they couldn't talk about it, they were afraid, I guess to mention it, so

now it's coming out. [whispers] *I don't know. NO* one talked about it to me, that's the real truth. I had a happy life. I used to have a play-house out there. My father was a carpenter. I tell you, God always provides for those who do good. I didn't have a whole lot, but if there was anything to be gotten, I got it. If there was anything to be gotten. My life was always happy. Now I'm not telling you no lies. No, I don't know any of that could have been, but [whispers and speaks very slowly] *I don't know anything about it.* My family was busy working and trying to provide for me, and my father was a carpenter, and a surveyor, he was in and out of Wilmington. Always jolly and happy. I don't know anything, just like I tell you. I wish I could help you with the 1898. I first heard about it a couple of years ago. Miss, if I heard it I never paid much attention to it. So, I've heard nothing about that 1898. And anything else I know, and probably reading it in the paper. Unh hunh.

The respondent explains that she had no knowledge of 1898 growing up, and only recently learned about the violence in 1898. She also took care to explain that her parents worked hard to provide for her, that they were too busy to tell her about the violence in Wilmington. She began addressing me as "miss" after we spoke about 1898, and I sensed she was very uncomfortable talking about this topic. In my field notes I wrote:

> Is she afraid to talk about this because her mother worked for powerful people in the community? Why does she keep saying "this is the truth"? Is it NOT the truth? In other parts of the interview, especially when describing the Wilmington Ten 1971 violence, she does not say "this is the truth."

I learned from earlier interviews that older black Wilmingtonians were still too afraid to talk about 1898 today. This interview confirmed that fear: either she had never heard about 1898; she was too afraid to talk about what she knew; or indeed she too finds it hard to believe that she had never heard about it and feels compelled to assure me "it is the truth." Nevertheless it was an uncomfortable topic for her and one that made her summon race-based deference practices of a Jim Crow era.

An African-American woman from the 1930–1937 political generation described how she learned about 1898:

> I remember older people, my mother, seem like my mother was a child, I know she would be talking about it. Now her mother, her mother remembered it well. But I didn't know her grandmother. I would hear them talk about the riot. And some people here in Wilmington, could tell you about it. Now that Love and Charity Hall where they burned down the paper, we used to have players, juvenile society, and we used to go in there to meet. I remember that well. You know Smith Creek

where they threw those people over board and cut their heads off. The only thing I can remember I know they said something about coming home, I don't know if it was her granddaddy and they were coming home down the street, and they could see something was going on, and they didn't know exactly what it was until they saw all the shooting. I don't remember all the details, and if she did tell me I don't remember it, but I can remember her saying it and some of what they said. The press said something about him talking about a black man and a white woman; some of the older folks say that it wasn't that. Then I heard them say that blacks had a lot of offices at that time, and this was what it was all about, they did not want them holding those offices. And they kept trying to find a way to get them out. And strange as it may seem, they said all black people were Republicans. And I had an uncle who remembers, who said he would beat you if you said anything bad about Republicans! [laughter] And they said that was really the main reason why they started the race riot, it wasn't about the paper, there were judges and offices, and they were just prominent, and this wasn't going to happen, and this is the way they—they kept holding meeting, holding meetings till they got it just the way they wanted it, and then they, the blacks were unexpected when they jumped them. Blacks didn't have guns or anything. Some got away, and some were killed. That's—now the man who had the paper was married to a Sadgwar, and I had a Sadgwar teach me. Many people were killed. I'm sure it was. They have never told how many people were killed. But look at the people, the ones that they threw overboard, the ones that they shot and pushed overboard, they were trying to get away and thrown in the river, and they shot them, how could you ever take a toll of them? You couldn't count them. And some people said that river looked like blood, a blood bath it was so red with how many people they shot. It was a lot of people. And then took them and put their heads on posts and all. I just don't see how people could treat a human being that way. [Whispering] I just got the feeling that people just had to get back to work and not think about it. And I often wondered that: How could they go back to work? But they just had to. To act like nothing happened. I think they had to get up, if I had a job for Mrs. So-and-So, I would just have to get up in the morning and go back to work. I imagine the city was so tore up, for a while I guess they didn't do anything. I guess. Cause more or less those people *knew* what they were going to do. They had it all cut and dried. And they knew the places they were going to target. And some of them, by the time they told them not to come back any more. Some of them they told them to go out of town and not to come back to Wilmington any more. And many of them left and never came back, some would come back in later years, some had no more use for Wilmington anymore. *Did you talk to your kids about 1898?* Really we never discussed it. Now I didn't know too much to tell them about the race riot. Some times we would just sit down, and things would come up about it. But I really didn't know too much to tell them about it. Seem like to me I would hear my husband talk about it. *Did you follow the 1998 centennial of the 1898 violence?* I did not go to any of those meetings. But I didn't go. I didn't have anything to do with it. Seem like people like to talk too much about that riot. There is something, I guess it's a part of history people are trying to forget I reckon. Now that's my version and I'm settled about that way. It's really not a nice thing that nobody even want to express it or talk about. It's just a mean thing for somebody to do and I don't know it just does something to you when you talk about it. It's just like a lot of things, like slavery, you know it happened, and there's nothing we can do about it, and it seems it just does something when you talk about it and all that. It just, then you wonder *why, why, why* would anybody want to do that? I know you worked people, and you weren't paying them, but why do you have to beat them and kill them? Cause they didn't have no choice but to work. And then they're working like dogs and then you go and beat them? Why? Cut their feet off and their toes off, and all kinds of things like that. I would want to know why they would want a memorial? Why? It's something I don't want to keep in my mind. Now some people want to but I don't. It's nothing that I want a memorial for, for a riot for somebody who's shooting me. Now to me, I just don't like it. Now some people just want to keep it going, but I think WHY? What's the point? I mean I don't. Well you know I was thinking WHY would anybody want to put up a memorial for a riot? I was talking to myself when I saw it in the *Star,* when I saw it, it was, it was saying it was going to be where the Martin Luther King, and now that don't fit in at all to me. Now he's up there him who's done something for the race to try and help, and now you're going to come down with a, a riot, where they tried to tear down people, I don't see where the two go together. I really don't. Now maybe they see something that I don't, but I don't see it. I really don't. I don't see why they want to remember it. It's a part of my history, and I know it's happened and you read and know it, but I don't want to think—I don't want to dwell on it. You know. I really wouldn't. Because that could have been avoided. I mean you could have done some other method, why didn't they go ahead and vote them out? Instead of killing them. That was just a mean thing to do. And then they did it and said that down in the basement they got together at First Baptist Church, and I was kind of surprised from them. The black church came out of that church! That sounds funny to me. And there is a tunnel at St. Stevens Church where the slaves come through. They had people come together, say they are not intelligence but they came together. It took a lot of mother wit to get together. Look at the Bellamy and the craft down town. They didn't have any education but they knew how to do it. They were just born that way. Just smart people. Some black people are intelligent people; I mean they are just smart. Just smart. The way I feel, I will tell you the truth, Wilmington does just what the law requires them to do. The law requires them to do certain things, I mean

to treat you right, I don't feel like—I feel like things would still be segregated. To a certain extent, I mean right now you can see it, you can
feel it. I know I've noticed it, and not only me, a lot of us had. So I
mean all they do is what they are required to do, and they have to. And
if they can get by without doing it and have a way of doing it where
they don't include blacks, they do it. That's the way Wilmington is.
That's why my kids left to get better jobs. You know in my time you
had to leave to get a decent job. And now it's almost the same identical thing. Young people they work, if they get a job here, they gotta,
they tell you right quick they got to do twice as good as a white to stay
on that job. I've heard them tell me that more than once, I've got to do
twice the work and be twice as good. If the land didn't say "you've got
to do thus" I don't think it would change, I really don't. And any time
a place you live in got to be made to treat a human being right, I'm
skeptical of it. Because just like—they had to be forced to treat you
right. That's my feeling. They had to get a law to force them to treat
you right. So naturally I feel like it's the law, that's all.

There are five key points raised in this narrative that resonate in narratives of
the three pre-World War II generations: First, the respondent learned about
1898 from older family members, particularly women; it is her understanding
that blacks held power in 1898; to her mind many deaths occurred and the
Cape Fear River was bloody from black deaths. Like the previous respondent,
this woman does not support the commemoration activities, but rather chooses
to forget. This respondent describes the fear and trauma of the event by trying
to fathom HOW victims who remained in Wilmington could continue—could
go back to work the next day as if nothing had happened: because they HAD
to. Though she says she did not tell her children much, she does indicate that
something about the 1898 was passed down. Lastly, and most importantly, this
respondent believes that Wilmington is still a segregated community. She tells
us that her children left to find better jobs, and that young black people in
Wilmington have to work harder and be 'twice as good' as white people. Blacks
are still not given respect in Wilmington today.

    A white woman from the 1938–1945 political generation told me very
nicely, yet curtly, that she had heard about 1898 growing up, but that she really did not have much to say about it:

> I heard about it growing up. We never learned about it in school, but
> I heard about it growing up. I heard about the shooting. They had to
> get rid of some blacks. I don't know that much about it. It was a bad
> time, that's all I know. *Did you follow the 1998 centennial activities?*
> I don't know anything about it. Don't have anything to do with it.

Like others in her generation, she did not support the 1998 centennial activities.

An African-American woman in the 1938–1945 political generation describes learning about 1898:

> Years ago a lot of the head officials in Wilmington were black. And that's what started that Wilmington fire, the head officials, banks and everything were headed by blacks. They tried to burn Wilmington down. But back then those days—they were bad. I heard about it as a child. Years ago. I heard about all that tension here. No black history in school, people talked about it though. It could have been in the 1890s 'cause it wasn't during my time. Years ago, blacks were in power. That's what sparked off the Wilmington fire, tried to burn it down. That's right. My mama used to tell me about it. She said, she was telling about different people who had high offices here in Wilmington and they ran the city, and some whites got mad about it, and Wilmington almost burned down. Blacks went north so they could get good money. And then they left Wilmington to go north. Blacks had a lot of power, a lot of money. And my mother's daddy was a mill-wright and knew how to keep up all that equipment out in the mill. That was a good job. Years ago, up there around Montague, they would place Negro heads on poles when they would kill them, up there in Pender County, and they stuck those heads on the stakes and that's the way they would keep others from going down in there. Years ago, you used to see on the maps, Nigger Head Road, up there near Montague, they called that Nigger Head Road. My mother and daddy lived on Long Creek. A lot of battles fought up there. *Did you follow the 1998 centennial commemoration of 1898 violence?* Never did. Never bother with things like that. I stayed away from that. Times are much better now. That's right. Don't you think? They have been a little change.

This informant learned about 1898 from her mother; and believed blacks were in power. Like the previous informant, the respondent references an event that is believed to have happened in 1832 on Negro Head Road (see Rose 1998). Local stories about "Nigger Head Road" describe an event where slaves' heads were put on poles outside of town as a warning to stay in line. Many variations on this story exist: sometimes it is outside Wilmington, sometimes in neighboring Pender County. Mariel Rose's (1998) research on an African American settlement called Pokomoke generated narratives about Nigger Head Road that mixed this gruesome imagery with stories about 1898 and the Bloody Cape Fear motif. In many of the interviews I collected, reference to Nigger Head Road and Bloody Cape Fear overlapped, sometimes as the same event. For the respondent above, as well as the previous informant, the macabre reference to Nigger Head Road is part of the employment of her narrative.

An African-American male in the 1938–1945 political generation describes when he learned about 1898:

My father was born right during the time, the year they had the riot here in 1898. That's when my father was born. In October 1898 and the riot was in November, and everybody, when he grew up everybody said "now see you gone and caused all that trouble by coming into the world" [laughter]. So he was born on North 9th Street. I was born at 9th and Wise. Very difficult time. He was too young to know anything. But he had older brothers and sisters, there were eleven in his family, and he had older brothers who were born in 1869, or somewhere along in there, and they were grown when all this happened. And when the riot started, they bailed out of here. Yea they bailed out. The Atlantic Coastline running down the track, it was a steam engine then, it made the sound [made sound of steam engine] and had to build up the steam before it got the speed going, and they were running for the train. And a lot of the young fellas they were jumping that train, getting out of Wilmington. Most likely a freight train, and they would jump in the box car, back in the back of that box car and stay there. Their mother she stayed here, my grandfather, they stayed here. She got word from them, they in New York. All in New York. And uh, so then, uh, I know when one of his brothers, when I was working for the railroad, employees of the railroad get passes on the train, free travel. So I had a pass and I told my dad, let's go to New York 'cause I've never been to New York. So I went to New York and I met my father's brother, his name is Harry. He stayed up there. And my father went to him "Harry you oughta come on home, back to Wilmington, I want you to see that place on the water," my father was working down there working on barrels, and uh the Sprunts were doing a whole lot of shipping stuff in barrels, and used to carry Papa, they called him papa daddy, give papa the lunch. I want you to see the place, see how they built it up. He looked at my father and said, "George, I'm not going back to Wilmington. I don't intend to go back to Wilmington. They are the meanest white folks I ever seen is in Wilmington, North Carolina. Ain't no place worse than Wilmington, North Carolina. Oh, no. I ain't going back to Wilmington. I rather be a lamppost in New York than be a man in Wilmington." That's what he said. That's how he felt. Right there. His mother died in 1914 and he wouldn't come back for the funeral. He sent messages and everything, telegrams. But he wouldn't come back, no he wouldn't come back. Now after his father died my father was still trying to get him to come back and he wouldn't come. And I didn't get the feeling about the riot, but when I heard him talk like that, I said "my goodness, yea." And the minister of my church, things got so bad round here he ran. He jumped the train too. Oh yea, whole families left. And they took the jobs. No jobs. And if you ain't got a job you were watched like a hot dog, and weren't trusted, no salary. During that time most people, black people, lived in a shot gun house. That's what we had all in Brooklyn. And that's why they built Taylor homes, and Nesbitt Homes were built for the whites, Taylor Homes built for the blacks. But all around Brooklyn there were these shot gun homes and poor living conditions. And water and sewage, all the poor things didn't have.

Our parents didn't talk about it. For one reason, I didn't know until I got older and started asking questions from older people in the neighborhood, and older people in the family. I had an older aunt; she was much older and I remember her very well and she was born in 1878, and she remembered all that stuff and she wouldn't even talk to her children. And she had eleven children just like her mama. You ask them questions they clam right up. Clam right up. And then I wondered "why"? And my older sister said to my mother, "How come you won't talk? Why won't you talk?" [Pause for effect] "There are some things good for you to know, some things not good for you to know." That's how they put it, because they didn't want to build hate. If you talk about all the bad things it's just hate. She said the only way for you to get along in life is not to hate but to love. And they never taught us. They never talked to us about it. And they never said, "Hate the white man, and hate this person," didn't talk about this and that. My father always told me to be dependable and always be trustworthy.

Hard times in Wilmington during that time, there, uh, Wilmington Ten. The integration of schools and all that kind of stuff. That was a hard time too. That kind of reminds you, the Wilmington Ten kind of reminds you of the riot of 1898, just in a different form. Uh, in 1898 the blacks in Wilmington, the white people, the blacks trusted the white people, they thought there were their friends, but they were their enemy and they didn't know it. The whites in Wilmington, they somehow hired someone in South Carolina to come and do their dirt for them. And therefore, when the riots were over in 1898 the blacks thought it was so and so and so and so. But later on, they found out more and more. They tried to say the black man caused it! The papers in Wilmington said the black man caused it! And then the paper came out and said black people and talking the black man and the white woman and all that kind of stuff. And it wasn't that, what it was they were trying to get the black, the black was the head of government. They were the City Council, the head of government, the judges, the lawyers were black and they wanted to get them out of power. So they got somebody else to do the dirt for them, so they still looked respectable to the blacks, you see. So that's, but uh. Now when the Wilmington Ten, Ben Chavis come in here, and organized those young blacks and they demonstrated. But he wanted to use force, and Martin Luther King said non-violence, and that's why he called for all that burning and looting and stuff, he went just the opposite of Martin Luther King and non-violence. Well then, it's a strange thing that officials of the city would not listen to reason and then were forced to integrate. Then they locked Ben Chavis up. This is just another repeat of 1898 but just come at a different type of force. You know I couldn't understand why I was in the service, I was in a black army. In Georgia, on the left side of the camp it was for blacks, and on the right side for whites. Now we all one army, we all going to fight one enemy. And why we separated? And when we went overseas, same thing, every where you went segregated, segregated. And then I said, uh, after something you grew up in. But I remember my mother was up in her nineties and sister was with her, and she was in the grocery store and the lady gave her some change, and she said "thank you ma'am." And my sister started screaming at her, "Why you call that child 'ma'am'?" She does not understand, one thing, she had to say "thank you ma'am" to child five and six years old, white!, And she was a grown woman. She still said "Thank you ma'am." My father's boss had two sons, Henry Hill Jr. and Harvey Hill Jr. and my father working down there, heard my daddy called the little boy "Mr. Hill," and the little boy's daddy didn't call me Mr. Evans, he didn't call my daddy Mr. Evans, he called him George. First name, never called him Mister. You got to look at the period of time you come in and the living conditions of your time and the way things are. And that thing is ingrained in you. And it's ingrained in me. I learned to live with it, and adjust myself to it. But a lot of my friends come along with me, couldn't stand it and they left. They were segregated up there, but they had a little more freedom.

Yea, I heard about that [1998 commemoration] but I didn't go out there to it. No, they try to have to get people's minds to think about the history and keep up with it, and they try to bring people together, and you got to be one to make any kind of life. No, I didn't go out there. We're not trying to fight a whole war. White man in Wilmington always swept that under the rug. And in these late years things are starting to come up, but they never talked about what they did in 1898. Now one thing they never did was sweep Confederacy under the rug! Now they bring that thing up front. Now time we say something, about black this or that they get offended! But they don't see how we're offended! What does the confederacy mean? Slavery! No "We don't mean anything, we don't mean anything!" What's in the heart, the issue of life comes out the heart. Yes sir. That's what I mean by, if you mean right Whites have kept 1898 quiet, what they did in 1898. Nobody talking about it.

Like others in these three political generations, this informant learned about 1898 from a family member, his father, who was born a month before the violence. The respondents' uncles fled Wilmington at that time, and we learn of the fear and trauma this event generated. Not even with the death of his mother would the uncle return to Wilmington. The respondent also describes the fear those who remained behind had, that they would not even tell their children about the event. His narrative also highlights the contradictions of the dominant narrative (they always swept that under the rug." And lastly, while this respondent served in the army during World War II and describes the contradictions of fighting for freedom, yet having little freedom at home, he also tells us these are things you learn to live with and "adjust myself to it."

For the political generations before and during World War II, there is a reluctance to memorialize the 1898 event. The organizing/evaluative principle found in these narratives is one of caution and consternation when talking about 1898. As the archival data shows, the suppression of the 1898 violence up to the late 1930s—early 1940s, coupled with the use of the dominant narrative as a cautionary tale in the early 1940s, created a climate of fear. Most in these three political generations wanted to forget and move on, unlike subsequent political generations. All the African Americans, but one, in these pre- WWII generations had learned about the 1898 event from family members growing up. The organizing evaluative feature of these narratives is the Bloody Cape Fear or other gruesome imageries of violence. We learn from these narratives that young African-American men left Wilmington at the time of the violence, and African-American women were left behind. Thus the storytelling in the private narratives of African Americans in Wilmington over generations was passed down by women. Whites in these pre-World War II political generations had knowledge of the event, although were very reluctant to share or elaborate on what they knew. While both blacks and whites in these generations wanted to forget about 1898, blacks more than whites, were more willing to ruminate and share the stories they had been told. Finally, black Wilmingtonians in these political generations puzzled and reflected on the lives of those affected wondering how they could continue and move on.

"1898 SUB-TEXT TO THEIR LIVES . . ."

An organizing/evaluative principle in the narratives of three post-World War II political generations (1946–1953, 1954–1961, 1962–1969), is embodied in a phrase coined by one respondent, the '1898 mentality' (quoted in Chapter Four page 133). Three of the fifteen (20 percent) respondents in these three political generations had not heard about the 1898 violence until the late 1990s (two white, one black). Nine (60 percent) had learned about the violence growing up from family members (eight black, one white). Three (20 percent) (all white) had heard about 1898 as young adults from friends. All respondents but two (86 percent (both whites) in these three political generations framed their narratives on an idea that people in Wilmington were encumbered with an '1898 effect,' a world view forged in the residue of the 1898 violence. Most of the post-World War II political generation respondents had lived outside Wilmington for some period of time during their lives, unlike the earlier political generations (during and pre-WWII) in which residency outside Wilmington did not occur, except for one respondent who served in the military during the war years.

A white woman in the 1946–1953 political generation explained:

I heard about 1898 long before they got their stuff going. When I first
came here I never thought about it. And I just never thought about it.
And I came here and saw the separate bathrooms and the separate
drinking fountains. And one thing. I don't know it's wrong. It's not
right. And I'm sure that being friendly with different people I heard
about it. I don't remember exactly when, I know it was the early 50s.
I guess I, you know, I. Well that 1898 that was terrible. They literally
cleaned the middle class out of this area. And 1971 was another. And
there were some not very nice elements mixed up in that. I knew Joe
Wright. They just, well, the teachers were prejudiced against the kids.
It was a mess from the beginning. But it wasn't right and I still get an
argument from everybody when I say it, but it wasn't right for them
to put those ten in jail. And then Ben Chavis turned out to be a big
pain-in-the-neck in a lot of ways, but, well, you know. Well, what's
happened is that the blacks are definitely separate from the whites.
There's no getting around it. And they want it that way. And I feel, the
only person, Barbara—but Barbara was the only black woman who I
really felt was a friend. I had other black women that I feel very close
to, but we don't have any social times together. But Barbara, she came
to our house, we went to her house. I think, you know, I think it's, I
don't know, I imagine it's self defense in a lot of ways. As a white person, you don't know how insulting you can be and not mean to. I
mean as whites we simply don't understand what they put up with
from one day to the next. And I mean it's nice to be white. *Did you
follow the 1898 centennial activities in 1998?* I felt like I was retread-
ing a lot. I went to the dialogues. I went to the different programs. I
don't think they ever accomplished much. I remember these two black
kids, and we were talking, you know, and they were, just, you know,
"what's the use." You know no matter what they did, no matter what
they said it wasn't going to change anything. And I felt, you know, it's
not really, it's not right. Because these were nice kids. These were not
kids standing on the street looking like bums and you know sort of
brazening it out with everybody. Nothing ever happens. I don't know,
I think in a way that living here (that's an underlying reason people
think the way they do. Nobody really tries to change anything. All the
new people are wealthy Republicans from the north who don't care.
They think they know everything because they've been here six years.
And they don't have to deal with the black problem. So. Well, it's, I
don't know. It's so slowly better that if you only got one life to live,
it's just too damn slow. Really.

For this respondent the segregated nature of Wilmington social relations has
something to do with the 1898 violence. This respondent participated in the
1998 centennial activities, but was unsure they made any change. She found
social change very slow to come to Wilmington.

A respondent in the 1954–1961 political generation, an African-American woman, recalled:

> The intimidation that was fostered on the black population with that riot has continued to roll down hill generation after generation after generation. I was taught nobody is better than me and I am better than nobody, and that has followed me all my life.

> My father would take me to visit elderly people he had met as a fireman for Atlantic Coastline. And that's how I got to meet former slaves, and talk to them and you simply had to ask to them what was it like when you were my age, and these people would begin to tell you that. But whenever you came up and started talking about anything connected to 1898, they would suddenly start looking around, or they would say, you know, that was just a bad time and we don't talk about it, which fueled my interest. I wanted to know more and more about it. So today, when you try to get some people to talk about it, they don't want to talk about it. Because descendants of the whites who were in charge during the time, basically are *still* in charge of the economy. That intimidation is still here.

> I think the first time I ever heard anything about it, there used to be a settlement across the river called Pokomoke. Well, okay, the majority of Pokomoke was torn down and demolished in the 30s, and there were a few houses spotted here and there. My father was a connoisseur of moonshine. He knew where a still was between Virginia and Tampa, Florida. And he liked to go to visit these places. And being an only child I was always with my parents. And my father took me over to Pokomoke, or what was left of it. And I remember those people sewing their own clothes, some of the most beautiful lace I ever saw. I just always wanted to hear these people talk about this stuff. And by going along with daddy I had a way to get in there—and they would start to tell you about it, and as I said, they would always start to look around, they were careful, they were afraid somebody was listening, because in that area, it was where, there were several of them, but the most well known was Nigger Head Road at Pokomoke, and once they put those heads on those spikes along that road then they had those people's minds. The younger children were told about it, you do this, you don't this, and you don't look at a white person when you're talking to 'em and this type thing. You keep your head down. I started to hear bits and pieces about this, but you just didn't, you had to be careful where you talked about it.

> The intimidation, the destruction of Wilmington's black community was erased, all of their property seized, nobody ever got anything from it, the folks that were left were so afraid that the same thing would happen to them that this is what they taught their descendants, and it was taught to me.

Blacks stood up for themselves more quickly in other places than they do here in Wilmington. And I am *convinced* it is because of the fact that [the] whole society was destroyed and the people were so afraid. I've lived in other places. You run into racism, but the blacks don't react to it the way they relate to it here. And the people here, the older ones especially still feel that they have to walk on eggshells. If they say anything at all they may lose the house they're in, or they may lose their job, or whatever. They can't get a loan from the bank, they won't be able to buy this car, or whatever. They don't react the same way as they do here. It's not just generational. It keeps going on. And the only way to get it to stop is to start with little children. And you have to get it out and no one wants to talk about it. The rest of them you really can't get them to talk to you. And one lady said she doesn't want to talk about it because she's afraid she'll lose her pension.

This respondent learned about 1898 from family members and friends in the community. She believes there is an '1898 effect' that has had a lasting impact on African-American Wilmingtonians in particular. She describes the hushed tones African Americans have used to talk about 1898, and that even today older blacks are very reluctant to discuss the event. To her mind, many of the same families who ran Wilmington in 1898 are still in charge of Wilmington today, and this contributes to the intimidation blacks in Wilmington have always felt. An organizing principle of this narrative is the loss of material possessions and its lasting influence on blacks in Wilmington.

A white woman in the same political generation had no knowledge of 1898 growing up in Wilmington. She explains:

Did you hear about 1898 growing up? Nothing. As a matter of fact, I've been thinking generally what I remember about black people period when I was growing up and when I was very young, it was practically nothing. It was very insular. We were not privileged, so I didn't see servants on a daily basis, I didn't feel isolated for that reason. It was really just a separate society. I can remember growing up with expressions like, "Acting like a nigger," "Sweating like one . . ." And all these sorts of things that you just accepted, but never really being face-to-face with a black person to know whether or not they were true. Do they really sweat? You know?

Even though weren't wealthy by any means, in fact we were fairly needy, we still could afford, I could remember when I was very young, we had a black woman come in to iron sometimes, so you see they must have really gotten, excuse the expression, slave wages, for us to have afforded it. And I can remember that when I did have my occasional face to face meetings with a black delivery man or woman who helped us iron, I never really connected that with the nigger stuff talk. It seemed like that they didn't know what it meant.

I think the biggest, the biggest surprise to me as an adult was when I went to high school, of course there was only one high school in the county, New Hanover, and I knew there was a black high school, it could have been on Mars—I had no idea where it was. And it was only as an adult that I found out it was just a few blocks from New Hanover. I had no idea. None. I could not have told you.

And I remember after school we would, because times were different and kids were allowed to roam around on their own a lot more, we used to walk downtown in the afternoons after high school and we would meet some black people going down town and we would try to avoid them because words were exchanged sometimes. I wouldn't do it but people would say nasty things, and I guess we always thought we would get beaten up or something and that was sort of an accepted thing too, along with black men always want to rape white women, and you can't be alone around a black man, oh it was so scary you know, there was only a black man and me (I'm sure he had a lot of interest in these pimply faced ugly little fat high school girls. But, anyway, we were all sure we were objects of all this.

I graduated in 1957. I went to Lake Forest Jr. High School and got bussed over there from Winter Park. And again, just sort of rode through but had no idea where people lived and how they lived. The City Market was still the city market then, and one of the favorite things to do to raise money, you know like today kids do car washes, was to have tag sales, or yard sales at City Market. And that was another place where we would come face-to-face with black people shopping on Saturdays. I can remember that the women still in the 1950s wore, what I now know was traditional African dress, head kerchiefs, head dresses, maybe not in the bright colors but they would tie their heads and [trails off]. You know, I think Wilmington was really lagging, it may still be, but lots of things didn't change for a long, long time.

The first I can really remember would have been probably reading the paper when there was a lot of publicity about it. I may have read or heard references to it, and it didn't mean that much to me.

My mother was a southerner, but not from here. So I wouldn't have got any traditional kind of stuff from them. And we didn't hear about it in school. I can remember the expressions, "Well, we should send them all back to Africa." And I never really did get it, that they were from Africa and we brought them from Africa. And all that, I don't know if I thought they moved to America to be slaves. I'm really embarrassed but I just never connected it.

This white respondent describes the separate lives whites and blacks led in Wilmington while she was growing up. There is no public reference to 1898 when this generation was 18–25 years old. While her black counterparts in this generation had heard about 1898 growing up, this white respondent had no knowledge of 1898 event until the 1990s.

An African-American woman in the 1954–1961 political generation describes the fear earlier generations of blacks felt about the 1898 event:

> I noticed, I found that the older people were afraid to talk about it. It was so negative on the families. If you took the man you took the breadwinner. So you went from a middle class person to a welfare recipient. They didn't have welfare then but you dropped down to that level. Many women lost their homes, their property. This is not written in books, and these people were so afraid that these people may do it again, and get me a second time. And so they passed the knowledge onto their children and their grandchildren to fright, or being afraid of the issue, or of people talking about the issue. So it, the black community became split when 1898 [1998 commemoration] started because some people didn't want to talk about it, some people wanted to revitalize it again for knowledge base, because many people were not aware of it, because it was a hush, hush thing, "We don't talk about this because they might come back and get us again." And you'll be amazed at what it did to families in terms of the bleakness. It did something to the overall personality of black people in Wilmington, that I can't get out here and work to my fullest potential cause I don't really know what is going to happen to me. Between that and the Wilmington 10, [it] just sort of killed Wilmington for a number of years. And people didn't want to say anything, and people didn't want to push for what they felt that they should have. Very complacent. There was fear, and the fear was so great, it something you just put on the back burner.

This respondent believes the fear the 1898 event instilled in African-Americans was transmitted through parents, specifically women who were left behind, to their children and this accounts for a collective disorder for blacks in Wilmington (Lira 1997). Additionally, she emphasizes the material loss for African Americans as a result of the 1898 violence.

An African-American male in the same political generation (1954–1961) expresses his belief in a lasting effect, explaining:

> I think 1898 has become part of the psyche, human beings, just like any other kind of animal, they are totally trainable. And that once you domesticate a horse or a dog, you don't have to domesticate the puppies. So they learned, and similarly, once people learn a behavior pattern you don't have to reinforce them anymore, once it is there its there. You know that experiment with fleas, you put fleas in a jar, and you put a top on it, and you can remove the top and they never jump higher than the top. So they are conditioned. And similarly here in Wilmington, you have a conditioning that you just don't talk about it. And if you look at 1898, and think about it, if you look at the names on the White Declaration of Independence, you can look in the yellow pages, they are here.

An African-American male, also from the 1954–1961 political generation, describes how he learned about 1898. He also explains that after
spending some time away from Wilmington, he was able to see "the real
deal" Wilmington when he returned:

> My dad did tell me about a riot that was in 1893, I'm not sure about the
> date, was it 1893, but the blacks used to run Wilmington, North
> Carolina. The blacks used to run Wilmington, North Carolina. And the
> whites ran them out. But I can't remember the exact date. I can't remem-
> ber now. My dad told me and what have you. Well he was just telling
> me that the blacks, the blacks had a position in Wilmington, North
> Carolina, and the whites ran them out. Like the Melrose down in
> Florida, yea, Rosewood. And blacks had position, owned different
> things, and they ran them out, ran them out in the woods, what have
> you, and the blacks have never been able to recover from that. Yea. I
> heard that from my daddy. But it's been more or less a hush, hush thing.
> I've heard a few talk about it, but not too many, not too many. It's been
> more or less a hush, hush type of thing. *But you have a feeling other peo-
> ple knew about it?* Oh definitely so, definitely so, definitely so!

> When I left Wilmington, and I came back to Wilmington I saw the real
> deal of Wilmington. Believe it or not, Wilmington—the white run
> Wilmington. You've got a few blacks, but this is a white man's town.
> You know. Schools, and this was my home town, and my mom being
> sick and what have you, I don't know that I would live in Wilmington.
> But like I said, I don't know, I got old, and go ahead and live. But this
> is a white man's town. *Is Wilmington different from other towns?*
> [heated] *I know so! I know so! I know so!* I'll tell you who runs
> Wilmington, the Camerons, the Sprunts, the Kenans, the Wise, that's
> where the chancellor lives now, and the Raeford Trask, all them peo-
> ple like that. And all the people who run Wilmington. THIS IS A
> WHITE MAN'S TOWN! You got a few blacks who went up the lad-
> der, there's always a few, a few get by, but every job believe it or not,
> that is paid any amount of money, you got more Caucasian than mi-
> nority on that job. ANY JOB, paying any amount of money, you got
> whites on that job. If I wasn't from Wilmington, North Carolina, and
> at my age, I don't know if I would live here or not. We have never been
> able to recover when that racist thing happened. When black people
> were in power. I can't really say, Leslie, I can't really say. I guess, I don't
> know. I really can't say. But we never were able to recover.

> Hey if my daddy had never told me I probably would never have known.
> He was kind of a Kunte Kinte, and I was able to read more about it, and
> I was able to tell my son. He told me so much stuff about that, but not
> on a daily basis. He just more or less told me what was told to him. My
> daddy was born in 1918. So anyway, that was before he was born. I
> guess his mother told him and he told me. See if he hadn't told me, I'd

have never knew that. See that was what he was telling me. What was told to him. Wilmington, like I say, just a few people in power and they pretty much do what they want to do.

I tell you what I did, believe it or not, the kids were small. I took the kids to Wrightsville Beach. I'll never forget it. And they was playing in the water and what have you, they were having a good time and laughing, they were kids, they don't know and what have you. And I could feel it, I could feel it. Leslie, you don't have to hit me to make me feel it. And them kids, they didn't want to, "No we got to go now, we got to go now," Leslie I could *feel it.* And they said "Hey some of this blackness is going to rub off in the water." And I told the kids I said, "Come on kids, let's go" and we left. We left it. Leslie I could feel it. "Why don't you go somewhere else?" Kids were having a good time in the water. They were about that size [shows photo] and I don't know if they know today why I left. I don't even know.

This informant describes the inhibited, hushed-hushed talk about 1898, and is pleased his father told him so he could pass it along to his son. He believes Wilmington, and specifically black Wilmington, never recovered from the trauma the event created. Blacks also never recovered from the material loss of 1898. For him, power is still situated in the same hands as it was in 1898. He tells us that Wilmington today is still a city for whites, and describes the lack of respect for blacks. If it were not for personal reasons he would move elsewhere. This respondent had no knowledge of the 1998 centennial activities.

A white informant in the 1962–1969 political generation described the 1898 effect that he felt existed in the black community:

What was happening, there was really a part of the historical continuum, if you will, from 1898, that sense of disenfranchisement and estrangement was still manifest in the students in their whole community, from what occurred in 1898. Working in the black community, it was very much a part of their history a part of their lives, it was in some regards like a sub-text in their lives, you know, and where they were and the fact that although the Civil Rights movement had occurred and affected them in many ways, this sense of disenfranchisement and I guess you could say emasculation that occurred in 1898 was still with them.

The organizing principle of this white respondent's narrative is around a lasting psychological effect on the African-American community due to the 1898 event, creating a feeling of 'estrangement.' This differs from the previous black respondent who framed his narratives in terms of loss of power, material resources and lack of respect.

An African-American woman in the 1954–1961 political generation who grew up in Wilmington yet had not heard about the 1898 event until 1996, also thinks there is a lasting effect on Wilmington from the 1898 event:

> Heard about it [1898 event] in 1996. Not taught in our history books didn't know anything about it. Period. So I got involved in that when a lot of people wouldn't. But we didn't know anything about it. In hindsight it was self serving, no reason to get black people riled up about this. It was a hundred years ago, just something that happened. I didn't know a damn thing about it. And I consider myself an educated person and didn't know anything about it. No, we didn't know anything about it. We did have power before then. And we lost all that. I guess there was a period from 1898 to when I knew in 1940 it was just Jim Crow. And you were kept down and we to this day suffer because of it. That is what is really critical and damning about it, the families that took control are still in control. And you had to swim up-stream all this time and then when you get upstream you don't get anything. You might get an opportunity to sit at the table with other folks, you might, if they feel like it.

> Because I sit on committees and boards, I get into situations where people would say, "We'll meet at the Country Club," and I would say, well I'm not going to the Country Club, I am not going to Cape Fear Country Club. We cannot hold a meeting there. A lot of things that white people do, they do out of matter of course. They're routine, they don't think about what it means, there is no need to think about it.

> Just think about what we would have been if we had the resources that white people have. But people don't realize that some of the things are just knives in our backs. And the most dangerous, I think, is just that it has become a part of your life that it has no impact to you, but it is killing you, it's bad.

This respondent's parents are from the political generations that repressed and chose to 'forget' the event (Paez, Basabe, Gonzales 1997). Despite never hearing about it, she believes 1898 has had a lasting effect believing that power in the community still resides in the same hands as it did in 1898. For this respondent, the loss of material resources has had a lasting, dangerous effect on the African American community. She also tells us about a contemporary form of Jim Crow, "Swimming up stream and then when you get there, you don't get anything—maybe an opportunity to sit at a table with other folks, if they feel like it." Whites do not consider their actions towards blacks as disrespectful or racist—they are 'routine' and a matter of course (Feagin & Vera 1995). What she describes is white privilege, "a lot of things that white people do, they do out of a matter of course . . . they don't think about what it means." Whites lack true knowledge about "the other" and the daily experiences of being non-white in America; this is part of white privilege–not having to know what it means to be non-white. At its core, this is about respect and rights (Savoie and Miller 2002).

Of these three political generations, the 1946–1953 cohort is the only one in which public reference to 1898, the last cautionary tale, occurred. Yet these three periods did mark a time of heightened and growing civil rights awareness both in Wilmington and the larger national arena. Most of the respondents in these political generations framed their narratives by pointing to the earlier generations' silence and fear, and how this fear has had an impact on Wilmington. The organizing principles of these narratives differed by race: blacks were more likely to frame their narratives around power, material loss and lack of respect.

WILMINGTON TEN POLITICAL GENERATION

Of the five respondents in the 1970–1977 political generation, three had heard about the 1898 event growing up in Wilmington, and of these three, one black respondent did not support the *1998 Foundation* activities, while two (one black and one white) did support the *1998 Foundation* activities and the 'new narrative' that emerged. Two white respondents had not heard about the 1898 event until 1998. Neither was familiar with the 1998 *Foundation* activities and consequently did not know very much about the 'new narrative.' All respondents in this political generation framed their narrative around the Wilmington Ten events, finding that relations in Wilmington are much better than they were when they were young adults. One white woman explains:

> I was at [one of the two Wilmington high schools] high school. I had lots of black friends. And the Wilmington Ten thing I didn't understand what was going on. You know like Vietnam, I didn't understand it. The Wilmington Ten were older people. They were militants; you could just see the way things changed. It was like a wave. They were resentful. There was a great big separation. In fact, we don't have high school reunions with blacks today. They wrote a letter to the person who was organizing our high school reunion, the first one, and said they would not be participating, and would no longer participate and would never participate. And they have always had their own reunion. You know I said, that's bad, because we had some black friends we would like to see. We graduated in 1971. And there was a big rift right down the middle, and it hurts. You know, it even changed my maid. She started wearing, she changed her clothes, she changed her attitude. We could hardly even recognize her. You know she was changing in her

thinking too. These events changed friendships. We never were consulted about it. About the whole thing. Our views were not taken into account. In other words, there was nothing. We were suddenly on the outside. I felt like that. What did we do wrong? What is this happening? Is this all based on something that happened 100 years ago, 1865 and here it is 1971? I had Dora [domestic helper] for a long time. She got paid good money, and she practically raised me. But her attitude changed during that time. I took her home one day with my daddy, and I saw how poor blacks were. She had a brick home and a chain link fence around her home. To own a brick home then meant you were doing well. So I felt like she was above all the others. I was happy for her. And the dress back then, oh it was like third world. It was like second hand-me downs. Dirty clothes. And it hurt. I didn't know until I got big enough to see the difference. I thought everybody had nice clothes and a big yard. I feel so much better for the race now. They didn't own cars when I was a little girl. No property. They've come a long way. But there is still prejudice. *Did you ever hear about 1898?* No I didn't hear about that until my husband talked about it a few years ago. Never heard about it growing up. Very hush, hush talking about that riot. I don't know why, I would like to know why?

The other white respondent in this political generation also had no knowledge of the 1898 racial violence:

I moved here when I was five. Never heard about, about 1898 until 1998. Not really any reference. Well I love history, and I had no idea the whole event had happened. We never talked about it in school; I don't know if we were more interested in boys, ballet, church and everything. Not an issue with us. I was not brought up in a discriminatory fashion by my parents. I was brought up to be respectful to everyone. Race relations are much better now. Things have settled down.

We spoke longer about the Wilmington Ten and race relations today in Wilmington, and I probed again about 1898. The respondent grew a bit frustrated saying, "We didn't grow up in a KKK background." When she said this, I realized I had heard this before—a moral equivalence with knowledge about 1898 and being a racist. A white woman in the 1962–1969 political generation told me, with the same incredulous look, "I never heard about 1898 growing up. Our family was not that way, we were taught to be kind to everyone. We never discriminated against blacks." It made me question whether respondents in the older white generations who would not elaborate on their knowledge about blacks felt they were crossing a line, a line of behaving in a way perceived to be racist simply by their knowledge of the 1898 racial violence.

Both African-Americans in this political generation had learned about 1898 growing up in Wilmington; one supported the 1998 *Foundation* activities and one did not. The respondent who did not support the 'new narrative' explains:

It was well known amongst all of the older blacks, especially the women, cause they talked about it all the time, because many of them lost fathers, uncles and great uncles and grandfathers, and as much [as] history tries to whitewash and suppress the truth on that issue. I had the pleasure of growing up with a grandmother who was born in 1893 and her sister-in-law and her aunts were well up into their 90s and 100s when I was a kid, so I not only knew about secondarily through them, but they were first hand victims of slavery, my aunt Rebecca was a child of slavery, and I spoke to her about it, she died at the age of 103, she never would accept running water or inside toilets, she did it that way until she died in the 80s. She was born in uh, let's see, it would have had to been in the late 1870s, and her mother and father were slaves. The 1898 was something, it wasn't something that they talked about all the time, but they would sit down and discuss it, especially with the children, and they wanted to pass on heritage, and they wanted us to be proud, they wanted us to know that we had been more than we were, or that what we appeared to be in this town. You know they tried to make you feel like nothing and nobody here, when in fact, if you were in another conducive and nurturing environment, the things you would do and were attempting to do folks would come right in and support. I was in a meeting in Chapel Hill up there last year, they had a group of lawyers, local bar and medical associations, professors at the university, the community leaders and business leaders, they were all sitting in one room talking about what they were going to do to make their city better, in certain parts of town that needed to be dealt with, and these were people from filthy rich to dirt poor all sitting in the same room. You see that's how you solve problems. You can't exclude and then say you inclusive. You know. It's an oxymoron. If you saying that you want me to be a part of it, then why aren't we a part of every process? You can't come to me and ask me what you think after you've done it. And then think that I'm supposed to feel a part of it. So, uh, hey. It's not very complicated to assess. There are people in this town, certain white people don't want to be a room with certain white people, certain black people don't want to be in a room, we're so divided, it's not just a racial divide, it's a class divide, it's a social and political divide, and it's all been orchestrated. Orchestrated. **When do you recall first hearing about 1898?** Probably, well I always loved to sit and listen to them tell stories, probably from the age of three or four, you know, I was like a sponge, I couldn't absorb enough of the knowledge they were imparting, cause I was always fascinated by that, even before I knew what history was I was fascinated by folklore, and stories. *Did you take part in the 1998 commemoration activities?* I was aware of it. I went to one event; it was a personal decision. I went to the initial meeting that they held at First Baptist Church, and I sat with them and when I saw where it was going I thought it was a mockery and disgrace to the memory of those people who were murdered and run from their homes, churches, their native land to somewhere else because they were good, solid productive affluent citizens. So no, to make a long story short, no I did not take place in the day to day rigamarole because it wasn't legitimate. It was not a legitimate organization. It's a farce. But the thing about that group, and I won't call names, but I spoke to people who were high up in that whole thing and they later admitted to me that they had been used, unbeknownst to them, but I told them in the beginning, I said, the only reason they are trying to incorporate this is to suppress any potential for riots or demonstrations. That's what it was for. They had a year of dinners, and cocktail parties, and lectures, at a time when people's lives should have been commemorated and validated and that we should have truly uh sat down and said "in every ill there is a root to that illness." Now we're dealing with the symptoms, and we're treating it symptomatically, and we're sitting over here sitting in a room together and when we leave we're not going to ever talk to each other again, but we're sitting here a in a room saying we shall over come and we have overcome, when clearly we don't know a thing about each other. *Healing can't take place until confession takes place.* See no one wants to confess what they've done here. Everybody wants to justify it. But there's no justification for killing, robbing, stealing, and pillaging anyone. This is the only city in the country and in the free world that was ever overthrown a legitimate government with the assistance of the state government and federal government who sat on the side and watched what happened. So what I'm saying is that there is a lot to answer for.

Like earlier political generations, this respondent learned about 1898 from family members, particularly women, and believes the lasting effects of 1898 are still present. The denial and distortion of history creates present-day symptoms of the malfeasance of 1898. He believes that in order to create lasting change, atonement and confession for past grievances will have to take place, which he sees did not occur with the development of the new narrative in 1998. In addition, he feels blacks in Wilmington get little respect, and knows that Wilmington differs from other cities, providing an example of ways in which city leaders can be inclusive and take note of material issues and problems facing African Americans. This respondent differs from others in this Wilmington Ten political generation, all of whom, except the one above, believed race relations in Wilmington had significantly improved since the 1970s.

The post-Wilmington Ten generations (1978–1985, 1986–1993, and 1994–2001) stand out in terms of the lack of knowledge about the 1898 event and little knowledge about the 1998 centennial commemoration. While half (3 black, 1 white) of the eight respondents in these three political generations had heard about the 1898 event from family members while growing up in Wilmington, three said they had heard it 'in passing' and they learned more about it during the 1998 commemoration activities. Of the other half, three learned about 1898 in 1998 and one respondent in the 1994–2001 political generation learned about the 1898 event during the interview, despite living in Wilmington through the 1998 centennial commemoration activities.

Of the eight respondents in the three post-Wilmington Ten generations, 38 percent supported the 'new narrative' and activities surrounding the commemoration and 12 percent did not. Fifty percent indicated they were unfamiliar with the 1998 activities. The organizing principle in the narratives for most post-Wilmington Ten political generation respondents is one of general equality:

> You know I think Wilmington is more accepting and I think they are fair to all the races and stuff. Especially compared to the smaller towns where they see it as black or they see it as white. You know there is no— it seems everywhere you go, all different mixes of people, movies, everywhere. They are more accepting of it.

A young white woman explains:

> The older I've gotten, I don't know. I look at it this way, if I'm walking down the road and see a black person I'll smile. And if they smile back, that's great. But if they don't, I feel this anger about it. I feel like, well you know, "What have I done?" I had nothing to do with any of that that happened back then. I'm not related to any of that. I understand that it hurts, and if it happened to my culture, I would be upset too, so I don't know. I don't get that racist feeling until their attitude. I work at [a restaurant]. Have a lot of nice people that come in there. For the most part they're black, but I tell you, and I'm working hard and table 8 starts snapping their fingers, and I'm a servant and they don't leave me a tip, those feelings come out. I felt used. It's like I'm supposed to serve them. Like now I'm supposed to serve them. They just want me to run around for them and don't leave a tip. They are really very friendly for the most part. But it seems like people in their—who went through civil rights 40s, 30s seem more hateful towards whites. But younger blacks are nicer. The only time I feel anger toward blacks is when they're mean to me. Otherwise, they're just like anybody else.

For this respondent the past should be forgotten, or at least people should 'move on'; she had nothing to do with past wrongs. If a black person is nice to her, she is nice in response. Yet if she is affected racially, no tip is left by a black person she feels used and invokes a racial ordering to her labor: "whites do not serve blacks; blacks do not order whites about." This respondent is clear about being a member of a socially privileged class, and expresses a display of white privilege. She says blacks are just like anyone else, until they are unkind, then they become 'black.' The respondent has clear expectations for blacks' behavior toward her that must differ from her expectations of whites' behavior. When blacks do not leave a tip she feels racist. A white who does not leave a tip is a jerk; a black who does not leave a tip makes her angry at *blacks,* not the individual.

CONCLUSION

In this chapter I examined when and how respondents learned about 1898 and whether or not they support the new liberal narrative. While 62 percent of the respondents had heard about 1898 during their childhood, primarily from family members or close family friends, 26 percent learned about the 1898 event from either the 1994 Gerard publication *Cape Fear Rising* or during the 1998 commemoration activities. Nine percent of the political generation informants learned about 1898 as young adults from people outside their families. One informant learned about 1898 during the interview.

I examined political generations to see if historical periods identified in the baseline archival data corresponded with narratives of contemporary informants. I found more patterns across several generations rather than within a single political generation, aside from the Wilmington Ten political generation. A finding consistent with the archival data is that pre-World War II experiences marked a period of great silence and repression in talking publicly about the 1898 violence and this fear is reflected in the narratives of these political generation informants. Three post-World War II political generations organized their narratives around the evaluative principal of an '1898 mentality' pointing to the fear of earlier generations and its effect on the community. These narratives reflect the changing attitudes found in the archival data—a greater sense of entitlement (O'Brien 1999) and growing demands for civil rights (Godwin 2000). The Wilmington Ten political generation framed their understanding of race based on their experiences in Wilmington during the racial violence in 1971. For most respondents in this political generation race relations had improved. The post-Wilmington Ten political generations' narratives reflect a growing disinterest in 1898 event, and a lack of interest and support for 1998 commemoration activities.

Forty-four percent of the political generation respondents were familiar with the 1998 commemoration activities and support the 'new narrative' as framed by the *1898 Centennial Foundation*. Fifteen percent of the political generation respondents indicated they did not know much about the 1998 activities and therefore do not really know if they support the 'new narrative' or not. Twelve percent had never heard about the 1998 commemoration activities or the *Foundation*'s work. Twenty-nine percent of the political generation respondents were familiar with the 1998 activities and did *not* support the new narrative emerging from the *Foundation*'s work.

Overall, the contemporary narratives describe a pattern of non-synchronous development based on race and generation. Black and white narratives in Wilmington have developed on relatively autonomous levels. Whites, overall, were less likely than blacks to have heard about 1898 growing up. Blacks were more likely than whites to have learned stories about 1898 violence from oral tradition in their families. Blacks were more likely than whites to provide narratives of terror, using gruesome imagery of Bloody Cape Fear or Nigger Head Road. The organizing principle of black contemporary narratives centered on lack of power, lack of material resources and lack of respect.

Critical historical events in Wilmington and national historical events shaped dominant and subordinate narratives about the 1898 racial violence. While the comparison of historical temporal locations of respondents revealed common narratives by generation, race was a more powerful indicator of narrative uniformity. The concept political generations was useful for this analysis as it focuses on the importance of history and events to sociological analysis (Zeitlin 1970:240). It also adds to Paige's model on elite narratives by providing a more historical dimension. Notwithstanding, the age/generational effect had less significance in the Wilmington case than it did for Zeitlin in the Cuban case. I saw greater coherency in the narratives between political generations rather than within political generations. Race, more so than generations, provided greater narrative uniformity.

In the next chapter I examine the findings presented in the previous chapters and draw conclusions using the concept of political unconscious. I close with a discussion concerning the ways narratives deny or repress history, and the implications for sociological research on race.

Chapter Seven
Do Narratives Matter?

As I write this conclusion (Spring 2002), people in Wilmington are in the midst of heated debates, again centered on race. While these current debates have not the magnitude of earlier racial violence in this city, they do reflect an underlying tension that is not resolved. As one respondent, an African-American male, told me recently:

> There is a truth to be told here. There are a lot of books out that told the history, but it doesn't deal with the current—see there's another massacre going on here. There's a new one every time the calendar turns. The massacre in 1898 didn't stop; it continued in '99, 1900, 1902. This massacre has been going on now for 103 years, see, it didn't begin and end in 1898. It's an ongoing phenomenon that has a new twist every year. It's the same thing but it's dressed up. This year we're going to spend the vast majority of our year talking about a woman who under normal circumstances would be recommended for counseling. We are going to keep this spin going for the rest of the year while HUD monies are being misappropriated, communities are decaying to the root, uh people are dying on our streets, uh, I mean it's so irrelevant to what the real issues are and the real problems are. But once again it's like I told you, it's a tool, it's a diversionary tool.

For this informant, stories—narratives—divert attention away from the real material conditions of people's lives. Narratives matter.

I turn now to a discussion of the significance of this research, elaborating on four key areas: 1) reflections on the theoretical exemplars for this research: Paige, Jameson and Zeitlin; 2) an elaboration on the function of narrative and ideology in light of my findings; 3) generalizing beyond the Wilmington case to the importance of narrative in other communities; and 4) policy implications arising from this research.

REFLECTIONS ON PAIGE, JAMESON AND ZEITLIN

This research moves beyond Jeffrey Paige's research on Central American coffee elite by examining both subordinate and dominant narratives and the cultural terrain where they interact. Paige's work examines elite narratives only. I revised his model by including the concept of hegemony, arguing that culture is a social site in which hegemonic control is continuously demonstrated and disputed. Based on the assumption that narrative is a contested terrain whereby subordinate as well as dominant narratives interact, I endeavored to better understand the hegemonic functions of narratives by seeking out narratives from various social categories.

In a hegemonic discourse, the dominant narrative is, in many ways, the only voice that is "heard" (Dowling 1984:131). I recall making notations in my field notes about feeling frustrated when, asking individuals for names of knowledgeable informants, I repeatedly would be offered the same list of wealthy Wilmingtonians. Academics and professionals in particular, would look at me askance when I explained I wanted to talk to 'ordinary folks.' Interestingly, it was not that easy to get the names of 'ordinary folks'—the people who make-up the majority of Wilmingtonians. Subordinated social groups provided contemporary counter-narratives to the dominant narrative. I found as I moved down the ladder of racial hierarchy in Wilmington, which is moving from those with greater prestige and status in the community to those with less, that the level of acumen and insight into Wilmington social structure and relations increased. Intuitively I knew this would be the case. Yet I noted time and again in my field notes how astounded I was at the level of shrewdness and insight of these informants. Some of the most profound commentaries on social inequality and the imperfections and contradictions of elite and the social structure they preserve came from informants who were intimately connected at the bottom of the hierarchy looking up. This was very important in understanding the contested terrain of narratives. While the hegemonic dominant narrative suppresses counter-narratives—it is the only one that we 'hear'—both Jameson (1981) and Genovese (1974) demonstrate that the dominant narrative remains bound in a dialogue with the discourse it has suppressed. What Paige neglects in his research, and what my research provides, is an examination of this contested terrain.

In the Wilmington case, the dominant narrative that developed immediately following the 1898 violence omits the political coup d'etat and responsibility for numerous deaths. Yet the dominant narrative remains bound in a dialogue with the subordinate counter-narrative through the process of omission and denial; through 'premature closure'—closing off inquiry before it leads to questions raised in the counter-narratives. For Jameson (1981:54) the omissions and suppression of counter-narratives represent a *strategy of containment*, "a way of achieving coherence by shutting out the truth about History." It is the Althuserrian 'problematic:'

> A problematic is the theoretical (and ideological) structure which both frames and produces the repertoire of criss-crossing and competing discourses out of which a text is materially organized. The problematic of a text relates to its moment of historical existence as much by what it excludes as by what it includes. That is to say, it encourages a text to answer questions posed by itself, but at the same time it generates the production of 'deformed' answers to the question which it attempts to exclude. Thus a problematic is structured as much by what is absent (what is not said) as by what is present (what is said) (Storey 1996:30).

I found that both the dominant narrative and the new contemporary narrative generated 'deformed' answers to the questions each attempted to exclude. The dominant narrative about 1898 racial violence offered 'deformed' answers to the questions it evaded via a repertoire of competing discourses, namely freedom and democracy. Likewise, the new narrative generates 'deformed' answers via reconciliation and culpability. The political unconscious is the collective denial of historical contradictions—— the repressed contradictions of history, the deformed answers. Resolutions in narratives come about, according to Jameson (1981:290), with resolutions of the contradictions in the social order. Narratives are ideological projects and are illuminated through examination of both the subordinate and dominant narratives.

I utilized Maurice Zeitlin's concept of political generations to examine the influence of historically significant events on narrative. To quote Zeitlin:

> The very concept itself is a statement of the hypothesis that social processes, relationships, norms and values are often inexplicable without reference to the events of the past, and that analysis limited to consideration only of contemporary relationships may be deficient in significant ways.

My findings demonstrate that the temporal location of respondents influenced the narratives of each political generation: historically significant events and omissions shaped and framed the narratives of Wilmingtonians. Again and again informants told me about the influences of their 'generation' on their behavior. For example:

> My generation has a learned behavior of 'don't yell too loud,' 'don't stand too far out front' they still might come get you.

And,

> But that's the way I was taught. Suck it up. Keep walking. Don't retaliate. That's what they told us years ago.

And in the quote at the beginning of Chapter Five:

> You got to look at the period of time you come in and the living conditions of your time and the way things are. And that thing is ingrained in you. And it's ingrained in me. I learned to live with it, and adjust myself to it.

Often these explanations would be provided to contrast the way respondents viewed the behavior of other generations.

Critical historical events in Wilmington and national historical events shaped dominant and subordinate narratives about the 1898 racial violence. While the comparison of historical temporal locations of respondents revealed common narratives by generation, race was a more powerful indicator of narrative uniformity. Across historical temporal locations, blacks in Wilmington are more likely than whites to have knowledge of the 1898 racial violence and to have learned about the violence from family members growing up. The findings in this research reveal that the both historical temporal location and race affect narratives.

NARRATIVE AS IDEOLOGICAL PROJECT

As an undergraduate student I remember reading Marx's explanation of ideology and the analogy he made with the inversion process of a camera obscura. This imagery of the inversion process always fascinated me. In Grahamstown, South Africa, I had the opportunity to see a 'camera obscura.' It was built in the late 1800s in a home, now a museum, of an English 'eccentric' who enjoyed astronomy and optics. The camera obscura is housed in one of the turrets of the house in a small room allowing a view of the entire city. Once inside the room one is, in essence, inside a camera—between the lens and the 'film.' The angle of the mirror which is situated on the turret, is adjusted and a moving miniature image of a section of town is reflected on a special glass in the center of the room. Section upon section of town is displayed as the rotating lens is adjusted. I was fortunate to be there on a sunny day, and so had a clear view of all the going-on's. The camera-obscura was used to locate people, before telephones I guess, whenever they were needed. It was dizzying for me—up in this tower trying to sort out which direction of town we were observing. It was like a movie—yet it was 'real life' being projected on a table. Nevertheless it was turned around—distorted. Real life turned around and distorted.

The dominant narrative created by the white elite in Wilmington immediately following the November 10, 1898, violence was, in essence, real life turned around and distorted. The white Wilmington elite fostered the ideology of white domination through motivated distortion of the event and the creation of a dominant narrative. The white elite used self-deception techniques of selective omission, blaming the enemy, fabrication, exaggeration and embellishment to create a positive image of itself (Baumeister and Hastings 1997:278). The organizing principle of the dominant narrative, as embodied in the "White Declaration of Independence" was the natural supremacy of whites over blacks. The overt white racist narrative that developed obscured the class interests of the ruling white elite. By focusing on racial superiority, the Wilmington white elite rid itself of its greatest enemy—Fusion politics—which was against the privatization of utilities and transportation, arenas where the leaders of the 1898 violence profited greatly. The dominant narrative was an ideological project that masked the underlying contradictions of history by suppressing the political coup d'etat, an undemocratic moment in the democracy of the United States. The events of November 10, 1898 represented what a class would do to preserve its interests—regardless of race. Sympathetic whites were exiled from Wilmington as well as affluent blacks. Counter-narratives, narratives that reveal that the narrators do not think, feel or act as they are "supposed to," have by and large been suppressed until the 1990s (Personal Narratives Group 1989:7).

The archival data and contemporary narratives demonstrate the way in which counter-narratives were suppressed over the years. Immediately following the violence in 1898, several anonymous letters to President McKinley as well as private letters and diaries describe the fear that some white and black Wilmingtonians felt in expressing publicly an alternative interpretation of events. Interviews by Edmonds in the late 1940s, by Nash in the early 1970s, by Prather in the early 1980s, and the contemporary narratives in this research mirror the sentiments expressed in these early counter-narratives. They provide counter-hegemonic insight illuminating the interests embedded in the dominant narrative.

Scholars of collective memory and traumatic events (Pennebaker 1997; Paez, Basabe and Gonzalez 1997; Lira 1997) argue that acts of violence generate a climate of fear that is linked to the inhibition of social sharing. Steinmetz (1992:503) argues that the absence of a narrative or story about events "may even make it difficult for individuals to produce coherent stories about their lives." Linde (1986:200) makes an important point:

The absence of such a discourse about what happened in Vietnam, which at least partly matches the experience of the participants and validates it, is responsible for at least some of the high rate of psychological disorders experienced by Vietnam veterans.

The findings from the contemporary narratives I collected reflect the research on traumatic events and collective memory. Several political generations spoke of an 1898 effect or the '1898 mentality' and in some ways equated this to a collective psychological disorder. Absent from the dominant narrative was an organizing or evaluative principle that in any way matched the experiences of the participants. Linde's (1986) argument is applicable to the new narrative as well. Through omission, the new (1998) narrative about 1898 fails to match and validate the experiences of the participants. Ironically, the new narrative's emphasis on inclusiveness and reconciliation effectively silenced narratives about reparations and, as the contemporary interviews show, a new form of Jim Crow. While the new narrative differs from the highly racialized narrative of white racism found in the dominant narrative, it is a narrative with an ideological purpose (Jameson 1981).

The new narrative emanating from the 1998 centennial commemoration of the 1898 racial violence embodies the values of American liberalism. These values: liberty, individualism, equality, and freedom, have been a part of the American belief system from the nation's beginnings. Yet 'color-blind' liberalism—everyone, regardless of skin color, is entitled to liberty, equality and freedom—is a result of the Civil Rights Movement of the 1950s and 1960s (Cochran 1999). This variety of liberalism has had widespread support among black and white Americans since the Civil Rights Movement and is based on the premise of individual freedom and equality of opportunity.

There is widespread belief among white Americans of all social classes that due to the success of the Civil Rights Movement, discrimination in most arenas is a thing of the past (Boston 1988; Feagin and Vera 1995; Sears, Henry and Kosterman 2000; Schuman, Steeh and Bobo 1985; Schuman 2000; DiTomaso 2001, Wacquant 2002). For Feagin and Vera (1995) this is a form of white racism, and I also argue, white privilege. White privilege can be understood in terms of the advantages of whiteness—especially the privilege of neither having to see discrimination nor to deal with it on a daily basis. Racism is seen as a system of racial oppression including ideas, institutions and practices that develop into lasting structures and widespread relations of domination (Feagin & Vera 1995). These patterns of highly racialized thought are long lasting and deeply entrenched in our society. In Chapter Five, I examined the way the new narrative combined elements of the dominant ideology with the subordinate narrative to produce an ideology that sustained ruling hegemony. I argued this could be viewed through the organizing principle of the narrative of reconciliation, embodied in the meta-narrative of liberalism. Liberal ideology is based on individualism and equality of opportunity. Addressing reparations implies that equality of opportunity does not exist; that is, someone who requires payment for past grievances must have been wronged in a way that requires redress. By not attributing blame ("no one living today"), the belief in individualism is preserved.

Counter-narratives circulate in Wilmington in response to the new (1998) narrative. The organizing principle of these counter-narratives centers on a critique of liberalism. They are the suppressed narratives about lack of respect and dignity, lack of opportunity, and being left out of the process. As exemplified by an African-American woman I interviewed:

> But really, the 1998 stuff [commemoration activities] just followed suit with what the nation does. Everyone says, 'get over it.' You can only heal if you can get angry. But see you're not allowed to get angry! Don't get angry or you make whites feel uncomfortable. You can't heal until you get angry and we don't get to do that part! To shout, scream, tear-up . . . you can't do that! We aren't being heard, but suppressed! They kill you—it's slow though—but it's murder . . . it's just murder. You know the dignity thing, that you can provide your kids—they make this difficult. It's the same 1898 mentality that has never been terminated.

For this woman, blacks in Wilmington are not allowed to shout, scream, or tear-up over a heinous racist event. The new narrative mutes voices that are not reconciliatory or that are unwilling to displace blame. As this woman intimates, the counter-narratives lack legitimacy—they go against the grain of liberalism. Telling the story of 1898 through the 1998 commemoration activities has moral authority—It revives the issues of freedom and liberty symbolized in the Civil Rights Movement, yet it stops short of creating meaningful change. The new 1998 narrative, like the dominant narrative before it, denies the history and the underlying conditions of the experiences of African-Americans in Wilmington and the United States. While not embodied in the *de jure* segregation historically symbolizing the Jim Crow period, there is a contemporary form of Jim Crow that confronts the lives of African Americans. An older African-American woman who worked as a domestic believes that not much has changed since the days of Jim Crow:

> And uh, then they go to Figure Island, and get a place and isolate it all from everybody else. That's what goes on in Wilmington. Segregation. You don't see no black people on Figure Eight Island. No blacks at Wrightsville Beach. You say it's integrated now, but some of these places,

no it's not either. It's definitely not. I don't know any blacks who go to Cape Fear Country Club and I know they know better than to go. And certain areas. Now there are some blacks out on Oleander, people with money have left, and when some blacks moved in they got right on up and left. And now when you take when blacks moved up to 6th and Queen they tried to get a sale on that [white] church but they couldn't so they had to stay. But see, that's uh a forerunner for the one at 3rd and Market. That's the sister church, for the poor people. I used to know a fellow who was a custodian to the one at 3rd and Market, and he said that anybody who joined the church if they were poor they sent them over to the church on 6th street [laughter] if you didn't have much money you had to go over the 6th Street church! We laughed about that, yea you got no money you are sent over to the other church! [Laughter] [Long Pause] It's false. There's nothing to it. It's just pretending They don't do any more than they have to do. Gore was here, do you see him mixing with blacks and whites? No he goes to Figure Eight. It goes on and on and on. It's just a pattern. You can take them right now the ones running for office. They used to lean to the blacks but they don't any more. They used to depend on the black vote but they don't now. People got to the point they don't even go vote. I worked for the polls for over 15 years, no body come to vote. Most of them say they didn't see nobody to vote for.

For this speaker blacks and whites are physically isolated from one another. She feels that nothing is done in Wilmington to address issues facing African Americans "they don't do anymore than they have to do." An African American man in his early sixties, who worked as low-skilled laborer, explains:

I've been to KFC, J.C. Penny, I'm standing there waiting, and the lady told her, "He was there before me." That shouldn't happen. Has it changed? No, it's just more or less sugar coated. You can't put up the sign, "you can't come in," no more. That's the only thing different. There's no sign that says well hey you can't eat here. There's no sign that says that. But I can walk in a store, and you can walk in a store, and 9 out of 10 that clerk will come to you first. You hear what I'm saying? I know what I'm saying now. Nine out of 10 they'll come to you first. I told a lady about this. I think they're programmed to think, "I'm better than that nigger over there." I went to this store, and, Leslie, believe it or not, this guy came in there, OK, I was standing there waiting, and this lady went straight to him, got his stuff and whatever they doing, then later on this other guy came in and she had me standing up there. I told her, I said, "You should have asked, 'Who's next?'" I'm not mad at you, but you should've asked. The bottom line, "who is next?" That's not so hard! You know what crossed my mind. Thousand things gone through my mind. 'Cause I been in this situation before. I've been called a nigger, right down town, been by myself, called me that, what have you. I've been on that job out there and get passed by, and they call me that, what have you. I'm used to it. But that's the way I was taught. Suck it up. Keep walking. Don't retaliate. That's what they told us years ago. But here, we're in the 21st Century, and you're putting a cover over this thing! And this thing is still there? You ain't fooling me, Leslie! You see what they do a weak-minded person say in their mind, "well we don't have to go to the back door no more to get food." But see that's a weak minded black person. You hear what I'm saying? No, you don't have to go to that door. But that thing is still there.

He expresses his frustration at contemporary forms of Jim Crow that confront his daily life: "No you don't have to go to that [back] door—but that thing is still there." Another example of this is expressed by an African-American businesswoman:

There is a Partners of Economic Inclusion to try to get black people included in some things and rightfully so. It should not have to exist. There is a Chamber of Commerce that ought to always have been doing this, what its mission is. Black people are not recognized as business people. We've always had florists, morticians, all these cooks have started to come together from white people's kitchens and opened catering services. And they're the best cooks in Wilmington. We have got one of the best cakes that white people use, because they *know* it is the absolute best. And you still don't get any respect. Sometimes and you know people *still* if you go into a store, people will watch you. But people will watch you like a hawk.

This businesswoman laments over the same lack of respect and dignity in her daily life, and the frustration that African Americans are not properly recognized as entrepreneurs. A college educated African-American businessman recently explained to me:

For as long as I can remember, and I was a young person here during the days of the Wilmington Ten, and it was truly heightened racial tensions, essentially this town has grown in an economic sense, but it hasn't grown very much socially. In fact, I think that we have transients coming in now at a higher rate that's bring about the marginal change, the nominal change, if it had not been for tourism and transitional reestablishment of residents, and people coming from the outside in, we probably, we'd still be in the same stagnant, discriminate, racist state back in 1898. But the interesting thing that even though we are in 2002, that a established core in the community, still calls all of the shots. Still makes a vast amount of the decisions that still bear negatively on black people, poor people, females, people not in their social spheres and cliques. And, consequently, you look in this town and look at the number of black educated people with college degrees, four year baccalaureates and higher and you look at the jobs that they have versus the jobs that their white counterparts who have high school or GED or even less, the positions that they hold, and so naturally that's going to bring about economic disparity, which brings about social classification and disparity, and then that brings about a higher degree of racial, social, economic, and political tension. So really the core of the denial is really the crux of all of the problems that we have here. Even here, we have this center across the street, we were one of the first people to come here and do any type of development, you have funds available with the city and county galore, but look at how that money is invested and who they allow to access it. We've never been able to be viable participants in the process, we pay tax dollars at every level, local, city, county, state and federal, and when we look at what we benefit from out tax dollars in this city and this county, I don't have to tell you how disparate those numbers are and how far apart they are. So when you talk about race relations, I don't want to give the impression that there aren't good white citizens in this town, cause they are, but they are so afraid to be good that they themselves squalor and hide in obscurity and won't present themselves strongly. Um, I mean, when they stand up they get ostracized and isolated, and they called all kinds of things, and you know what I'm talking about, uh, they try to make the impression that any black man that, well let's say this, if you're befriended by the powers that be in this community, chances are you not going to be a strong black man that stands up for strong principles, that doesn't go along with the flow of personal benefit and who truly has an undying and abiding desire to see social and economic and political change in this town, so that life can be better for everybody.

For this informant, the egregious wrongdoing in 1898 had a long-lasting effect in Wilmington. He speaks of a contemporary Jim Crow in which blacks lag behind economically, socially and politically. In his mind, blacks are unable to do well in Wilmington unless they sell out and turn their backs on inequality. The 'core of denial' is to not address the inequality that remains in Wilmington. This interview, along with those in Chapters Five and Six, reveal a counter-narrative in Wilmington today that is primarily about lack of respect, lack of opportunities, physical isolation, and being denied part of the process. The new liberal narrative born out of the 1998 commemoration ceremony lacks support among many blacks, from all class categories, because it does not legitimately reflect lived experiences: it implies that there is not a cumulative effect to the 1898 violence.

DiTomaso's (2001) research on white views on race and politics in the United States finds that most whites in her study benefit from structural advantage (networks, resources, 'benefit of the doubt') in their day-to-day experiences, yet do not attribute these advantages to their whiteness nor even realize they are advantaged—"structural advantage is invisible to them, usually forgotten, or minimized or discounted" (2001:2). Most whites, she finds, hold a strong belief that everyone has opportunity, and thus do not think much about inequality. DiTomaso (2001:6) argues:

> . . . the conflict and discomfort that would present itself if whites believe themselves to be unfair and inegalitarian is addressed by a strong ideology regarding "equal opportunity" and "colorblindness" by which whites have convinced themselves that the advantages they enjoy are the result of their having the motivation to use opportunities that come along, just like everyone else. There is also a fairly general presumption that whatever racial problems existed in the past are now "resolved" by formal civil rights. This form of white egalitarianism is reinforced by the day to day experiences in the life histories of the white interviewees. Because they themselves perceive that they faced challenges, obstacles and uncertainty in their own efforts to "get ahead," and because they believe that opportunity is available to anyone who is willing to take "advantage" of it, then whites believe that anyone who does what they have done can have the same life advantages that they have come to enjoy. . . . there is a disconnection between the kind of structural advantage that they receive and the way they make sense of it in their everyday lives.

The juxtaposition of this new form of white racism and the findings in the counter-narratives of African-American Wilmingtonians portrays the national dilemma on race relations facing America. Wacquant (2002) argues in his article, "From Slavery to Mass Incarceration," that the cultural values of equal opportunity and 'hard work' implicitly describe white, suburban and deserving families. In contrast, dark-skinned, urban, undeserving underclass of "loafers and leeches" represent the 'polar opposition' of whites in the US today (2002:60). Wacquant (2002:57) includes a critique of the policies of 'carceral affirmative action' towards African Americans, which he argues denies access to cultural capital, excludes blacks from social redistribution, and bans black males in particular from political participation via 'criminal disenfranchisement.' The prison, he finds, has increasingly become the dividing line between those "morally anchored in conjugality and work, affluence and opportunity for all" and those on the "dark side of the American dream (Wacquant 2002:60)." The early ideological racism of black natural inferiority embodied in the historical periods of colonial formation of the United States, throughout the period of slavery and then the legally enforced discrimination of the Jim Crow system, has been replaced by a new form of racism typified in the cultural inferiority of African Americans (see Sears, Sidanius and Bobo 2000; and Feagin and Vera 1995). A white businessman told me recently, "Blacks don't want to work—they don't work!" And expressed in this interview collected by Feagin and Vera (1995:150) in response to the question, "What do you think blacks need to do to become truly equal?"

The white respondent replied:

> For them to be as successful as we are, they are going to need to adopt
> our values. Be part of our system of whatever . . . Not values exactly,
> but, it is like, it is just that thing, like wanting the money but not want-
> ing to actually show up, being reliable. The basic things we try to teach
> clients, or a high school kid about work, you know, like you need to be
> there, you need to work hard, so I guess it is the work ethic.

Blacks lack the cultural values, specifically a work ethic, and need to be
more like whites: if you work hard you can acquire the American dream.
Liberal ideology tells us that there is equal opportunity for all. Yet the
counter-narratives expressed in the contemporary interviews of African-
American Wilmingtonians contest that ideological belief.

What will happen next in Wilmington? How will the dominant narrative
mutate and change? In 2001, Hugh MacRae II, grandson of the leader of the
Secret Nine, commented in a public radio broadcast about 1898 violence:

> Being in the Secret Nine, as near as I can understand, is doing often what
> groups of businessmen do today, they get together and figure out how
> they can get more of their representatives in political position, how they
> can support their candidates and get them in place.

MacRae reckons the Secret Nine of 1898 differs little from today's political
networking (Are we supposed to forget the planned political coup d'etat and
racial violence?). MacRae also comments later in the program:

> I was amazed to find out from black business leaders that they felt that
> they had an uphill battle to be included in the business activities or to
> develop a small business of their own. It's hard to make a success in this
> world, competition is fierce, and often I think the white businessman,
> because for generations he's been more involved, if he runs into difficul-
> ties he just says, well I'm running into difficulties and that's the way the
> world is. I think so often the black businessman might say, I'm running
> into difficulties and it's because I'm black. And maybe you read too
> much into this, that it's because you're black.

This quote echoes the presumption expressed in the interviews collected by
DiTomaso—that "everyone has the same opportunities" and "if they would
just try as hard as I have" then they would make it (2001:17). According to
MacRae, being a black businessperson does not make running a business
more difficult. Yet in the quote preceding it, MacRae describes the structural advantage (networks and resources) of groups "getting together to
support their candidate." As Feagin and McKinney (2003) argue, it is part

of the denial of the seriousness of racism in the United States. I think this quote beautifully illustrates the disconnection between structural advantage and lived experiences argued in the DiTomaso (2001) research. It also represents the disconnect in Wilmington between the new liberal narrative of 'individualism and equal opportunity,' and the counter-narrative of 'lack of opportunity' and 'lack of respect.' Paige (1997:358) also found a similar disconnect in the narratives of Central American coffee elite:

> In Central America it is the contrast between the lived experience of the majority of the population and the stories told about these experiences by the coffee elite that reveal the denials and distortions of those stories.

I turn the discussion now to two other communities with violent racial pasts that affirm the power of narratives and allow us to generalize beyond the Wilmington case.

"THE INESCAPABLE CENTRALITY OF NARRATIVE"

Frequently, people ask me about my research. I usually explain that it is research into the stories surrounding the 1898 racial violence in Wilmington. So often the tone of the conversation abruptly changes. People begin to whisper, telling me about a family that was involved or knowledge about a descendant of a conspirator. Recently a fellow changed his tone completely during our conversation and began talking in code as if a three-year-old was present and should not hear what the adults are talking about. He spoke of a family he knew who was connected in some way to one of the leaders of the Secret Nine. He nodded to a building where someone worked, not willing to utter their name in public, concluding with a smile "they don't like to talk about it much." I am always struck by the need to whisper and the secrecy that still surrounds the event today—even after a year-long commemoration series, countless public lectures, and numerous newspaper articles. The conspiratorial and secretive manner in which 1898 racial violence is frequently expressed is the remnant of the influence of the dominant narrative. I believe it represents, to borrow a phrase from Sewell, (1992:487) "the inescapable centrality of narrative."

Research on two other events in United States history underpins the importance of narrative: 1919 Elaine, Arkansas and 1921 Tulsa, Oklahoma. Stockley's (2001) recent book *Blood in Their Eyes,* examines the events in 1919 that led to the 'Elaine massacres of 1919' in which five whites were killed and "estimates of African American deaths, made by individuals writing about the Elaine affair between 1919 and 1925, range from 20 to 856

(Stockley 2001:xiv)." A group of black sharecroppers in the Elaine, Arkansas area had organized, through the Progressive Farmers' and Household Union, to circumvent the exploitive price gouging by merchants and planters in the area. The group organized to buy land and create farming cooperatives, and hired legal representation to assist in their efforts. Violence erupted on September 30, 1919 during an organizational meeting at a black church in Hoop Spur, in which armed black farmers were standing guard outside the church. A car with white gunmen drove up and opened fire on the church. In the exchange one white man was killed, and an unknown number of African Americans in the church were killed and wounded. Reports spread rapidly through the Arkansas-Mississippi delta area that blacks were rioting in Phillips County and white troops from Arkansas, Mississippi, and Tennessee converged on the area. According to Stockley's research, a three-day period of looting and killing ensued in which whites ransacked the homes of black union members and killed African Americans in the area. Reports of black corpses were published in local, state and regional papers. A master's thesis written in 1927 reports ". . . . cutting off the ears or toes of dead negroes for souvenirs and the dragging of their bodies through the streets of Elaine are told by witnesses (Stockley 2001:xxiii)." Stockley writes:

> As early as the second day of the Elaine massacres, the white power structure in the Delta, including the media, began to formulate an explanation of the events that was psychologically irresistible to almost everyone, including the governor and the black elite of the state. Though the details would continually be refined, one theme was constant: *there had been no lynchings* [emphasis original]. Over the years, as evidence began to mount that something horrible had indeed occurred in Phillips County, a fallback position would emerge and be adopted by future investigators: *what happened in Phillips County in the fall of 1919 depends on what version one believes—the black account or the white account* [emphasis original].

The similarities to the Wilmington case are numerous. In February 2000, I read with interest a *New York Times* article about the silence surrounding the Elaine Arkansas event and a conference organized at the Delta Cultural Center in Helena Arkansas (Phillips County seat) to commemorate the Elaine violence. The article described a white version of the event and a black version of the event, both of which were not discussed publicly. An historian at Arkansas State University, along with her graduate students, has instituted the Elaine Riot Project to provide information about the "slaughter." Stockley writes

(2001:xv): "The tragedy of the Elaine massacres is not only that they occurred, but also that we are ignorant of them today."

Research on racial violence in Tulsa, Oklahoma, in 1921 also bears strong resemblance to the Wilmington case. In Tulsa, the black community of Greenwood or "Black Wall Street" was burnt to the ground and an estimated 300 African American lives were lost, 10,000 made homeless, and considerable amount of property lost (Brune 2002). Ellsworth (1982) writes:

> Perhaps the most lasting effects of the riot are the twin oral traditions—one set white and the other black—which it has generated in Tulsa decades later. The collective white "memory" of the riot in Tulsa has revealed both realism and fantasy, but in all cases it has been subdued in one way or another. Those whites who were involved in the riot have been reluctant to discuss it—especially in the presence of a tape recorder—or have minimized their role. Fifty-seven years after the event, several white Tulsans allowed copies of old photographs of early Tulsa to be made, but adamantly refused to permit riot photographs to also be copied. White Tulsans too young to remember the event, or who were born after it, have often been able to spin tall tales about it . . . It has been said in the city, by both blacks and whites, that the story of the riot has been "hushed up" . . . The race riot is, for some, a blot on the city's history and something not to be discussed, much less proclaimed (Ellsworth 1982 104; 106–107).

Like the Elaine, Arkansas and Wilmington cases, stories about racial violence in Tulsa developed non-synchronously. Tulsa attempted to address the silence surrounding the violence. In 1997, the State of Oklahoma formed the Tulsa Race Riot Commission to investigate the violence and assess the culpability of the state and city for the damage done to the Greenwood area in 1921. The commission located 130 survivors of the destruction and in its 2001 report recommended that the survivors be given reparations. Although historians and legal experts agree that the state of Oklahoma and city of Tulsa are responsible for most of the damages and loss of life in Greenwood, the state does not agree. The Oklahoma Governor, Frank Keating, believes the findings in the Commission's report do not assign blame for the riot to the state, and therefore reparations will not be forthcoming. Indeed the Governor cites an Oklahoma state law prohibiting the state from making reparations for "past crimes committed by its officials or on the state's behalf (Brune 2002:2)." Before the March 2001 Tulsa Race Riot Commission's report was released, a Tulsa talk-radio host's comments on reparations were:

> Are you kidding? Everyone knows that what happened 80 years ago was a bad, awful thing. But our people are saying, "If this is leading to

money . . . the answer is no. We had nothing to do with it. We're not paying any reparations" (Montgomery 2001).

This reflects the liberal ideological belief of individualism—"we had nothing to do with it." In a recent article in *The Nation,* an investigator in Tulsa's human rights office is quoted saying: " . . . people in Oklahoma don't talk about reparations, because it comes too close to broaching the topic of racism, one that many Tulsans stay as far away from as possible." One organization, the Tulsa Reparations Coalition, is investigating ways to sue the city of Tulsa on behalf of the survivors. One survivor is quoted saying:

> I often think about that riot, and when I'm asked whether I favor reparations, I say, "Yes, I certainly do!" . . . If Japanese Americans got reparations for their suffering during World War II, we black Tulsa Race Riot survivors deserve it for our suffering in 1921 (quoted in Brune 2002:3).

This reparations voice is also about respect—if others have been compensated, respect us enough to compensate us also. Narrative analysis provides a tool to understand social relations. In each of these communities— Wilmington, Elaine, and Tulsa—the stories about racial violence are 'inescapably central.' For Wilmington and Elaine, the silences have only recently been confronted. In Tulsa, stories about suffering and reparations contest a liberal ideology about 'moving on.' The political unconscious of these communities are the repressed narratives that reflect the underlying symptoms of the contradictions of historical oppression. Like Paige's three Central American agro-industrial elite narratives from El Salvador, Costa Rica and Nicaragua, the three race narratives from Elaine, Tulsa, and Wilmington repress the underlying conditions of racial oppression.

Narratives connect subjects to social relations and provide social scientists with a way to do empirical research about social life. In addition to examining institutional ways to create social change (Sampson, Squires, Zhou 2001; Sears, Sidanius and Bobo 2000; Jennings 1997) this research points to the necessity of narrative analysis in theories about social change. An important component of narrative analysis is the focus on agency (Denzin 2000; Andrews, Sclater, Squire, and Treacher 2000; Bradbury and Sclater 2000). Narratives represent the interests of dominant groups and provide a powerful mechanism to control subordinates; they are also moral statements about the way things ought to be. Yet as much as dominant narratives may constrain action, "social groups are still able to use narrative effectively to challenge power and create social change (Jacobs 2000:23)." Narratives may form the basis of new social movements as ideological frames (Snow and Benford 1992; Gamson 1992).

Covin (1997:272–273) examines narratives of the Brazilian Black Consciousness movement and their use in creating a counter-ideology "capable of sustaining itself in the face of the hegemonic ideology." He finds that "these narratives provide a living memory for participants in the movement, a memory which both sustains and directs their actions." My research examines counter-narratives of social actors that may be used as resources to promote and create social change, particularly racial change. Narratives represent a social site which is continually being both established and contested and allows us to theorize about ways to make constitutive social change.

IMPLICATIONS FOR POLICY

I believe it was when I was in second grade that the slogan "Give a hoot, don't pollute" was developed to address littering. It was a national campaign, like others in the history of our nation, which provided a narrative about civic duty and littering. We were taught in schools about littering and pollution, and signs along the highways reminded us of the penalties associated with littering. I recall the power of this campaign, and the moral connotations I associated with being a 'litterbug.' Even to this day I am repulsed and incensed at the thought of littering. I was reminded of this while living in southern Africa during the independence of Namibia in 1990 from South Africa. There was a 'nation-building' campaign, a curriculum developed in schools, and signs and slogans developed with the intent to build a new nation. There was moral authority invested in the social creation of the stories on unity in the new nation. I wonder how powerful these stories were for children who received them in their curriculums. Are they as powerful as the 'give a hoot, don't pollute' story I learned?

Feagin and Vera (1995) allude to an educational component for Americans to combat white racism. Based on the findings in this research, I believe an educational policy initiative to provide a cultural intervention in the school curriculums of each state is necessary to address the absence of historical knowledge of violent racial events. In North Carolina, students are not taught about the statewide white supremacy campaign nor about the 1898 violence in Wilmington. To my knowledge, respective curriculums on racial violence do not exist in either the Oklahoma or Arkansas public school curriculums. Adopting the curriculum at the state level would be requisite to avoid local interests preventing its implementation.

North Carolina state history is a key component of the 8th grade curriculum. In appendix three, I provide a model for an 8th grade curriculum supplement that examines the social, political, economic, and historical conditions of the 1898 Wilmington violence. It provides more than just a lesson in history; rather I have developed a week-long component that integrates interdisciplinary activities in core curriculum studies. Using sociological concepts, learners examine the context of the violence in their state. This would require states to adopt the curriculum and offer workshop training to teachers to implement the material in their classrooms. Since the material is geared for 8th grade learning and existing core curriculum requirements, this would be an easy component to incorporate into the standard course of study. This would be one step, and I believe a necessary one, to facilitate social change. An educational component may result in the creation of a new counter-narrative, and combined with existing counter-narratives may, as Covin (1997:278) argues, create "spaces where oppressed groups can articulate their own critiques and vision of society."

FINAL THOUGHTS

Late autumn is a season in which my family gets a good laugh at my expense. It is pecan season, and it is true, I have been called obsessive. It is, however, a pastime I relish, and have learned to ignore the jokes and giggles from those I love. A veteran pecan picker-upper (a good ten years of my childhood was devoted to perfecting the technique) I am able to spot pecans from a fair distance. As others who share this obsession know, it is not always an easy task. It is, indeed, an art or maybe a science. Of course when the big wind blows—which it always does at the end of pecan season—anyone can find pecans (actually sunlight is not even required, I know I have many times harvested pecans in the moonlight after such a wind). However, before the big wind blows, skill, patience and just the right tilt of the head *and* necessary illumination from the sun is required. Indeed I always marvel at how two people, walking down the same path, can either see, or miss altogether, the pecan right in their track. It's all in the lighting and shadows that pecans are found.

Why such a tangent in an essay on narratives? Because it has occurred to me that in order to create social change we can learn a lot from the pecan harvesting metaphor: looking, tilting the head, the lighting and the shadows—all reveal various perspectives on obtaining something really nourishing. Something that is already there. In the case of narratives, examining the sun-drenched dominant narratives, or finding the subordinate narrative hiding in the shadows—a turn of the head, a second glance, these are required strategies to find the nut, the kernel, the fruit that, to my mind, is like gold. I think we often walk down the same path together, yet don't see the same terrain. And without a big wind, we require some special skills. Adding the underutilized concept of narratives to the toolbox we sociologists carry around with us will move us a step closer, I believe, to creating constitutive social change.

Declaration of White Independence

Believing that the Constitution of the United States contemplated a government to be carried on by an enlightened people, in that its framers did not anticipate the enfranchisement of an ignorant population of African origin, and believing that the men of the State of North Carolina who joined in form in a the Union did not contemplate for their descendants a subjection to an inferior race,

We, the undersigned citizens of the city of Wilmington and county of New Hanover, do hereby declare that we will no longer be ruled, and will never again be ruled, by men of African origin. This condition we have in part endured because we felt that the consequences of the war of succession were such to deprive us of the fair consideration of many of our countrymen,

We believe that, after more than thirty years, this is no longer the case.

The stand we now pledge ourselves to is forced upon us suddenly by crisis and our eyes are open to the fact that we must act now or leave our descendants to a fate too gloomy to be borne.

While we recognize the authority of the United States, and will yield to it if exerted, we would not for a moment believe that it is the purpose of more than 60,000,000 of our own race to subject us permanently to a fate to which no Anglo-Saxon has ever been forced to submit.

We, therefore, believing that we represent unequivocally the sentiment of white people of this county and city, hereby for ourselves, and representing them, proclaim:

1. That the time has passed for the intelligent citizens of this community, owning 95 per cent of the property and paying taxes in like proportion, to be ruled by Negroes.

2. That we will not tolerate the action of unscrupulous white men in affiliating with Negroes so that by means of their votes they can dominate the intelligent and thrifty element in the community, thus causing business to stagnate and progress to be out of the question.

3. That the Negro has demonstrated, by antagonizing our interest in every way, and especially by his ballot, that he is incapable of realizing that his interest are and should be identical with those of the community.

4. That the progressive element in any community is the white population, and that the giving of nearly all of the employment to Negro laborers has been against the best interest of this county and city, and is sufficient reason why the city of Wilmington with its natural advantages has not become a city of at least 50,000 inhabitants.

5. That we propose in the future to give the white men a large part of the employment heretofore given to Negroes, because we realize that white families can not thrive here unless there are more opportunities for the different members of said family.

6. That the white men expect to live in this community peaceably, to have and provide absolute protection for their families, who shall be safe from insult from all persons whomsoever, We are prepared to treat the Negroes with justice and consideration in all matters which do not involve sacrifices of the interest of the intelligent and progressive portion of the community. But we are equally prepared now and immediately to enforce what we know to be our rights.

7. That we have been, in our desire for harmony and peace, blinded to our best interests and our rights. A climax was reached when the Negro paper of this city published an article so vile and slanderous that it would in most communities have resulted in lynching of the editor. We deprecate lynching, and yet there is no punishment provided by the laws adequate for this offense. We therefore owe it to the people of this community and of this city, as a protection against such license in the future, that the paper known as the *Record* cease to be published, and that its editor be banished from this community.

We demand that he leave this city within twenty-four hours after the issuance of this proclamation, second, that the printing press from which the *Record* has been issued be packed and shipped from the city without delay, that we be notified within twelve hours of the acceptance of this demand. If it is agreed to within twelve hours, we counsel forbearance on the part of all white men. If the demand is refused, or if no answer is given within the time mentioned, the editor, Manly, will be expelled by force.

8. It is the sense of this meeting that Mayor S.P. Wright and Chief of Police J.R. Melton, having demonstrated their utter incapacity to give the city a decent government and keep order therein, their continuance in office being a constant menace to the peace of this community should forthwith resign.

The Story of the Wilmington, N.C., Race Riots by Col. Alfred M. Waddell

Leader of the Reform Movement and Now Revolutionary Mayor of Wilmington, *Colliers Weekly*

MY ACTIVE connection with what has been termed the Revolutionary Government commenced when the Campaign Committee called upon me to make a speech stating my views; and I would like to say, in this connection, that some of the daily press representatives who have given an account of my speech selected two paragraphs standing alone. They came to the conclusion that I was a violent revolutionist. I said in my speech: "If there should be a race conflict here (which God forbid!), the first men who should be held to strict accountability are the white leaders, who would be chiefly responsible, and the work should begin at the top of the list. I scorn to leave any doubt as to whom I mean by that phrase. I mean the Governor of this State, who is the engineer of all the deviltry and meanness." That is one part of the speech. I also said: "We will not live under these intolerable conditions. No society can stand it. We intend to change it, if we have to choke the current of the Cape Fear River with carcasses." That is the other paragraph which some of the press representatives took out.

All the rest of the speech, which was chiefly a statement of facts, was omitted. Those paragraphs disconnected from the text, were sent out as my speech. When the crisis came, there was a universal demand that I should take charge. Last week, at the mass meeting, they made me chairman by acclamation, and also chairman of the Citizens' Committee of Twenty-five.

Demand was made for the negroes to reply to our ultimatum to them, and their reply was delayed or sent astray (whether purposely or not, I do not know), and that caused all the trouble. The people came to me. Although two other men were in command, they demanded that I should lead them. I took my Winchester rifle, assumed my position at the head of the procession, and marched to the "Record" office. We designed merely to destroy the press. I took a couple of men to the door, when our demand to open was not answered, and burst it in. Not I personally, for I have not the strength, but those with me did it. We wrecked the house. I believe that the fire which occurred was purely accidental; it certainly was unintentional on our part. I saw smoke issuing from the top story. Some one said the house was afire. I could not believe it. There were a number of kerosene oil lamps hanging round. They were thrown down and smashed, and the kerosene ran over the floor. It is possible that some fellow set it afire with a match. Immediately there were shouts when the fire occurred. "Stop that fire! Put it out! This won't do at all!" I at once had the fire alarm bell rung. We saved the wooden buildings next to the "Record" office, and soon had the fire out. I then marched the column back through the streets down to the armory, lined them up, and stood on the stoop and made a speech to them. I said: "Now you have performed the duty which you called on me to lead you to perform. Now let us go quietly to our homes, and about our business, and obey the law, unless we are forced, in self-defense, to do other wise." I came home, On about an hour, or less time, the trouble commenced over in the other end of town, by the negroes starting to come over here. I was not there at the time. I was here in this part of town. But we began immediately to turn out and prepare. And right here I want to say this about my part: I never dreamed the time would come when I would lead a mob. But I want to say, too, a United States Army officer, a prominent man, was here, and saw the whole performance. He said: "I never witnessed anything like this before. It is the most orderly performance I ever witnessed!" Then they got seven of the negro leaders, brought them downtown, and put them in jail. I had been elected mayor by that time. It was certainly the strangest performance in American history, though we literally followed the law, as the Fusionists made it themselves. There has not been a single illegal act committed in the change of government. Simply, the old board went out, and the new board came in—strictly according to law. In regard to those men who had been brought to the jail a crowd said that they intended to destroy them; that they were the leaders, and that they were going to take the men out of the jail. I ordered a force of military around the jail. I said to the people: "My position has been radically changed. I am now a sworn officer of the law. That jail and those people must have protection." I went out and appealed to the people in different parts of the town. They realized the situation and told me I was right, and that they would stand by me.

I stayed up the whole night myself, and the forces stayed up all night, and we saved those wretched creatures' lives. I waited until next morning at nine o'clock and then I made the troops form a hollow square in front of the jail. We placed the scoundrels in the midst of the square and marched them to the railroad station. I bought and gave them tickets to Richmond, and told them to go and to never show up again. That bunch were all negroes. Then they had taken other fellows that they sent out, and had them some-where protected. They took them under guard to another train—there were three whites in that party—and sent them off also.

Rumors fly here and there that the negroes are arming. There is no truth in that. They are utterly cowed and crushed, and are not going to in-terfere with anybody. I have sent messengers of both races out into the sur-rounding woods, where, it is said, fugitives are in hiding, begging the people to come back to their homes, and to rest assured they will be protected in their persons and property. A great many have come in, and I expect more will come to-night.

The negroes here have always professed to have faith in me. When I made the speech in the Opera House they were astounded. One of the lead-ers said: "My God! When so conservative a man as Colonel Waddell talks about filling the river with dead niggers, I want to get out of town!"

Since this trouble many negroes have come to me and said they are glad I have taken charge. I said: "Never a hair of your heads will be harmed. I will dispense justice to you as I would to the first man in the community. I will try to discharge my duty honestly and impartially." No one knows bet-ter than I that this has been a serious matter, but it has, like all such affairs, its humorous side. After the crisis had passed, an old negro came complain-ing to me about his jack-knife which he wanted me to get back for him. It seems it had been taken from him during the fracas. Then another negro came, complaining that some cattle had been penned up, and he wanted them "tu'nd loose."

The pendulum swings from the most tragic incidents to the most triv-ial. I have been bombarded with every kind of petition and complaint, both for protection against imaginary trouble, and for what I consider would be persecution—that spirit of cruelty that a revolution always develops; people who want to gratify their animosity and personal spite.

As to the government we have established, it is a perfectly legal one. The law, passed by the Republican Legislature itself, has been complied with. There was no intimidation used in the establishment of the present city government. The old government had become satisfied of their inefficiency and utterly helpless imbecility, and believed if they did not resign they would be run out of town . . .

Appendix Three

8th Grade Educational Component on Racial Violence in Wilmington, North Carolina 1898 to Supplement North Carolina Department of Education "North Carolina— History of an American State" Syllabus

KeyActors in North Carolina 1894–1900	Social Conditions 1894–1898	North Carolina White Supremacy Campaign 1898	Racial Violence in Wilmington, North Carolina 1898	Consequences

• Populist Movement
• Populist Party
• Republican Party
• Democratic Party
• Fusion Politics
	• Demographic Data
	• Black/White Differences
	• Occupation/Wealth Tables
	• Urban Residency Patterns
		• Role of Newspapers
		• Manly Editorial
		• Race, Class and Gender
		• Wilmington, NC 1898 White Supremacy Campaign
		  — Secret Nine
		  — Anne Russell's play: "No More Sorrow to Arise"
			• Waddell's Speech
			• Letters to President McKinley
			• Letters of B.F. Keith to Senator Marion Butler
			• Jane Cronly's Account
			• Collier's Weekly
			• White Declaration of Independence
			• WHQR Public Radio production of Wilmington Racial Violence/Historical Reconstruction released 11/14/98
				• Establishment of Jim Crow Laws 1900
				• Overview of Social Conditions 1900
				• Demographic Change
				• Demise of Populist Movement

Each component provides lessons and activities for students to explore key concepts via interdisciplinary activities for North Carolina Grade 8 Standard Course of Study including each of the following: English Language Arts (2001) Goals 1, 2, 3, 4, 5; Social Studies (1996/97) Goals 1,7,8 and Skills I, II, IV; Mathematics (1999/2000) Goals 1,3,4; Computer Technology Skills (1998/99) Goals 1, 2, 3; Information Skills (1999) Goals 1, 3, 4, 5. Contact **Leslie Hossfeld** for complete syllabus with lesson plans, activities and evaluation/ assessment component at hossfeld@uncp.edu Key sociological concepts: social stratification; race; class; gender; inequality; lifechances; quality of life; narrative; counter-narrative.

Notes

NOTES TO CHAPTER THREE

1. The grass roots organization that organized the Centennial commemoration event.

NOTES TO CHAPTER FOUR

1. *Wilmington Messenger,* October 25 1898.
2. Ibid
3. See Bishir 2000 page 145.
4. An excellent source on Wilmington political maneuvers during this period is McDuffie's (1979) *Politics in Wilmington and New Hanover County NC 1865–1900: The Genesis of a Race Riot.*
5. See Kirshenbaum (1998) and Gilmore (1996) for analysis of gender, white supremacy and Jim Crow.
6. Historians termed the period after Reconstruction to 1894 the period of "Redeemer" or "Bourbon" Democrats; see McDuffie (1979); Edmonds (1951).
7. For the most part, the word Negro was not capitalized by white writers during this period. Since this appears to be the normative practice of white writers of the time, I have omitted the marker [sic] for each incorrect capitalization usage.
8. See appendix three for entire document.
9. According to Edmonds' (1951:168 n.44;45) 1945 interview with Judge Armond Scott, who mailed the letter, "it was unthinkable for any Negro to enter the white settlement to deliver the letter that night for fear of loss of life; consequently he mailed it."
10. Rountree memoir
11. According to Hayden (1936:18) military units came to assist the white supremacy campaign, including: The Fayetteville Light Infantry; the Kinston division Naval Reserves; and the Sampson Light Infantry. He also notes that many military organizations telegraphed offering their services, some as "far South as New Orleans."
12. Prather (1984:149) quotes from *The Wilmington Messenger* 27 November 1898 that "Bevies of pretty girls stood on the platform outside and tearfully begged cartridges for remembrance." The Hayden (1936:9)

publication also mentions 'souvenirs.' The handwritten amendments by
J.A. Taylor read "Bunting was captured by Hugh MacRae and myself at
the Beverly Scott house, which premises are now occupied by J.O. Carr,
and two pistols were found buried in his yard. One of these was given to
Capt. Jame McBryde and the other to Liet. Smith of the Maxton Guards,
which I am sure they will always preserve as souvenirs." In an interview
I conducted a respondent told me, "I did house painting when I was in
college, and I met a man whose dad handed him a bullet that day from
the race riot. And he gave me one. But I think my ex-wife has it. His dad
handed him a bullet! Can you believe it?"

13. Letter from B.F. Keith to Senator Marion Butler, November 17, 1898.
    Photocopy from Marion Butler Papers in the Southern Historical
    Collection at the University of North Carolina Library, Chapel Hill,
    North Carolina; Manuscript Number 69 File 26, William Madison
    Randall Library Manuscript Collection. (Handwritten letter. Omissions
    reflect illegible handwriting.)

14. Letter from B.F. Keith to Senator Marion Butler, December 8, 1898.
    Photocopy from Marion Butler Papers in the Southern Historical Collection
    at the University of North Carolina Library, Chapel Hill, North Carolina;
    Manuscript Number 69 File 26, William Madison Randall Library
    Manuscript Collection. (Handwritten letter. Omissions reflect illegible
    handwriting.)

15. November 13, 1898, Letter to President McKinnley, National Archives,
    Record Group 60

16. 13 November 1898, Letter to President McKinnley, National Archives
    Record Group 60

17. Kirshenbaum 1998:25

18. Cited in McDuffie 1963:171

19. In Connor and Poe, *The Life and Speeches of Charles B. Aycock* 1912:232

20. Cited in Bishir (2000:43)

21. An interesting aside, the Secretary of Navy at the time was Josephus Daniels,
    former editor of the Raleigh *New and Observer* and instrumental player in
    the state-wide white supremacy campaign of 1898.

22. Wilmington Morning Star, 12–10–1936; January 7, 1937; December 29,
    1936

23. *Wilmington Morning Star* 2 December 1991

24. Cited in Scott (1979) based on U.S. Bureau of Labor Statistics, *A Statistical
    Summary of the Wilmigton Area: New Hanover County* (Washington, D.C.
    1943).

25. The 1940 population of Holly Ridge was 28, growing to 110,000 by 1943
    (*Wilmington Star News* 2 December 1991).

26. *Wilmington Morning Star,* December 2, 1991.

27. The December 2, 1991 *Morning Star* article also discussed the need for ad-
    ditional electricity due to the expansion and growth of the area. This was
    supplied by the Tidewater Power Company, "an independent company that
    bought power wholesale from Carolina Power and Light. CP&L absorbed
    Tidewater after the war."

28. Reaves 1998:367; *Wilmington Morning Star,* December 2, 1991; *Wilmington Morning Star* July 12, 1943.
29. *Wilmington Morning Star* July 12, 1943.
30. Cited in Scott (1979:109).
31. Reaves (1998:270) reports of other Jim Crow bus violations in Wilmington during the war years: in October 1940; April 1941; and December 1941.
32. According to 1985 tax records collected in *Who Owns North Carolina?* Bruce and Louise Cameron own the most land acreage (6287 acres) in New Hanover County, above the federal government (3565 acres).
33. Governor Broughton papers, Box 82, Race Folder, North Carolina State Archives
34. See *Public Addresses, Letters and Papers of Joseph Melville Broughton* edited by David L. Corbitt, 1950, State of North Carolina.
35. US Census Bureau 1950
36. Hogue was the same attorney quoted during the 1941 fray between black soldiers and black citizens. Additionally, I was unable to find coverage of the 6 March meeting in the *Wilmington Morning Star.*
37. Interview from Thomas 1980:41.
38. A symbolic location, as it was founded in 1898 by the Daughters of the Confederacy, and is housed in the old Wilmington Light Infantry armory. One rumor claims that the Gatlin gun used in the 1898 racial violence is housed in the basement of the Museum.
39. Prather's book, along with Edmond's chapter on the violence, are perhaps two of the better sources covering the event. Prather's book jacket has quotes from historians of the caliber of John Hope Franklin and C. Vann Woodward lauding the research.
40. *Wilmington Morning Star*

NOTES TO CHAPTER FIVE

1. Anthony (1999:50) notes that one of the goals outlined during the first Education Committee meeting in January 1997 was the rededication of Hugh MacRae Park. Hugh MacRae, the leader of the Secret Nine responsible for the coup d'etat and 1898 violence, donated the land to New Hanover County in the 1920s to be used as a White's Only park. Hugh MacRae II, his grandson, was scheduled to rededicate the park, without the racial exclusion, during a celebration at Greenfield Lake in 1999. Although Mr. MacRae attended the event he never made the rededication announcement.
2. The *1898 Foundation, Inc.* first called itself the *1898 Centennial Commission* yet changed its name in early 1997.
3. See McLaurin (2000) for narrative of commemoration activities, also *The 1898 Centennial Foundation* publication by director Bolton Anthony (1999) *Confronting Dangerous Memories* which outlines the formation of the organization and its activities.
4. Approximately 1000 in attendance.
5. The 1898 Foundation contracted Dr. Margaret Mulrooney, a visiting professor of history at the University of North Carolina at Wilmington, to

write a history of the 1898 event. In addition to the version that appears on the 1898 website, Mulrooney wrote a lengthier version of the event that provides the names of the Secret Nine and an interpretive account of the 1898 violence. The version that is used and promoted by the 1898 Foundation, however, is the shorter version provided in this chapter and does not address the loss of African American lives nor mentions the names of local white leaders involved in the coup. In a telephone conversation with Dr. Mulrooney (December 2003), I learned that the lengthier, interpretive version she wrote was available on the 1898 website as a link (not as the primary historical account) for a period of time, then was removed. Only the abbreviated version is provided today.

6. "Moving Forward Together" is a slogan the 1898 Foundation used on much of its printed material.

Bibliography

MANUSCRIPTS, DOCUMENTS AND PRIVATE PAPERS

Cronly Family Papers, William R. Perkins Library, Duke University. "Account of the Race Riot in Wilmington, N.C. in 1898," by Jane Murphy Cronly.

Governor J. Melville Broughton Papers, Box 82, Race Relations Folder, North Carolina Division of Archives and History, Raleigh, North Carolina.

Glancy, Michael. "Source Documents for the Wilmington Riot of November 10, 1898" Special Collections. William Madison Randall Library, University of North Carolina at Wilmington. Special Manuscript MS 69

Harry Hayden File. Local History Room. New Hanover County Public Library, Wilmington, North Carolina.

Louis T. Moore Collection. Local History Room. New Hanover County Public Library, Wilmington, North Carolina.

Shipbuilding File, World War I. Local History Room. New Hanover County Public Library, Wilmington, North Carolina.

Shipbuilding File, World War II. Local History Room. New Hanover County Public Library, Wilmington, North Carolina.

Wilmington Ten File. Local History Room. New Hanover Public Library, Wilmington, North Carolina.

NEWSPAPERS

Raleigh News and Observer
Union Labor Record
Wilmington Daily Record
Wilmington Journal
Wilmington Messenger
Wilmington Morning Star

PUBLISHED COLLECTIONS

Corbitt, David. (ed)1950. Public Addresses, Letters, and Papers of John Melville Broughton, Governor of North Carolina 1941–1945. Raleigh: Council of State of North Carolina.

DISSERTATIONS, THESES AND RESEARCH PAPERS

Cody, Sue. 2000. After the Storm: Racial Violence in Wilmington, North Carolina and its Consequences for African Americans 1898–1905. Masters Thesis: University of North Carolina at Wilmington.

DiTomaso, Nancy. 2001. "The American Non-Dilemma: White Views on Race and Politics." Paper delivered to Sociology Department North Carolina State University January 2001.

Dosher, Craig 2000. Reactionaries, Reformers, and Remembrances: The African American Segregated School Experience in Wilmington, North Carolina: Masters Thesis: University of North Carolina at Wilmington.

Frankel, Linda. 1986. Women, Paternalism and Protest in a Southern Textile Community. Dissertation, Harvard University.

Glancy, Michael. 1973. The Wilmington Riot of 1898. Research Paper: University of North Carolina at Wilmington.

Kornegay, Ralph. 1969. The Wilmington Riot, November 10, 1898. Masters Thesis: Appalachian State University.

Kraft, Andrew Clinton. Wilmington's Political-Racial Revolution of 1898: A Geographical and Cartographic Analysis of the Wilmington North Carolina Race Riot. Honors Paper: University of North Carolina at Wilmington.

McDuffie, Jerome A. 1979. Politics in Wilmington and New Hanover County, North Carolina, 1865–1900: The Genesis of a Race Riot. Doctoral Dissertation: Kent State University

McDuffie, Jerome A. 1963. The Wilmington Riots of November 10, 1898. Masters Thesis: Wake Forest College.

Scott, Ralph. 1979. Welding the Sinews of War: History of the North Carolina Shipbuilding Corporation. Masters Thesis: East Carolina State University.

Thomas, Larry R. 1980. The True Story Behind the Wilmington Ten. Masters Thesis: University of North Carolina at Chapel Hill.

PAMPHLETS AND TRANSCRIPTS

Anthony, Bolton. 1999. *Confronting Dangerous Memories.* Executive Summary of the 1898 Foundation. Wilmington, North Carolina.

Hayden, Harry. 1936. *The Story of the Wilmington Rebellion.* Wilmington, North Carolina. Local History Room, New Hanover County Public Library.

The Centennial Record, Wilmington: 1898 Centennial Commission, December 1998.

The North Carolina Shipbuilder 1942–1946. Local History Room, New Hanover County Public Library.

WECT Communique. Transcript of March 29, 1971 program with Kenneth Murphy; Wayne Jackson; Golden Frinks; Milton Fitch; Charles McLean, North Carolina NAACP Director. Local History Room, Wilmington Ten File, New Hanover County Public Library.

JOURNAL AND NEWSPAPER ARTICLES

Bertaux, Daniel, and Kohli, M. 1984. "The Life Story Approach: A Continental View," *Annual Review of Sociology,* 10:215–37.

Boltanski, L. and Thevenot L. 1999. "Sociology of Critical Capacity," *European Journal of Social Theory* 2(3) 359–377.

Brune, Adrian. 2002. "Tulsa's Shame," *The Nation,* March 18, 2002.

Covin, David. 1997. "Narrative, Free Spaces, and Communities of Memory in the Brazilian Black Consciousness Movement," *The Western Journal of Black Studies* 21(4) 272–279.

Hall, Stuart. 1985. "Signification, Representation, Ideology: Althusser and the Post-Structuralist Debates," *Critical Studies in Mass Communication* 2(2) 91–114.

Hart, Janet, 1992. "Cracking the Code: Narrative and Political Mobilization in the Greek Resistance," in *Social Science History* 16:4 (Winter) 631–668.

Hopkins, Fred. 1997. "Ferro-Concrete Shipbuilding in Wilmington, North Carolina, During World War I," *Steamboat Bill,* Summer 115–126.

King, Wayne. 1978. "The Case Against the Wilmington Ten," *New York Sunday Times Magazine,* Section 6, December.

Kirschenbaum, Andrea. 1998. "The Vampire That Hovers Over North Carolina:" Gender, White Supremacy and the Wilmington Race Riot of 1898," *Southern Cultures* 4(3) 6–30.

Levi-Strauss, Claude. 1955. "The Structural Study of Myth," *Journal of American Folklore,* 68:428–444.

Linde, Charlotte. 1986. "Private Stories in Public Discourse: Narrative Analysis in the Social Sciences," *Poetics* 15:183–202.

Maines, David. 1993. "Narrative's Moment and Sociology's Phenomena: Toward a Narrative Sociology," *Sociological Quarterly* (34)1:17–38.

Montgomery, Rick. 2001. "Panel Wraps Up Inquiry Into Race Riot in Tulsa," *Kansas City Star,* February 23, 2001.

Maynes, Mary Jo. 1992. "Autobiography and Class Formation in Nineteenth-Century Europe: Methodological Considerations," *Social Science History* 16:4, 517–537.

McLaurin, Melton.2000. "Commemorating Wilmington's Racial Violence of 1898: From Individual to Collective Memory," *Southern Cultures* 6(4) 35–57.

Mishler, E.G. 1995. "Models of Narrative Analysis: A Typology," *Journal of Narrative and Life History,* 5(2) 87–123.

Nash, June. 1973. "The Cost of Violence," *Journal of Black Studies.* 4(2) 153–183.

Richardson, Laurel. "Narrative and Sociology," *Journal of Contemporary Sociology,* (19) 1, 116–135.

Rose, Mariel.1998. "Pokomoke: A Study in Remembering and Forgetting," *Ethnohistory* 45(3), 543–573.

Schuman, H. and Scott, J. 1989. "Generations and Collective Memories," *American Sociological Review* 54, 359–381.

Sewell, William. 1992. "Narratives and Social Identities," *Social Science History* 16:3 Fall, 479–488.

Snow, David and Benford, R. 1988. "Ideology, Frame Resonance, and Participant Mobilization," *International Social Movement Research* 1, 197–217.

Somers, Margaret. 1992. "Narrativity, Narrative Identity, and Social Action: Rethinking English Working-Class Formation," *Social Science History* 16:4, 591–629.

Steelman, Bennett. 1994. "Black, White and Gray: The Wilmington Race Riot in Fact and Legend," *North Carolina Literary Review* 2, 70–82.

Steinmetz, George. 1992. "Reflections on the Role of Social Narratives in Working-Class Formation: Narrative Theory in the Social Sciences," *Social Science History* 16:4, 489–516.

Swidler & Ariditi. 1994. "The New Sociology of Knowledge," *Annual Review of Sociology,* 20, 305–329.

Wacquant, Loic. 2002. "From Slavery to Mass Incarceration," *New Left Review* (13) January-February.

White, Hayden. 1982. "Getting Out of History" *Diacritics* (12) 2–13.

BOOKS

Adamson, Walter. 1980. *Hegemony and Revolution.* Berkeley: University of California Press.

Andrews, M. Sclater, S.D., Squires, C., and Treacher, A. 2000. *Lines of Narrative.* London: Routledge.

Aptheker, Herbert. 1992. *A Documentary History of the Negro People in the United States, Volume II.* New York: Citadel.

Arrighi, G. 1978. *The Geometry of Imperialism.* London: New Left Books.

Arrighi, G. and Silver, B. 1999. *Chaos and Governance in the Modern World System.* Minneapolis: University of Minnesota Press.

Baumeister, R. and Hastings, S. 1997, "Distortions of Collective Memory: How Groups Flatter and Deceive Themselves," in Pennebaker, J., Paez, D., and Rime, B. (ed). 1997. *Collective Memory of Political Events.* Mahwah, New Jersey: Lawrence Erlbaum Associates.

Bellilli, G. and Amatulli, M. 1997, "Nostalgia, Immigration and Collective Memory," in Pennebaker, J., Paez, D., and Rime, B. (ed). 1997. *Collective Memory of Political Events.* Mahwah, New Jersey: Lawrence Erlbaum Associates.

Bendix, R. and Lipset, S.M. (Ed). 1966. Class, Status, and Power; Social Stratification in   Comparative perspective.

Billlings, D. 1979. *Planters and The Making of a "New South."* Chapel Hill: University of North Carolina Press.

Bishir, C. 2000. "Landmarks of Power: Building a Southern Past in Raleigh and Wilmington, North Carolina, 1885–1915," in Brundage, W.F. (ed). *Where These Memories Grow.* Chapel Hill: University of North Carolina Press.

Block, S. 1998. *Along the Cape Fear.* Dover: Arcadia Publishing.

Boston, T. 1988. *Race, Class and Conservatism.* Boston: Unwin Hyman.

Bradbury P. and Slater, S.D. 2000. "Conclusion." in_*Lines of Narrative,* by Andrews, Sclater, Squire and Treacher (Ed), London: Routledge

Brundage, W.F. (ed). 2000. *Where These Memories Grow.* Chapel Hill: University of North Carolina Press.

Cecelski, D. and Tyson, T. 1998. *Democracy Betrayed.* Chapel Hill: University of North Carolina Press.

Clifford, J. and Marcus, G. eds. 1986. *Writing Culture.* Berkeley: University of California Press.

Chafe, William H. 1981. *Civilities and Civil Right: Greensboro, North Carolina, and the Black Struggle for Freedom.* Oxford University Press: New York.

Cochran, D.C. 1999. *The Color of Freedom: Race and Contemporary American Liberalism.* New York: State University of New York Press.

Connor, R.D. and Poe, C. 1912. *The Life and Speeches of Charles Brantley Aycock.* Garden City: Doubleday, Page and Company.

Conti, J. and Stetson, B. 1993. *Challenging the Civil Rights Establishment.* Westport: Praeger.

Craib, Ian. 2000. "Narratives as Bad Faith," in *Lines of Narrative,* by Andrews, Sclater, Squire and Treacher (Ed), London: Routledge.

Das, V., Kleinman, A., Lock, M., Ramphele, M. and Reynolds, P. (ed). 2001. *Remaking a World.* Berkeley: University of California Press.

Davis, Robert Con. 1983. *Lacan and Narration.* Baltimore: John Hopkins University Press.

de Lauretis, Teresa (ed). 1986. *Feminist Studies/Critical Studies.* Bloomington: Indiana University Press.

deCertau, Michel. 1984. *The Practice of Everyday Life.* Berkeley: University of California Press.

Denzin, N. 2000. "Narrative's Moment," in *Lines of Narrative,* by Andrews, Sclater, Squire and Treacher (Ed), London: Routledge.

Dowling, W. 1984. *Jameson, Althusser and Marx.* Ithaca: Cornell University Press.

Dray, Philip. 2002. *At the Hands of Persons Unknown: The Lynching of Black America.* New York: Random House.

Eagleton, Terry. *Against the Grain.* London: Verso.

. 1981. *Walter Benjamin Towards a Revolutionary Criticism.* London: Verso.

Eaton, Hubert. 1984. *Every Man Should Try.* Wilmington: Bonaparte Press.

Edmonds, H. 1951. *The Negro and Fusion Politics in North Carolina.* New York: Russell & Russell.

Ellsworth, Scott. 1982. *Death in a Promised Land.* Baton Rouge: Louisiana State University Press.

Evans, W. M. 1966. *Ballots and Fence Rails.* Chapel Hill: University of North Carolina Press.

Feagin, J. and Vera, H. 1995. *White Racism.* New York: Routledge.

Feagin.J. and McKinney, K. 2003. *The Many Costs of White Racism.* New York: Rowman and Littlefield Publishers.

Gamson, William. 1992. *Talking Politics.* Cambridge: Cambridge University Press.

Geertz, Clifford. 1973. *The Interpretation of Cultures.* New York: Basic Books.

_____. 1988. *Works and Lives.* Stanford: Stanford University Press.

Genovese, Eugene. 1974. *Roll Jordan Roll: The World the Slaves Made.* New York: Pantheon Books.

Gilmore, G. 1996. *Gender and Jim Crow: Women and the Politics of White Supremacy in North Carolina 1896–1920.* Chapel Hill: University of North Carolina Press.

Godwin, John. 2000. *Black Wilmington and The North Carolina Way.* Lanham: University Press of America.

Gramsci, Antonio. 1971. *Selections From the Prison Notebooks.* New York: International Publishers.

Gurevitch, M. Et al. (Eds). 1982. *Culture, Society and the Media*. London: Methuen.

Hadden, Salley E. 2001. *Slave Patrols Law and Violence in Virginia and the Carolinas*. Cambridge: Harvard University Press.

Halbwachs, Maurice. 1992. *On Collective Memory*. Chicago: University of Chicago Press.

Hall, Bob. 1986. Project Director. *Who Owns North Carolina? Report of the Landownership Project conducted under the auspices of the Institute for Southern Studies*. Durham: The Institute.

Harris, David. 1992. *From Class Struggle to the Politics of Pleasure*. London: Routledge.

Holloway, John. 1979. *Narrative and Structure*. Cambridge: Cambridge University Press.

Homer, Sean. 1998. *Frederic Jameson, Marxism, Hermeneutics, Postmodernism*. New York: Routledge.

Igartua, J. and Paez, D. 1997. "Art and Remembering Traumatic Collective Events: The Case of the Spanish Civil War," in Pennebaker, J., Paez, D., and Rime, B. (ed). 1997. *Collective Memory of Political Events*. Mahwah, New Jersey: Lawrence Erlbaum Associates.

Iniguez, L., Valencia, J. and Vazquez, F. 1997, "The Construction of Remembering and Forgetfulness: Memories and Histories of the Spanish Civil War, in Pennebaker, J., Paez, D., and Rime, B. (ed). 1997. *Collective Memory of Political Events*. Mahwah, New Jersey: Lawrence Erlbaum Associates.

Jacobs, R. 2000. "Narrative, civil society and public culture," in Andrews, M. Sclater, S.D., Squire, C., and Teacher, A. *Lines of Narrative*. London: Routledge.

Jameson, Frederic. 1981. *The Political Unconscious Narrative as a Socially Symbolic Act*. Cornell University Press.

Jennings, J. 1997. *Race and Politics*. London: Verso.

Lee, L. 1984. *New Hanover County: A Brief History*. Raleigh: Division of Archives and History Department of Cultural Resources.

Lieblich, Amia, Tuval-Mashiach, Rivka, Zilber, Tamar. 1998. *Narrative Research*. Thousand Oaks: Sage.

Lira, E. 1997, "Remembering: Passing Back Through the Heart," in Pennebaker, J., Paez, D., and Rime, B. (ed). 1997. *Collective Memory of Political Events*. Mahwah, New Jersey: Lawrence Erlbaum Associates.

Lowe, Lisa, 1996. *Immigrant Acts: On Asian American Cultural Politics*. Durham: Duke University Press.

Lukes, S. 1974. *Power: A Radical View*. London: MacMillan.

March, J. and Olsen, J. 1976. *Ambiguity and Choice in Organizations*. Bergen: Universitetforlaget.

Marques, J., Paez, D. and Serra, A. 1997, "Social Sharing, Emotional Climate, and the Transgenerational Transmission of Memories: The Portuguese Colonial War," in Pennebaker, J., Paez, D., and Rime, B. (ed). 1997. *Collective emory of Political Events*. Mahwah, New Jersey: Lawrence Erlbaum Associates.

Martin,Wallace.1986. *Recent Theories of Narrative*. Ithaca: Cornell University Press.

Marx, Karl. 1963. *The Eighteenth Brumaire of Louis Bonaparte*. New York: International Publishers.

Miles, M. and Huberman, A.M. 1994. *Qualitative Data Analysis*. Thousand Oaks: Sage.

Miller, Nancy. 1991. *Getting Personal Feminist Occasions and Other Autobiographical Acts*. New York: Routledge.

Mishler, E.G. 1991. *Research Interviewing: Context and Narrative*. Cambridge: Cambridge University Press.

Moore, Barrington. (1966). *Social Origins of Dictatorship and Democracy: Lord and Peasant in the Making of the Modern World*. Boston: Beacon

Mumby, Dennis (ed). 1993. *Narrative and Social Control: Critical Perspectives*. Newbury Park: Sage.

Myerson, Michael. 1978. *Nothing Could Be Finer*. New York: International Publishers.

Nash, Christopher. 1990. *Narrative in Culture*. London: Routledge.

Neuman, Lawrence. 2000. *Social Research Methods*. Boston: Allyn and Bacon.

O'Brien, Gail. 1999. *The Color of the Law: Race, Violence and Justice in the Post-World War II South*. Chapel Hill: University of North Carolina Press.

Odum, Howard W. 1943. *Race and Rumors of Race: Challenge to American Crisis*. New York: Negro Universities Press.

Paez, D., Basabe, N., and Gonzalez, J.L. 1997, "Social Processes and Collective Memory: A Cross-Cultural Approach to Remembering," in Pennebaker, J., Paez, D., and Rime, B. (ed). 1997. *Collective Memory of Political Events*. Mahwah, New Jersey: Lawrence Erlbaum Associates.

Paige, Jeffrey. 1997. *Coffee and Power*. Cambridge: Harvard University Press.

Pemberton, J. 1994. *On the Subject of "Java."* Ithaca: Cornell University Press.

Pennebaker, J., Paez, D., and Rime, B. (ed). 1997. *Collective Memory of Political Events*. Mahwah, New Jersey: Lawrence Erlbaum Associates.

Pennebaker, J. and Banasick, B. 1997. "On the Creation and Maintenance of Collective Memories: History as Social Psychology," In Pennebaker, J., Paez, D., and Rime, B. (ed). 1997. *Collective Memory of Political Events*. Mahwah, New Jersey: Lawrence Erlbaum Associates.

Perrow, Charles. 1986. *Complex Organizations: A Critical Essay*. New York: Random.

Personal Narratives Group (ed). 1989. *Interpreting Women's Lives*. Bloomington: Indiana University Press.

Peterson, Richard (ed). 1976. *The Production of Culture*. Beverly Hills: Sage.

Polanyi, Livia. 1985. *Telling The American Story: A Structural and Cultural Analysis of Conversational Storytelling*. Norwood: Ablex.

Polkinghorne, Donald. 1988. *Narrative Knowing and the Human Sciences*. Albany: State University of New York Press.

Prather, H. Leon. 1984. *We Have Taken a City*. Associated University Presses.

Propp, Vladimir. 1968 (translation). *Morphology of the Folktale*. Austin: University of Texas Press.

Reeves, William (ed). 1998. *Strength Through Struggle*. Wilmington: New Hanover County Public Library.

Reisman, C. 1993. *Narrative Analysis*. Thousand Oaks: Sage.

Ricoeur, Paul. 1984. *Time and Narrative, Volume 3*. Chicago: University of Chicago Press.

Rime, B. and Christophe, V. 1997, "How Individual Emotional Episodes Feed Collective Memory," in Pennebaker, J., Paez, D., and Rime, B. (ed). 1997. *Collective Memory of Political Events*. Mahwah, New Jersey: Lawrence Erlbaum Associates.

Roberts, H. 1981. *Doing Feminist Research*. London: Routledge.

Sampson, R., Squires, G. and Zhou, M. 2001. *How Neighborhoods Matter: The Value of Investing at the Local Level*. Washington: ASA.

Sassoon, Anne (ed). 1982. *Approaches to Gramsci*. London: Writers and Readers Publishing Cooperative Society.

Savoie, A. and Miller, S. 2002. *Respect and Rights: Class, Race and Gender*. New York: Rowman and Littlefield.

Schuman, J., Belli, R. and Bischoping, K. 1997, "The Generational Basis of Historical Knowledge," in Pennebaker, J., Paez, D., and Rime, B. (ed). 1997. *Collective Memory of Political Events*. Mahwah, New Jersey: Lawrence Erlbaum Associates.

Sears, D., Sidanius, J. and Bobo, L. 2000. *Racialized Politics*. Chicago: University of Chicago Press.

Shull, Steven. 1993. *A Kindler, Genler Racism?* Armonk: M.E. Sharpe.

Shuman, H., Steeh, C. and Bobo, L. 1985. *Racial Attitudes in America*. Cambridge: Harvard University Press.

Silverman, David. 2000. *Doing Qualitative Research*. London: Sage.

Skocpol, Theda (ed). 1984. *Vision and Methods in Historical Sociology*. Cambridge: Cambridge University Press.

Steedly, Mary M. 1993. *Hanging Without A Rope: Narrative Experience in Colonial and Postcolonial Karoland*. Princeton: Princeton University Press.

Stockley, J. 2001. *Blood in Their Eyes*. Fayetteville: University of Arkansas Press.

Stone, Lawrence. 1981. *The Past and the Present*. Boston: Routledge & Kegan Paul.

Storey, John. 1996. *Cultural Studies and the Study of Popular Culture*. Athens: University of Georgia Press.

Strinati, Dominic. 1995. *An Introduction to Theories of Popular Culture*. London: Routledge

Therborn, Goran. 1980. *The Ideology of Power and the Power of Ideology*. London: Verso.

———. 1978. *What Does the Ruling Class Do When It Rules?* London: New Left Books.

Thompson, John. 1984. *Studies in the Theory of Ideology*. Berkeley: University of California Press.

Thompson, John. 1990. *Ideology and Modern Culture*. Stanford: Stanford University Press.

Tilly, Charles. 1998. *Durable Inequality*. Berkeley: University of California Press.

Toolan, Michael J. 1988. *Narrative A Critical Linguistic Introduction*. London: Routledge.

Tuttle, William. 1970. *Race Riot Chicago in the Red Summer of 1919*. New York: Atheneum.

Tyson, Timothy. 1998. "Wars for Democracy," in Cecelski, D. and Tyson, T. *Democracy Betrayed*. Chapel Hill: University of North Carolina Press.

Walters, Suzanna D. 2000. "Wedding bells and baby carriages; heterosexuals imagine gay families, gay families imagine themselves," in Andrews, M. Sclater, S.D., Squire, C., and Teacher, A. *Lines of Narrative*. London: Routledge.

Wellman, David. 1977. *Portraits of White Racism*. Cambridge: Cambridge University Press.

Wolkowitz, Carol. 2000. "Papa's bomb: the local and the global in women's Manhattan Project personal narratives," in Andrews, M. Sclater, S.D., Squire, C., and Teacher, A. *Lines of Narrative*. London: Routledge.

Zeitlin, Maurice. 1970. *Revolutionary Politics and the Cuban Working Class*. New York: Harper and Row.

Zizek, Slavoj. 2001. *Enjoy Your Symptom!* New York: Routledge.

. 2001. *Did Somebody Say Totalitarianism?* London: Verso.

_____. 1997. *The Plague of Fantasies*. London: Verso.

_____. 1993. *Tarrying with the Negative Kant, Hegel, and the Critique of Ideology*. Durham: Duke University Press.

_____. 1989. *The Sublime Object of Ideology*. London: Verso.

Index

Wilmington Ten 15, 19, 26, 27, 85–94,
        124, 126, 132, 143–147,
        159
Winsten, Francis 51
Wolkowitz, Carol 11
Wrightsville Beach, NC 54

Z

Zeitlin, Maurice 7, 14–15, 19, 152–154
Zhou, M. 6, 166
Zilber, Tamal 10, 11
Zimbabwe 1
Zizek, Slavoj 10